Transformations of the State

The influence of the state on the trajectory of human lives is more comprehensive and sustained than that of any other organizational construct. It steers the economy, fights crime, provides education, regulates traffic, sustains democracy, enters wars, guarantees social welfare, builds streets, provides water, collects taxes, and deploys some forty percent of the gross national product. *Transformations of the State?* defines the multi-faceted modern state in four intersecting dimensions: *resources*, or control of the use of force and revenues; *law*, or jurisdiction and the courts; *legitimacy*, or the acceptance of political rule by the populace; and *welfare*, or the facilitation of economic growth and social equality.

The remarkable feature of the twentieth-century nation state was that it focused the activities of those four dimensions at the national level, merged them in one tightly woven fabric that was so plush and well-suited to the post-WWII era that people nowadays look back on that period as the golden age of the state. But what has become of that Golden-Age State and its national interweaving of functions in the decades since the seventies? Is its fabric worn out, is it unraveling? Will it be rewoven and restyled – perhaps as one gigantic world state of uniform pattern, or perhaps in the miniature, as a multitude of semi-sovereign regional governments? Or will the fibres simply separate, each following its individual fate in postmodern fashion, the rule of law moving into the international arena and the nation state clinging to its resources, while the intervention state comes completely unspun and goes every which way? What is the future of the state? In *Transformations of the State?* political scientists, lawyers, economists and sociologists take a sample of OECD nation-states, and search for answers to these questions.

Non est potestas Super Terram que Comparetur ei Iob. 41. 24.

liberté, egalité, fraternité

UN
EU

ECJ
WTO
OECD

Salus publica suprema lex esto

Pursuit of Happiness

Save the Whales

Transformations of the State?

Stephan Leibfried
and
Michael Zürn,
eds.

Transformations
of the State?

Edited by
Stephan Leibfried
and Michael Zürn

PUBLISHED BY THE PRESS SYNDICATE OF THE UNIVERSITY OF CAMBRIDGE
The Pitt Building, Trumpington Street, Cambridge, CB2 1RP United Kingdom

CAMBRIDGE UNIVERSITY PRESS
The Edinburgh Building, Cambridge CB2 2RU, UK
40 West 20th Street, New York, NY 10011-4211, USA
477 Williamstown Road, Port Melbourne, VIC 3207, Australia
Ruiz de Alarcón 13, 28014 Madrid, Spain
Dock House, The Waterfront, Cape Town 8001, South Africa

http://www.cambridge.org

First published 2005

Printed in the United Kingdom at the University Press, Cambridge

A catalogue record for this book is available from the British Library

ISBN 0 521 672384

The cover illustration is taken from the original etching in Thomas Hobbes' *Leviathan* of 1651. Cambridge
University Press and TranState are grateful to Lucila Munoz-Sanchez and Monika Sniegs for their help in
redesigning the original in such a way that it illustrates what *Transformations of the State?* might be all
about. The inscription at the top of the original frontispiece reads *Non est potestas Super Terram quae
Comparetor ei. Job 41. 24.* – There is no power on earth which can be compared to him, and, in the Bible,
refers to the seamonster Leviathan.

Contents

European Review, Vol. 13, Supp. No. 1, 1–36 (2005) © Academia Europaea, Printed in the United Kingdom

A NEW PERSPECTIVE ON THE STATE

1 Reconfiguring the national constellation

MICHAEL ZÜRN and STEPHAN LEIBFRIED

The influence of the state on the trajectory of human lives is more comprehensive and sustained than that of any other organizational construct. We provide a definition of the modern nation-state in four intersecting dimensions – resources, law, legitimacy, and welfare – and review the history and status of each dimension, focusing on the fusion of nation and state in the 19th century, and the development of the 'national constellation' of institutions in the 20th. We then assess the fate of the nation-state after the Second World War and, with western OECD countries as our sample, track the rise and decline of its Golden Age through its prime in the 1960s and early 1970s. Finally, we identify the challenges confronting the nation-state of the 21st century, and use the analyses in the following eight essays to produce some working *hypotheses* about its current and future trajectory – namely, that the changes over the past 40 years are not merely creases in the fabric of the nation-state, but rather an unravelling of the finely woven national constellation of its Golden Age. Nor does there appear to be any standard, interwoven development of its four dimensions on the horizon. However, although an era of structural uncertainty awaits us, it is not uniformly chaotic. Rather, we see structured, but *asymmetric* change in the make-up of the state, with divergent transformations in each of its four dimensions. In general, nation-states are clinging to tax revenues and monopolies on the use of force, such that the resource dimension may change slowly if at all; the rule of law appears to be moving consistently into the international arena; the welfare dimension is headed in every direction, with privatization, internationalization, supra-nationalization, and defence of the national status quo, occurring at various rates for healthcare, pensions, public utilities, consumer protection, etc. in different countries. How, and whether, the democratic legitimacy of political processes will be ensured in such an incongruent, if not incoherent and paradoxical state is still unclear.

Se vogliamo che tutto rimanga come è, bisogna che tutto cambi.
If we want things to stay the same, they are going to have to change.
(Giuseppe Tomasi di Lampedusa [1896–1957], *The Leopard* 1960 [1958].[74]

τὰ πάντα ῥεῖ
Ta panta rei. Everything is in flux. Heraclitus (535–475 BC)

Political theorists have traditionally sought to define the state in terms of a single crucial function or trait. In Thomas Hobbes' (1588–1679) *Leviathan*,[51] written at a time when war was the rule and peace the exception, the state's purpose is to overcome the natural tendency toward a 'warre, as if of every man, against every man'[51:88] that rendered 'the life of man solitary, poore, nasty, brutish, and short'.[51:89] The book's frontispiece[15,16,80] has informed our idea of the state for almost four centuries. It depicts a gigantic king with a body made up of faceless citizens, a worldly sword and a bishop's staff in his hands, and a benign smile on his face, as he looks out over a peaceful but barren countryside. A few centuries later, Max Weber[124] (1864–1920), one of the fathers of sociology, put the emphasis on the sword, exchanged the ecclesiastical staff for secular moral legitimacy, and deemed the state's 'monopoly of the legitimate use of force' the crucial function of the state; and the notorious constitutional lawyer Carl Schmitt[110] (1888–1985) defined the power to rule in a state of emergency or other exceptional circumstance as the central characteristic of statehood. But today's modern state, at its apogee in continental Europe, is really a 'polimorphous beast'[126] that represents far more than these one-dimensional definitions can encompass. The state regulates the labour market, steers the economy, fights crime, and provides some form of education; it regulates traffic, provides a framework for democracy, owns businesses, enters wars and makes peace treaties, creates a reliable legal structure, supports social welfare, builds streets, provides water, imposes military service, maintains the pension system, collects taxes and deploys some 40% of the gross national product, represents national interests and generally regulates daily life down to the smallest detail. Such a multi-faceted entity clearly requires a multi-dimensional definition.

We define the modern state in four, intersecting, dimensions. The *resource* dimension comprises the control of the use of force and revenues, and is associated with the consolidation of the modern *territorial* state from scattered feudal patterns. The *law* dimension includes jurisdiction, courts, and all the necessary elements of the *rule of law*, called 'Rechtsstaat' or constitutional state in German-speaking countries where it is most closely identified with the widely held concept of the state. *Legitimacy* or the acceptance of political rule came into full bloom with the rise of the *democratic nation-state* in the 19th century. And *welfare*, or the facilitation of economic growth and social equality, is the *leitmotif* of the *intervention state*, which acquired responsibility for the general well-being of the citizenry in the 20th century.

The remarkable feature of the modern, 20th-century nation-state was that these four dimensions were merged and their activities concentrated at the national level. Only the nation-state or its designated subunits controlled the military and police, and had a monopoly on extracting revenues from the citizenry. Only it could guarantee the rule of law. Political legitimisation processes such as elections and public discourse focused first on the national level. The responsibility for ensuring welfare, balancing social inequalities and creating infrastructure for economic development all lay with the nation-state. It had evolved four dimensions and fashioned them into a tightly woven fabric – a multi-functional state that combines the Territorial State, the state that secures the Rule of Law, the Democratic State, and the Intervention State, and which we connote with the acronym TRUDI.

How did TRUDI respond to the challenges of the late 20th century? How is it coping with the 21st? Is TRUDI worn out, is it unravelling? Can, and will, it be mended or rewoven – perhaps transformed into one gigantic world state with a uniform pattern, or restyled into semi-sovereign, sub-national, regional governments? Or will the threads of TRUDI simply separate and follow individual fates in post-modern fashion, with the rule of law moving into the international arena while the nation-state clings to the resources of the territorial state, and the intervention state comes unspun and goes every which way? What is the future of the state?

In the German constitutional debates of centuries past – likewise concerned with the transnational trajectory of state-building – the young philosopher Georg W. F. Hegel (1770–1831), called the scholars of his time to task when he said, 'was nicht begriffen werden kann, ist nicht mehr.'[47] What cannot be comprehended, ceases to exist. In 2003, faced with so many incomprehensible and elemental uncertainties about the future of the nation-state and the values it embodies, a team of political scientists, lawyers, economists and sociologists established the TranState Research Centre[a] with funds from the German National Science Foundation (Deutsche Forschungsgemeinschaft). In this volume they review and synthesize the extant literature on the state, and the most recent results of their own efforts at comprehending 'the state of the state' in the new millennium, taking the western nation-states of the OECD as their sample.

In continental Europe, the state has been a prominent component of social and legal theory for centuries, and across the political spectrum, with democracy

---

[a] TranState is located in the state of Bremen, Germany, with twelve research projects at the University of Bremen, two at the International University Bremen and one at the University of Applied Sciences Bremen. In total it comprises about 65 researchers working on 15 projects for a period of 12 years (reviewed every four). Extensive information about TranState and all of the projects is available at http://www.state.uni-bremen.de/.

tacked on as an afterthought in the late 19th and early 20th century. In the US, it was the state that was the afterthought, improvised in the wake of revolution and democracy, and viewed thereafter as a necessary evil. Democracy then tended to obscure the growing state apparatus and confuse its role, and it was not until the 1980s, in works such as *Bringing the State Back In*,[30] that political theorists really started taking the state seriously in the US. While, in the US, the state is often perceived as a camouflage for a large collection of agencies beholden to special interests, Europeans tend to see the state as a generally benevolent autonomous institution. Both perceptions, when taken to the extreme, as is often the case, are surely myopic.[66]

In this first chapter, we review the history of the fusion of nation and state as it emerged in the Western world during the 19th century, and describe the development of the modern nation-state's 'national constellation'[b] of institutions in the first half of the 20th. We then provide a broad, but integrated, perspective that has been lacking in the political research of both Europe and the Anglo-American world, by tracking and assessing the fate of the nation-state after the Second World War, paying particularly close attention to the last three decades. We identify some of the current challenges confronting the nation-state and, in this context, introduce the eight essays that follow, making use of their analyses to produce some working hypotheses about its current trajectory and future.

The national configuration of the state in its Golden Age

The influence of the state on the trajectory of human lives is more comprehensive and sustained than that of any other organizational construct. And yet any perfunctory consideration of the modern state will reveal that it has always had, even during its Golden Age, an ambivalent nature. It is the citizen's most trusted friend, and most dreaded enemy. States are the most frequent violators of human rights, and yet only the state can guarantee these rights. The state's defence apparatus provides protection from outside interference, even while it poses a threat to other states or, in times of domestic unrest, to its own citizenry. That the state is simultaneously the main promoter of economic growth, and its greatest obstacle, can be witnessed in the reform debates over pensions, health policy, public utilities and education that are currently raging in every OECD country. Seen from this perspective, the historian Wolfgang Reinhard's[98:49] dictum would appear to be the rule: 'He who knows how the state operates no longer believes in the state'.[96,97]

---

[b] In 1998, Jürgen Habermas[42] (English 2001) regarded the emerging configuration of institutions in western nations as a 'post-national constellation', and yet the pre-existing 'national constellation' that was his implicit norm had not yet been fully examined.

Despite these conundrums of state power, basic social values such as peace, legal security, individual liberty, political self-determination and social welfare have, to varying extents, become hallmarks of the modern state. The historian Eric J. Hobsbawm[53] idealized the democratic welfare-state's most prosperous period in the 1950s and 1960s as the 'Golden Age' of modern times, and the philosopher Jürgen Habermas expanded on, and further popularized, the concept.[c] In an even larger sense, and in retrospect, we might call the national configuration of the state that existed in the 1950s, 1960s and into the 1970s the Golden Age of TRUDI, as these basic social values were fully incorporated in its four dimensions and their institutions.[103]

The resource dimension – the modern territorial state

The modern state presupposes control over key material resources within its territory; in its modern form, this includes monopolies on the issue of currency,[20] the power of taxation and the use of force. In the medieval order, several feudal rulers might well have used force and collected taxes in the same territory. But conflicts between rulers led to the development of monopolies on the use of force within distinct territories, beginning in France and England in the 16th century, becoming the norm throughout Western Europe by the end of the 18th, and culminating in Germany and Central Europe during the 19th. The monopolization of force within a territory went hand in hand with territorial control of the collection of taxes. The financial resources thus gained helped the state to strengthen and stabilize control over the means of force, making it readily available for use, both against domestic opposition within the state's own territory, and against other nation-states that were likewise engaged in the consolidation of resources.[27,39,120] Together these resources paved the way for the eventual development of the other dimensions in the fledgling territorial states – for the rule of law and accompanying social order, which, in turn, accommodated individual freedoms, and for the growth of welfare as an 'entitlement state'.

Initially the control of resources was simply engaged in by territorial rulers, and it was only during the 19th century that a normative basis was introduced. The process of institutionalizing the use of force and power to tax occurred throughout Europe, but at different paces and in different forms. Bureaucratic constraints and institutions waxed and waned, and the monopoly of power and taxation were tied to the rule of law, untied, and then retied, with the monopoly of force losing its tentative moorings to the rule of law time and again – in Nazi Germany, Mussolini's Italy, Franco's Spain, Horty's Hungary etc. In today's OECD nations,

---

[c] In 2001 Jürgen Habermas gave a lecture in Hamburg titled 'Why Europe Needs a Constitution'. For the text and the public response see amongst others http://www.newleftreview.net/NLR24501.shtml; http://www.germanlawjournal.com/article.php?id = 82 (accessed September 15, 2003).

there are still enormous differences in the resource dimension of statehood between nation-states. The once closely coupled relationship between the use of force and fiscal extraction has, in general, slackened. One obvious distinction is that between centralised and federal states.[35,76] In central states both are monopolized by the central tier of government, and federal states have developed several varieties of federalism whereby the state and the central tiers share these resources.

The legal dimension – the rule of law and sovereignty

During the 16th century, a process began which would effectively restrict the powers of rulers, internally and externally, by legal means, and transform the crude 17th-century territorial monopoly of force into what Max Weber called a monopoly of the *legitimate* use of force,[124] the cornerstone of Western legal tradition.[11]

The principles of secular international law began to fall into place as a result of the religious wars of the 16th and 17th centuries. Beginning with the Religious Peace of Augsburg of 1555, and formalized in the Westphalian Peace Treaty of 1648, the exclusive right of each state to rule within its own borders was recognized by all other states. These were the events that inspired Hobbes' political philosophy, and *Leviathan*, which laid out the first systematic theory of the sovereign state, was published in 1651. Over the course of the next few centuries, this mutual recognition of the sovereign status of states by other states matured into what we might now describe as external sovereignty. External sovereignty gave the state the right to exclusive rule within its territory; to legitimately bar other states from interfering in its territory; and to international recognition as a governing unit with rights equal to those of other states.[84] It allowed the rulers of territorial states to exclude both the Emperor and the Pope from the effective execution of powers in their territories, and effectively marginalized competition from northern Italian city states and northern European city leagues like the Hansa.[114]

As the precepts of external sovereignty became established in the international arena, internal state rule was progressively legalized. Step by step, the rule of law superseded tyranny, and the powers of the state were differentiated and separated. In the spirit of Montesquieu,[74] the territorial states established the separation of powers, and lawmaking, the application of law, and the judicial enforcement of the law were placed under different authorities. With its monopoly of the use of force, the state was then able to consolidate and acquire exclusive rights to these legal powers. This, in turn, positively affected the economy.[87] The state's increasingly legalized monopoly of rule on a given territory guaranteed a degree of legal certainty and predictability[d] that was unheard of in the 14th and 15th

---

[d] Michael Stolleis[115:27f.] points out that the word '*ragion*' in the term *ragion di stato*, or 'reason of state', is historically associated with the necessity of state-building as visualized by Hobbes and personified in the frontispiece of *Leviathan*, comes from the same linguistic root as '*ragione*' which means calculability.

centuries, and which eventually made it possible to secure the legal equality of all citizens.

These internal and external components of the rule of law meet when there is a generally accepted, nationally defined judicial institution that can resolve legal disputes between state institutions, as well as conflicts between national and international law. National constitutional courts and their parliamentary equivalents have thus become the most tangible and universal symbols of the rule of law in modern times.

From the 16th century onwards, the law dimension of the state, like its resource dimension, developed different forms in the nation-states of the OECD world. The best known distinction is that between states like Germany and France, with their tradition of *droit civil*, and states like Great Britain or the United States that follow the common-law tradition.[22] *Droit civil* restricts the judiciary to the application of the law and the precise implementation of the will of the lawmaker. In the common-law tradition, the judiciary itself has a law-making function. In continental Europe, the state generally plays a large role in regulating societal relations: here, 'politics and law meet' and are, in the words of the German constitutional judge and scholar Udo DiFabio, 'chained to each other in the institutions of the state'.[24] In the Anglo-Saxon world, on the other hand, societal self-regulation – at its extreme in the wild-west 'adversarial legalism' of the US[62] – is more dominant.

The legitimation dimension – the democratic nation-state

The emergence of the democratic nation-state in the 19th and 20th centuries inaugurated TRUDI's far-reaching legitimation dimension. Common institutions are legitimate in the *empirical sense* if the governed demonstrate a certain degree of voluntary compliance with collectively binding, socially accepted rules. Legitimacy in the *normative sense* requires the democratic constitutionalization of the form of government – that the empowerment to make laws is constitutionally limited and based on due process, and that those affected by these laws have participated in a meaningful way in generating them. With the development of TRUDI, the democratic constitutionalization of the state became the most important, although not the only, source of political legitimacy in the *empirical sense* as well. As Hasso Hofmann[54] recently described, this process took place exclusively within the nation-state.

A precondition for the development of a legitimate government is the existence of a political community formed by citizens who are loyal to the state and the laws it promulgates. The territorial states of the 17th and 18th centuries did not necessarily coincide with political loyalties, and in order to acquire such legitimacy, states shifted their territorial boundaries, either by uniting smaller states, as in Germany and Italy, or, as was more often the case, splitting up larger ones as in the Hapsburg Empire.[1] A national political community could often be shaped from the extant local and regional loyalties in territorial states by appealing to unifying ethnic and cultural identities. In the 19th century, the introduction of compulsory school attendance and military service[52] encouraged the development of national loyalties. At the same time, the spread of mass media both connected and reshaped thinking in local and regional communities to such an extent that they began to distinguish themselves as an 'imagined' national community with common political interests.[4]

The growing concurrence of political loyalties and state territorial borders in Western and Central Europe during the 19th and 20th centuries[36] marked the turning point from the old world of territorial states to the modern world of nation-states.[23] It strengthened the geographical character of a political order and government.[78] The nationalism that accompanied this process was an institutional principle that went more or less hand in hand with democracy. Both were based on the normative principle of self-determination: nationalism maintains that a national political community should not be shaped by foreign forces, whereas democracy requires individual self-determination, and both depend on political autonomy.[48]

The rise of the bourgeoisie in the 18th century, and their increasing insistence on participation in government in return for supporting the aristocracy and clergy, laid the foundations for new democratic principles. The ideas that the state belongs to society and that the monopoly of the use of force is contingent on the democratic constitutionalization of the polity were developed during the American and French revolutions. The late 19th and early 20th century saw the general democratization of the nation-states of Western Europe and North America and the emergence of institutionally protected societal participation in government.[94]

Whereas all states in today's OECD world experienced democratization, there were important differences in the range of institutional forms available for it.[76,108] Thus, one can distinguish between parliamentary democracies and presidential systems, centralized and federal democracies, and systems based on representation versus more direct democratic ones. Furthermore, one can differentiate between majoritarian democracies, in which political decisions are made in parliaments based on majority rule, and consociational[e] democracies[75], in which decisions are settled by 'amicable agreement' between the various political parties and the major 'social partners', such as unions

---

[e] The term 'consociational democracy' was introduced by the Yale political scientist Arend Lijphart at the end of the 1960s and defined as 'government by elite cartel designed to turn a democracy with a fragmented political culture into a stable democracy'.[75:216] It dates back to Johannes Althusius' (1557–1638) use of 'consociatio' in his *Politica Methodice Digesta* (1603).

and employers. The democracies of the OECD also differ in the way the state interacts with interest groups: in a corporatist relationship, interest groups – usually unions and employers – can effectively bring state activity to a halt if they do not approve of it, whereas in a pluralist relationship the state keeps interest groups at arm's length and can proceed even if not all social actors are in agreement.[70]

The welfare dimension – the intervention state

Since the late 19th century, the state has been expected to fulfil a variety of tasks, recently analysed in great detail by Peter H. Lindert,[77] far beyond the limited role of 'nightwatchman'[99] in the laissez-faire economy advocated by Adam Smith (1723–1790). In order to be militarily prepared to defend itself against other states, the 'early modern'[79] or 'absolutist' state needed a national economy that would allow for efficient production and trade, and provided workers with the relevant basic skills. It laid the foundations for a national market economy by removing market barriers and standardizing weights and measures within its borders, and by investing in infrastructure and education, and operating its own industries.[19,121] The state took on regulatory tasks such as factory inspections, industrial health and safety, and town and country planning, and encouraged extensive exchange of knowledge between 'backward' and 'advanced' states, with countries such as the UK, the US and Germany all fitting one or the other designation at some time or in some particular task.[50,102]

The late 19th-century state was also expected to ensure the fair and equitable distribution of wealth within society. The Industrial Revolution inflated the ranks of the working classes, and they were no longer willing to accept the glaringly unequal distribution of wealth within the new industrial society. Modern welfare policies were implemented whereby the primary distribution of income by the market could be corrected by state-sponsored secondary distribution. In many cases the primary distribution of wealth in society was and is itself channelled by state regulations such as systems of collective wage bargaining, minimum wages, and tax structures. This is often overlooked, but it actually makes certain varieties of capitalism good anchors for the welfare state. After 1945, the Keynesian version of the welfare state gave the state the additional responsibility of ensuring continuous economic growth, economic stability and full employment.[32]

In the fully developed interventionist state, the state takes responsibility for each and every one of its citizens.[67,68,81] It is, according to Wolfgang Streeck, characterized by three types of state interventions.[116] *Market-making* interventions regulate market and production processes. *Market-braking* interventions supply human resources, infrastructure and basic services, known as public utilities in the US and UK, *service public* in France, and *Daseinsvorsorge* in Germany.[f] *Market-correcting* interventions redistribute income via the welfare state, macro-economic policies and various micro-economic forms of risk absorption.

Like the other three dimensions of the state, the interventionist states of the OECD world developed different forms. Most typologies classify these according to their market-correcting welfare state components,[68] which developed according to the different religious, cultural and legal traditions, and the particular distribution of power in the society of each country.[29] They differentiate the conservative welfare regimes typical of continental Europe, the social democratic regimes of Scandinavia, and the liberal ones of the USA and, with certain reservations, Canada and the UK.[26,28] A characteristic southern European welfare regime, and a 'radical' model typical of Australia and New Zealand, have also been proposed. These welfare regimes can be distinguished by the relative importance they assign to the central welfare producers, i.e. state, market, and family; their different requirements for access to welfare services and payments, i.e. citizenship, need, employment, etc; their levels of support and modes of financing; and, connected to the latter, the degree to which they are able to maintain the social status of clients, and how much they pressure clients to join the labour force. Welfare regimes throughout the OECD world have different key factors, particular sectors that were and are central to the national sense of social well-being, e.g. Germany's pension system, the UK's national health system, and France's education system.

The constellation as a whole – TRUDI

As 'the post-World War II settlement'[57] matured in the 1960s and 1970s, the four dimensions of the modern state converged and became prominent at the national level. The result was what we have labelled TRUDI. Most states outside the OECD world, as well as some recent OECD members like Mexico and Turkey, have either failed to acquire or are still in the process of developing all of these four dimensions. Here we have straightforward empirical evidence that the successful state does in fact require the development of the resource, legal, democratic and welfare dimensions, and that TRUDI is more than a theoretical construct. In most of the states outside the OECD world only one dimension is fully developed,[9] and in a few, commonly referred to as 'failed states',[105,106] none is sufficiently developed.[g]

---

[f] For an English presentation of the German 'Staat der Daseinsvorsorge' of Ernst Forsthoff see Arthur Jacobson and Bernard Schlink.[59] For a German–French comparison of the divergent legal infrastructure for the privatization of public utilities see Johann-Christian Pielow.[93]

[g] In Berlin, Thomas Risse is leading an initiative to establish a large Research Centre on the issue of failed states, which would complement the work of the Bremen TranState Research Center functionally and geographically.

Colombia, for example, lacks a protected state monopoly on the use of force and fiscal extraction, and it also lacks an institutionalized form of democracy and a fully developed intervention state. It is what the political scientist Robert H. Jackson[58] calls a 'quasi state', wherein the only quality that makes it a state at all is its legal status as a sovereign state. Taiwan lacks recognition as a sovereign state, but has a fully developed resource dimension, is on the way to becoming a full-fledged legitimation state with a developing national political community, and has a burgeoning welfare dimension.[100:241-335] Saudi Arabia, on the other hand, is recognized as a sovereign state under international law and has a fully developed resource dimension, but clearly lacks the separation of powers required for the rule of law and the democratic underpinnings of a legitimation state. In other states such as Argentina and the Philippines[83] political elites are democratically legitimized but not constitutionally embedded. Whether or not some or all of these states will continue to develop their four dimensions – and if so, to what degree that development either depends on, or produces, a convergence of those dimensions into a national constellation – or whether such states will simply leap forward into some unforeseen post-national constellation, remains to be seen.

Despite the failure of many nations to achieve it, the fully developed TRUDI of the OECD world, with its variable institutional arrangements, is viewed as an exemplary model of the modern state by the median voter in all parts of the world.[61] Substantial deviations from this model in any of TRUDI's four dimensions are typically seen by those affected as deficiencies or aberrations.

For our purposes of examining the status and future of the nation-state, the crucial characteristic of TRUDI was the convergence of all four dimensions of the state in a *national* constellation[b] where they strengthened, supported and stabilized each other. Monopolies on the use of force and tax extraction, the myriad functions of the intervention state, the trappings of democratic legitimation, and national constitutions[41] and their judicial systems are all firmly rooted in *national* institutions. And the very essence of the nation-state, its legal sovereignty, has a double presence at the national level in that territorially bound governing entities must both recognize and be recognized by other territorially bound governing entities as sovereign states.

Challenges to the Golden Age state

The national constellation of the Golden Age was a unique and enduring political structure whose existence was dependent on two conditions of central importance for the modern state: the congruence of social and political space, and the simplicity and manageability of societal interactions, which lent itself to paternalistic state control. The most serious challenges and threats to the structure of the nation-state stem from the disappearance of these two conditions.

According to the principle of *congruence*, territory, people and effective government go hand in hand,[60] and state sovereignty spans the territory in which the individuals of a community of people interact with each other. The territorial units so constituted must be separated from each other by 'clear and precise demarcations', to use the words of Carl Schmitt.[109] In more sociological terms, one might say that the space in which intensive societal transactions and interactions occur must be the same as the space which that same society regulates politically. As long as social activities such as the post and telecommunications, pollution, the production and consumption of culture occurred within national borders – in what J. A. Hall dubs 'complete power containers'[45] – it was possible to regulate them through national measures.

It is precisely this congruence of social space with political space that is threatened by what is commonly called globalization.[49] There is extensive literature describing how the emergence of global markets[13] has enabled businesses to elude political control, disempowering national politics and putting the nation-state in what Thomas Friedman has referred to as a 'golden straitjacket'.[34] According to these studies, transborder economic and social transactions are growing rapidly while political intervention remains confined within national boundaries.[64] This implies that flourishing global markets are either making a handful of cunning multinational Chief Executive Officers (CEOs) very rich, or leading us into a global consumer paradise. Regardless of one's interpretation, many studies concur that technological and political developments over the past two or three decades have caused an unprecedented decline in the significance of space as an obstacle to social interaction. As transactions become less place-bound, the spatial congruence of political and social activity is threatened.[129,130] In many central areas of human activity, the borders of social transactions now lie beyond the borders of any nation-state, and yet the majority of political institutions and regulations aspire to function only within nation-states. Ulrich Beck notes that 'society and state are still conceived, organised and lived ... as if they had stayed in congruence'.[10] This weakens the capacity of national policies to achieve the desired political outcomes and has far-reaching effects on the notion of what constitutes legitimate government.

Other important challenges for the nation state lie in the growing complexity of many areas of human interaction – be they economic, scientific, cultural or religious – which makes them increasingly incomprehensible to outsiders. The state cannot possibly keep up with change in all of these societal subsystems, or acquire the expertise and information necessary to control them effectively. In order to be successful in such an environment the state must transform its traditional hierarchical, patriarchal image and share responsibilities with private or civil society actors. The state may still cast a large regulatory shadow over many such activities, even increasing its reach in some areas, but it now requires the help of private actors to do so.[h] The separation of telecommunications from the postal services in many European states, and its subsequent privatization in the global market is just one example of this development.[82,90,107]

Even in the core areas of state regulatory activity – the straightforward exercise of state power through prohibitions, permits, and other binding orders – hierarchical forms of government are becoming increasingly rare and the state often cooperates as *primus inter pares* with non-state actors.[112] So extensive are such arrangements becoming[25] – including everything from private pension schemes and toll roads, to the American outsourcing of prisons or military functions, and there are even suggestions that the state could get rid of public debt by selling *all* its property to private actors and leasing it back – that some scholars refer to a 'public management revolution'.[86,118] Whatever one's views on these issues, such a regulatory trend can hardly be overlooked.

What other changes have been triggered by the disappearance of the conditions that nurtured and supported TRUDI through its Golden Age? Do these changes constitute a complete transformation – do we need a new conceptualization of what comprises a state? What is the future of the state in an era of globalization and increasing subsystem autonomy? Before taking up these questions, four conceptual notes are in order.

First, to avoid excessive abstraction, the fully developed TRUDI of the OECD world of the 1960s and 1970s will serve as the *status quo ante* for our analysis and comparisons, as our historical starting point. It is this particular constellation of the state that most analysts see as the apogee of 400 years of development, and which we take as the norm against which to measure change.[i]

Second, it is not analytically productive to dichotomize the prospects of the state as is typically done in debates about its future. Attempts to discern whether the state as a whole will be strengthened or weakened by its new circumstances do not account for the multifaceted character of TRUDI. A multidimensional understanding of the state[17] suggests that one dimension, or even a single component of a dimension, may be 'strengthened' while another dimension or component is 'weakened'.

Third, we must clarify what 'strengthened' and 'weakened' actually mean. Here, it is helpful to distinguish between *organizational* and *territorial* changes.[63] An organizational change in any dimension of TRUDI is one in which the relationship between state and society changes. The question, then, is whether

---

[h] This is also true in the international sphere and sometimes leads to an exercise of private power on an international basis.[46,101]

[i] The issue of how the many different states of the world came into being, many of them as split-offs, is another one altogether, and is addressed by Alberto Alesina and Enrico Spolaore.[1]

we're seeing an expansion of state power – i.e. the acquisition of new responsibilities and autonomy for national institutions – or privatization, with the state relinquishing responsibilities to non-governmental entities such as private markets,[19,31,122] the voluntary sector,[5] and families, heading, in the extreme case, towards a society dominated by unregulated market relations. A change in the territorial sense is a change in the relationship of the national to other political levels, whether international or regional.[6] The national level is weakened by 'denationalization'[129] when the national institutions of any of TRUDI's dimensions relinquish their political responsibilities, tasks, resources, or the administration of political processes and command of political loyalties to international or regional institutions – internationalization or subnationalization, respectively.

Changes in TRUDI, then, can occur along two axes, organizational and territorial, and the combined effect is not necessarily a simple strengthening or weakening of the state. Table 1 shows the possible combinations of transformative change relative to TRUDI as it existed during its Golden Age, including everything from transnationalization – a combination of privatization and internationalization – to a strengthening of the Golden-Age TRUDI, with its national configuration of institutions and responsibilities. This scheme accounts for all the theoretically possible changes of the *status quo ante*, even those that seem, in these times, the least likely, such as increased socialization of private sector activities, which was known as 'nationalization' in the early 20th century. Such a scheme can be used to examine the empirical results from studies of change in western political landscapes without prejudicing them toward any particular direction of change. Rather, the direction of change is determined directly by the empirical findings. We can look at change – if any – in each of TRUDI's four dimensions, and then synthesize the results to see more clearly how the nation-state as a whole is being reconfigured – thus countering the literature's militant tendency towards too much aggregation and oversimplification. In addition, all change is measured against the historically unique national constellation of TRUDI's Golden Age, thus countering the social scientist's propensity towards over-abstraction with the historian's specificity.

The fourth conceptual problem lies in determining just how much and what kind of change constitutes a *transformation* of the state. After all, a good amount of change is inherent in the status quo, or as the French are fond of saying, *Plus ça change, plus c'est la même chose*. More change, more of the same.

It is important to note here that critical, *transformative* changes are marked by the changing nature of the state and *not* by that of the specific policy of origin. A revolutionary change in social policy, such as the introduction of a dynamic pension scheme or a shift to a 'supply-driven' policy, can also be a revolutionary change for the state, in this case because the political system is accepting or

Table 1. Change in TRUDI – from the national to the post-national constellation

ORGANIZATIONAL CHANGE	TERRITORIAL CHANGE		
	Subnationalization	*Status quo ante*	*Internationalization*
Privatization	Localization	Liberalization (Deregulation)	Transnationalization
Status quo ante	Regionalization	STATUS QUO ANTE / TRUDI's national constellation	Internationalization
State expansion	Fragmentation	Socialization (Nationalization)	Supranationalization

Note: See also the article of Robert O. Keohane and Joseph S. Nye,[70:13] where a similar three-by-three matrix is employed. Their matrix refers to 'typical actors' like 'multinational corporations' rather than 'processes' like 'transnationalization'.

reneging on its guarantee of the social welfare of all its citizens. But a revolutionary social policy change such as throttling early exit into pension insurance, or indexing or de-indexing monetary transfers, might also involve *no* significant change in the general state make-up. And it is even possible that a relatively minor social policy change results in crucial changes for the state; this may be the case with the recent German labour market reform (Hartz IV) that merged federal Unemployment Insurance and communal Social Assistance, short-circuiting the finances between these tiers of government and introducing permanent turbulence into the General Federal Revenue Sharing system, which is the bedrock of German federalism. As Jakob S. Hacker[44] and Wolfgang Streeck and Kathleen Thelen[117] have pointed out, small changes can form part of processes such as displacement, layering, drift, conversion, and exhaustion that take place in tiny increments but lead to massive system-wide change. So we see that while policy research is not necessarily dealing with state transformation, state transformation must nevertheless pass through the needle's eye of policy research, where we can distinguish transformative from 'more-of-the-same' or business-as-usual policy change.

A certain degree of liberalization in the welfare dimension of a single country, such as the privatization of postal and telecommunication services in Great Britain, may constitute a significant change for that country, but does not necessarily represent a transformation of *the* intervention state as a functional concept and structure in the western world. A transformation of one of TRUDI's dimensions requires change that is *epidemic*, a diagnosis we make with some confidence if the majority of the countries in our OECD sample have experienced significant change in that dimension. But just how much change must be observed? We've seen that in each dimension of TRUDI there is a certain *corridor of variation* within which a number of institutional forms have developed and policy patterns routinely change and vary. A transformation would mean that the size or shape of the *corridor* itself – the nature or range of routine variation – has changed. A corridor may have narrowed or widened, or the ceiling may be lower, or it may have moved to another location or become unstable to the point of caving in altogether. For example, if different regime types mix and converge into one homogeneous type, there is less variation and the corridor narrows; a decrease in the social relevance of regimes means the ceiling becomes lower; a structural rearrangement of regimes means the corridor has moved, and general turbulence and uncertainty in policy-making means it has become unstable.

Finally, there is one last requirement for determining precisely what constitutes a transformation of *the state*. The transformation of one dimension does not necessarily result in a transformation of the nation-state as a whole. Here we must look for the *configurative effect* of the transformation, if and how it might strengthen or destabilize the national constellation and the way in which the four dimensions have traditionally strengthened and supported each other.

The unravelling Golden-Age state – hypotheses and findings

Our working hypotheses assume, firstly, that *important* shifts are taking place in the different dimensions of the modern state, i.e. we are in an age of transformation that began in the 1970s.[14] Secondly, we propose that the shifts are in different directions, that the very fabric of the state is unravelling, with its central components drifting apart and refashioning themselves in a variety of new and radically different patterns. It is not a single transformation of the state that we are witnessing, but a plurality of divergent changes in each of its dimensions, transformation*s* in the plural, which may interact in the unravelling just as they did in the weaving. However, not every shift in state structures, every wrinkle in the fabric, amounts to an unravelling. The transformations of the state do not follow the fourth-century metaphysical doctrine of the gloomy Greek philosopher Heraclitus: not everything is in flux. We can distinguish different kinds and degrees of change, and dynamic forms of stability. Unravelling occurs only if important shifts in *different* directions take place in different dimensions of the state, only if the change is asymmetrical or divergent. Changes that take place in parallel in the different dimensions would not unravel the state's fabric, but rather restyle it in some integrated fashion at a new level, be it a 'world state' or a 'regional state' – the sort of archetypically symmetrical state that Hobbes imagined in *Leviathan*. If our hypothesis is correct, change in the four dimensions of the state should be divergent.

The resource dimension – the modern territorial state

At first glance, TRUDI's most ancient dimension, its material base, would appear to be holding true, staying in place with little observable change[128] while the fabric unravels around it. Neither the monopoly on fiscal extraction nor the monopoly on the use of force appears to be weakened at its core in any of the OECD countries. International organizations, such as the EU and the United Nations, despite their increasing responsibilities, have little direct access to nation-states' resources. The EU, which is extremely active in the intervention dimension and determines the substance of about half of all bills considered by national legislatures, receives about 1% of the European gross domestic product in the form of members' fees, while the tax revenues of its member states are, on average, around 40% of their respective Gross Domestic Products.[95,123] Likewise, although both the grounds for military intervention and the number of interventions authorized by the United Nations have increased markedly over the past 15 years, the military resources at the UN's disposal are extremely limited and implementation lies in the hands of a few powerful nation-states.

Although international and supranational institutions have not gained direct control of nation-state resources and this dimension remains relatively intact in the core OECD countries, it is increasingly threatened by the appropriation of the resources of failed states outside the OECD world. These areas provide violent societal actors with more and more opportunities to become established and gain local control of the means of force and often of the means of fiscal extraction. Organized crime, Mafia-like structures, and transnational terrorism[105] pose new threats to security and fuel demands for change in the OECD world. In the next essay, Jachtenfuchs shows how these sorts of threats have provoked new collaborative relationships between the police forces of EU countries, as well as broader, cooperative military intervention policies from the United Nations. The nation-state still has the final word in terms of whether and how the police and military are put to use, but their daily operations are being coordinated, and standards for their use are being set, at the international and supranational levels. So while national sovereignty over the means of force is not in question, the autonomy of nation-states with respect to its employment is constrained and directed by international consensus and coordination.[j]

Genschel's contribution in this volume shows that the fiscal components of the resource dimension are experiencing a similar loss of autonomy. Although globalization, the free movement of capital, and increased international competition for capital, have triggered the reshaping of national fiscal policies,[72] internationalization *per se* has been less significant here and change has been more in the organizational than the territorial sense. The number of bilateral treaties has increased hand in hand with the internationalization of markets, but proposals to create a multilateral regime for taxation have gone unheeded. Endeavours to harmonize fiscal policy at the international level have met with limited success over the past 40 years, and even at the European level such programmes remain in their infancy.[38] Recently, the OECD started a rather successful 'Project on Harmful Tax Practices' to force tax havens outside the OECD to trim down their attractiveness for tax evaders from OECD member states. But programmes to redistribute fiscal revenue between countries by international agreement are

---

[j] The decision of the US to go to war with Iraq without the approval of the UN Security Council, and against the opposition of the majority of its members, throws into question the idea that national autonomy is actually constrained by international consensus. Given that this unilateral intervention has been extremely costly for the US and its allies, and the United States' recent attempt at rapprochement with the UN, it remains to be seen whether the American action and the crisis it generated has indeed weakened the multilateral approach to security, or whether, in the long run, it will strengthen sectors of the US political elite and public that warned the US not to 'go it alone' in world politics. The Harvard international relations specialist Joseph S. Nye[88] and the doyen of the historians of international diplomacy Paul W. Schroeder[111] were particularly outspoken on this issue.

limited to some 1% of the European Gross Domestic Product, and though there is increased harmonization between national tax systems in Europe, attempts to introduce an EU tax system have so far failed.

At present, globalization's biggest challenge for national fiscal policies takes the form of tax competition between leading economies in the West, the transformation economies of Eastern Europe, and the leading and fast-developing economies of Asia. Catching-up nations have such a strong incentive to lure new investments with lower taxes that it is nearly impossible to reach consensus and contain such competition by international agreement. Instead, the globalization pressure has created a near-epidemic of national fiscal policy adjustments, which have in fact converged, narrowing the corridor of variation for this component of the resource dimension. Genschel's studies show that, so far, tax competition has not resulted in a race to the bottom in aggregate tax revenues. But it has imposed serious constraints on the national capacity to increase tax revenue in response to rising spending requirements, and created pressure to cheapen and 'de-tax' labour, despite chronically high levels of unemployment.[37] Fiscal responsibility for the welfare state, which was formerly shared by workers and employers, is becoming the responsibility of workers only, something Fritz W. Scharpf once referred to as 'one-class socialism' – an example of lowering the ceiling of the fiscal corridor, even while it converges and narrows. This shrinking corridor also tends to limit the state's range of options for generating tax revenue and maintaining budgets: it bars increases in capital taxes, income taxes and company-based social insurance contributions, and shifts the emphasis to options like value-added taxes and privatization of insurance that are particularly unpopular and politically visible.

A certain degree of privatization in response to budget constraints can also be observed in the resource dimension, including the privatization of prison services and of sections of the military in the US, and of military training sites in the UK. Private security services are a growth industry throughout the OECD world, but they do not yet threaten the state monopoly on the legitimate use of force.

Globalization is clearly tugging at the threads of TRUDI's resource dimension, and we have noted a number of significant changes in response. But we have also seen that there is a good deal of resistance to internationalization of resources in most nation-states, the trend toward privatization is limited to a few countries and not epidemic, there is enough fiscal elasticity and national bickering about fiscal policies to keep the epidemic of corridor-shrinking adjustments under control, and none of these changes appears to be having significant configurative effects on the national constellation as a whole. We cannot rule out that these developments represent the leading edge of transformative change, but, to date, it appears that TRUDI's territorial state remains relatively intact, with nation-states maintaining their sovereignty – if not complete autonomy – over the use of force and fiscal extraction.

The legal dimension – the rule of law and sovereignty

While national constitutional courts and parliamentary systems remain effective guarantors of the domestic rule of law, European and international institutions have increased in importance in the last 30 years. The European Court of Justice (ECJ), the European Court of Human Rights, the World Trade Organization (WTO), the United Nations and the World Bank all, to varying extents, monitor nation-states for adherence to both international (legal) standards and their own national constitutions. The rule of law now appears to be doubly secured, from within and without[k] – a situation that has been described as 'governance through a global web of government networks'.[113] As Joerges and Godt point out in their contribution to this volume, the ECJ gained its special, law-based supranational role at the end of the Golden Age, after two decades of inching towards 'integration through law'. Paradoxically, the ECJ itself is now challenged by the WTO, and although international trade conflicts are primarily resolved at the WTO-level, the ECJ has, to date, resisted submitting formally to the new authority. Joerges and Godt point out both striking parallels and differences between the ECJ and the WTO. Unlike the ECJ, the WTO was in full force within months of its creation in 1994. But, at the international level, legalization, let alone and constitutionalization, are significantly less advanced than at the European level, with the international rule of law being much more politically embedded than the European one.

External mechanisms for ensuring the rule of law are a double-edged sword for the legal dimension, as they can result in a considerable restriction of the external sovereignty of nation-states. Respect for fundamental human rights is increasingly considered a pre-requisite for acknowledgement as a sovereign state by other states. When supranational monitoring determines that a state has violated these international norms within its borders, that state now loses the unconditional sovereignty it had acquired when it was first recognised as such. It is disqualified from the exclusive right to rule on its territory and to legitimately exclude other states from ruling there, and it loses its status as a recognized governing organization with rights equal to those of other states. Such disenfranchisement

---

[k] In the national lawyers' perspective one might see a more *ambivalent* 'double anchor': The rule of law could be seen as challenged by processes taking place inside and outside the nation-state: The twofold supervision from within and without challenges the position of the nation-state as the highest authority for law-making and for interpreting legal norms. By the same token, denationalization and globalization create new authorities, fresh governance structures, which are themselves difficult to hold accountable.

was almost unheard of in the past, a rare and temporary condition imposed only in the wake of war.

Over the past few decades there has also been an increasing tendency to augment disenfranchisement with sanctions that range from sending observers or placing special conditions on the receipt of financial aid, to economic boycotts and military intervention. Mechanisms at the international level thus serve as coercive instruments for upholding the rule of law as determined by the international community, with consensus overriding unanimity and the right of a state to veto, undermining traditional principles of international politics. In their new role as external guarantors of the domestic rule of law, international institutions are also transforming national sovereignty from a permanent status to a conditional one.[33,43,55]

The international dimension of the rule of law is strengthened by the increasingly widespread use of quasi-juridical procedures for the implementation of international agreements. In the past 15 years, over 20 new units for international arbitration have been established,[3,104] the most well-known being the International Criminal Court and the Dispute Settlement Body of the WTO. Nation-states have thus lost their control over the interpretation of international agreements, which, once made, develop a dynamic that can be completely beyond the reach of any state's jurisdiction. In this volume, Zangl demonstrates that such changes are not mere formalities, but rather new forms of dispute settlement that effectively internationalize or supranationalize the interpretative authority of international law. The ECJ in particular is so well established that national constitutional courts have seen the balance of proof shift against them,[2] and they have been integrated in a multi-level constitutional court system.

What is more, some issue areas are increasingly determined by transnational rules that in turn also exhibit typical characteristics of internationalization. The international merchant law (*lex mercatoria*), but also the *ICANN* – the private Californian organization with authority over the world wide web (*lex informatica*) – and the large international sport federations (*lex sportiva*) have also, partly with the support of state courts, developed transnational legal forms that function outside the realm of the nation-state, as the handling of doping in national and international sports events makes apparent.[101,132]

Is the nation-state still the highest authority for law-making and for interpreting legal norms?[69] The role of the nation-state in securing the rule of law has most certainly diminished. International legal norms now complement domestic mechanisms for securing fundamental rights while quasi-judicial procedures are used to interpret international norms. In this new version of the rule of law the state's sovereignty is conditional on its observance of fundamental rights, and it submits to an international interpretation of the law, and to transnational legal regimes that function in parallel to the national legal system. These regimes have emerged in addition to the well-known European, supranational legal structure.

The legitimation dimension – the democratic nation-state

In this volume's contributions on the topic, it is apparent that the nation-state is still the locus of processes of democratic legitimation. Peters *et al.* show that public discourse on political issues still takes place primarily within national communities, and is only observed at the European level in a few exceptional cases. Hurrelmann *et al.* show that the meta-discourses, which indirectly assess the democratic legitimacy of political decisions, refer most often to the nation-state. The 'cosmopolitan democracy' championed by Daniele Archibugi, David Held[7] and others, is clearly a long way off.

This does not, however, mean that the democratic legitimacy of nation-states is unaffected by globalization or associated changes in TRUDI's other dimensions. The studies by both the Peters and Hurrelman groups present empirical evidence confirming Robert A. Dahl's[21] 1994 observation that, while the means of democratic legitimation are firmly entrenched in national political communities, there is growing public criticism of the performance of democratic institutions in parliamentary democracies. Although criticism and vindication of political processes are focused on the nation-state, the perception that traditional democratic institutions and their actors are no longer responding adequately to the problems at hand must be viewed in light of the enormous intervention potential of international organizations, which themselves lack the means for obtaining legitimacy to act.[91]

The lack of democratic processes beyond the nation-state, and the growing importance of international organizations, raises questions about international processes in the normative sense, i.e. their justness, propriety, and legitimacy. Although the major public debates still take place within the national context and national elections are the most important mechanisms for provoking discussions and forcing resolutions, it may well be that developments in the international sphere require *direct* legitimation. International politics, which was traditionally limited to a relationship between nations and their statesmen, is beginning to be scrutinized with the normative criteria for a sound political order that nation-states employ.[131] Even though the European Union plays a largely regulatory state role,[18] it is now subject to Europe-wide elections, a European Parliament, and an emerging European Constitution that gently interferes with the traditional chains between nation-state and constitution. International institutions such as the World Trade Organization and the International Monetary Fund are now being called to task on issues of justice, and there are increasing demands that non-governmental organizations (NGOs) be allowed to participate in their decision-making processes.[85] An international conference that does not include protests by NGOs questioning the legitimacy of the decisions made by government representatives is now rare, so in an informal sense they are already participating. Likewise, international agreements are being increasingly submitted to direct legitimation in national elections and referenda, where the electorate must continuously pass verdict on the necessity to protect national autonomy, taking a stand on the protection of national sovereignty and democracy.

While there are as yet no strong indications of democratic processes taking place beyond the nation-state, many scholars see an increase in challenges to nation-state legitimacy by ethnic and other minorities within its borders,[1] and certainly there is a growing perception among the mainstream voters of western societies that national institutions are inadequate, and that normative evaluation of international institutions and their policies by the national and transnational citizenry is necessary. With these processes running in the same direction, an eventual transformation or destabilization of the legitimation dimension seems likely. While we do not intend to revive, at the international level, Jürgen Habermas' 1973 diagnosis of a legitimation crisis of late capitalism, problems of legitimation in this age of transformation can be ignored no more.

The welfare dimension – the intervention state

In purely quantitative terms, the intervention state has clearly shifted from the national to the international arena. In the course of globalization, the effectiveness of national borders as filters or membranes has declined, and it is becoming increasingly difficult to shield national societies and policies from external societal and political developments, especially within the European Union. As a result, cross-border political processes and international regulation have increased significantly. This is particularly apparent in the European Union, where a large share of national parliamentary business concerns the implementation of Community law and international agreements. Never have international aspects of national policies been so important. In Germany, for example, the 74 sections of the Foreign Office used to handle such issues, but the government now requires 336 sections across all its ministries, and, of those, 281 also deal with issues outside of Europe.[26] And never before have international political regimes and organizations played such a significant role in domestic social policies. The removal of e-market barriers, the standardization of products and measurements, environmental regulations, product safety, not to mention many of the other

---

[1] This contestation addresses national identity and the ethnic or multicultural challenges to it. A wide-ranging debate rages here, involving authors like Samuel P. Huntington[56], Will Kymlicka[73] and Brian Berry,[12] pointing to Golden Age (and earlier) imperial roots and more recent international migration patterns as the backdrop for these 'endogenous' problems.

classical intervention state issues from the 18th and 19th centuries, are now regulated by international institutions – a process also signalled by the fact that domestic reform debates on a broad front have meanwhile converted the OECD as an institution into a transnational intervention state referee.[8]

This quantitative shift to the international arena, however, is only one side of the coin. On the other side we see privatization dominating the sphere of public utilities while social policies effectively remain mainly with the nation-state. During the Golden Age, *public utilities* such as railways, postal services, air transport, electricity, gas and water works were public enterprises. They were financed by charges rather than taxes, and with the higher-income services often subsidizing the poorer ones, ensured equal service across the country, in the city and in the countryside. Starting with telecommunications in the 1980s, branch after branch of these public structures crumbled and was privatized.[90] Here, territorial competition and both direct and indirect supranational prodding played more of a role than organizational concerns: EU regulation,[40] privatization and deregulation in the Anglo-American world, and domestic attempts to cut state spending and equalise prospects for dissimilar enterprises, all contributed to radically increased competitive pressure in the new global and continental markets. Private, multinational companies, regulated by the state, formed in branches of public utilities that were originally national or regional.

Two essays in this volume deal with the *welfare state* in the core OECD states. It is the intervention state's most prominent component, occupying over half of its 40% take of the Gross National Product, a considerable sum by any reckoning, with an equally large potential for transformative change. These studies find evidence that welfare states have undergone significant organizational change, but not in the direction – toward privatization – that one might have expected. Rothgang *et al.* find instead that different types of healthcare systems are being combined into one mixed type, such that the options for either a purely public system like the UK's National Health Service or a purely private, US market-style system have disappeared. Obinger *et al.* see a similar mixing, or blurring of regime types in the welfare state as a whole. Both studies find evidence of extensive international cross-fertilization between policy areas, either the importation of single policy instruments, such as the use of managed care or healthcare co-payments as incentive mechanisms to control service usage, or of general policy-reform approaches such as Activation Politics for labour market reform.

In terms of the level of state intervention, public health expenditures are decreasing – although public plus private health expenditures are increasing – while overall welfare state expenditures are on the rise and national trends in expenditure levels are converging in all social policy sectors. Our preliminary analysis of a sampling of policies thus shows a slight convergence of regime types on an uplifted plateau of state intervention, this latter mostly due to the catching-up processes of late-developing welfare states in countries such as Spain and Greece. In contrast to the public-utilities component, the welfare state is clearly being reformed more in the organizational than the territorial sense, the main issue being how to organize the provision of welfare on the national level. The intervention state components whose development throughout the 19th and much of the 20th century was parallel, in both a philosophical and a bureaucratic sense, are now on completely divergent pathways: privatization plus supranationalization in the case of public utilities, *status quo* defence with a decreasing corridor in the case of welfare state policies, and internationalization of the rest.

Thus, there are clearly signs of epidemic change for the intervention state, but they point in different directions for its different components. In some cases the regime corridor is narrowing ('blurring of regimes', mixed types); in others the corridor is being destabilized by massive privatization, often promoted by the EU.[71] How these changes affect the configuration of TRUDI is unclear, not least because the public-utilities component moves in a different direction than does the welfare state itself, not to mention education and labour market policies. It is a major challenge to even gain a synthetic or cohesive perspective of this huge, schizophrenic chunk of state activity.

The constellation as a whole – the future of TRUDI

This overview of the trajectories of change in each of TRUDI's four dimensions has provided evidence in support of the hypothesis that the once finely woven national constellation of the nation-state is, in fact, in the process of unravelling, that each thread, each dimension of the state is headed in a different direction. Even within the welfare dimension there are signs of unravelling, with substantial sectors breaking out of the geographical constraints of the national constellation, while the welfare state component remains within the jurisdiction of the nation-state. Its role as provider is shrinking, while its regulatory role in the domain of private markets increases. The rule of law appears to be moving consistently into the international arena. Although domestic institutions for guaranteeing the rule of law are still essential, they are now embedded and supported by institutions outside of the nation-state, to the extent that international lawyers like Anne-Marie Slaughter speak of 'a networked social order'.[113] The resource dimension, on the other hand, has seen relatively little transformative change; although state sovereignty has changed from a permanent to a qualified condition, TRUDI still holds firmly to its tax revenues and its monopoly on the use of force. Given such paradoxes and incongruities in the make-up of the state, it is difficult to foresee what sort of structures might ensure that political decisions are democratically legitimated.[m]

---

[m] For other general surveys of the 'state of the state' see several recent volumes edited by Joseph S. Nye and John D. Donahue[89]; Linda Weiss[127]; T. V. Paul *et al.*[92]; and by Miles Kahler and David A. Lake.[65]

What is striking, in the final analysis, is that no *standard* development for the state as such can be identified. There is no standard 'post-national constellation' in sight, no symmetrical pattern to the institutions emerging from the four unevenly unravelling dimensions, and little uniformity to the developments within them. The threads of the Golden-Age TRUDI are unravelling by different processes, at different speeds and in different directions throughout the OECD world, and they will not necessarily be rewoven into an attractive or even serviceable fabric. We cannot even predict whether TRUDI will *have* a follow-up model.

Rather, we are moving toward a situation of structural uncertainty. The citizenry that cloaked the grand corpus of the state in the frontispiece of Hobbes' *Leviathan* is turning away, floating off into the unknown international realm, or climbing down from its old refuge in search of a new haven. The most forward-looking literature of the day lacks insight into the future, discussing denationalization or post-national constellations, the road that lies behind us and what we should hang onto – but not the road we're on, nor the one that lies ahead and what we may encounter. The very term 'post-national' defines a new constellation only in the negative, as what has ceased to exist. At most, there is the broad concept of a devolution of the nation-state as a whole, proceeding on to a mediated 'state without sovereignty', similar to the federal subunits in the US (states) or Germany (*Länder*) in the 19th century.[115:26] The European Union is the only exception here, in that it offers its members the possibility, at least, of integration, sets it as a goal without forcing it or cementing it into its structure. But the EU model of a supranational state is not suitable for the whole of the OECD world, and has itself been under strain since the 1990s. In the post-TRUDI age, it seems, we are doomed to Max Weber's[125] version of politics as 'slow, strong drilling through hard boards, with a combination of passion and judgement'. We can only watch the gradual spinning, thread by thread, of individual patterns and solutions, which will eventually, with the hindsight of the 21st century, weave the fabric of a recognizable post-national politics.

Will the post-national state protect us from organized crime and transnational threats? How will this be organized? Who should have a monopoly on the legitimate use of force? Can the monopoly be broken up or shared among several tiers, and still work to ensure a stable legal framework and predictable relations? How can deviations be effectively sanctioned? How can politics be legitimated when democratically controlled decisions made at nation-state level are transferred to the international and societal level? Who should be responsible for guaranteeing social equality in a post-national constellation? How can redistribution be organized and the necessary resources secured? What, in the end, will become of our fundamental social values, such as peace and security, legal certainty and individual liberty, political self-determination and social welfare?

If we wish to conserve the values protected by the national constellation of the Golden Age, we may well need to conceive a post-national Silver Age,[119] a truly multi-lateral world order in which social responsibility is embedded at the international level. Of the two seemingly oxymoronic epigraphs that head this chapter it may be Giuseppe Tomasi di Lampedusa's semi-autobiographical novel that offers the wisest advice. *The Leopard* is the story of a Sicilian prince who attempts to protect his family's aristocratic values during the period of social and political upheaval that accompanied the unification of Italy at the end of the 19th century. Early in the novel, the prince's young nephew, caught up in the struggle for an electoral republic and trying to alert his complacent uncle to the changes taking place around them, says: 'Unless we ourselves take a hand now, they'll foist a Republic on us. If we want things to stay as they are, they'll have to change. D'you understand?'

Ironically, the island in the Mediterranean that the Lampedusa family, in reality, once owned, is now inundated with economic refugees trying to enter post-national Europe. As we shall see in this volume, this flood of humanity from failed and failing states is transforming Europe's immigration and police policies, and is just one of many changes that are challenging multi-tiered Europe. In these uncertain times, at the dawn of the 21st century, it is not an aristocratic way of life that we would protect, but the core values of our Golden-Age nation-state. And yet, one thing is abundantly clear: if we want to safeguard those values, the national constellation of institutions that guards them will have to be configured anew.

Acknowledgements

We are grateful to Susan Gaines, Berit Dencker, Vicki May and Dörthe Hauschild for transsubstantiating this text into English, with special thanks to Susan Gaines for 'reforming' it and 'finding TRUDI' in the process – and to Ulrich K. Preuß for advice on Carl Schmitt. Our thanks also to Bernhard Zangl, Bernhard Peters, Markus Jachtenfuchs, Peter Mayer, Christian Joerges and many others in the TranState research programme, who provided much of the raw material for this overview in regular discussions since 2000.

References

1. A. Alesina and E. Spolaore (2003) *The Size of Nations* (Cambridge, MA and London: MIT Press).
2. K. J. Alter (2001) *Establishing the Supremacy of European Law. The Making of an International Rule of Law in Europe* (Oxford: Oxford University Press).

3. K. J. Alter (2004) *Agents or Trustees? International Courts in their Political Context* (Bremen: University of Bremen, TranState Research Center, WP 8/04).

4. B. R. Anderson (1991) *Imagined Communities. Reflections on the Origin and Spread of Nationalism*, revised edn (London: Verso; 1st edn 1983).

5. H. Anheier and R. Wuthnow (1991) *Between States and Markets. The Voluntary Sector in Comparative Perspective* (Princeton, NJ: Princeton University Press).

6. C. K. Ansell and G. di Palma (Eds) (2004) *Restructuring Territoriality. Europe and the United States Compared* (Cambridge: Cambridge University Press).

7. D. Archibugi and D. Held (Eds) (1995) *Cosmopolitan Democracy. An Agenda for a New World Order* (Cambridge, UK: Polity).

8. K. Armingeon and M. Beyerler (Eds) (2004) *The OECD and European Welfare States* (Cheltenham, UK: Edward Elgar).

9. B. Badie (2000) *The Imported State. The Westernization of Political Order* (Stanford, CA: Stanford University Press).

10. U. Beck (2000) *What is Globalization?*, translated by P. Camiller (Cambridge, UK and Malden, MA: Polity Press); the passage cited is at p. 115 in the German original: *Was ist Globalisierung?* (Frankfurt a.M.: Suhrkamp).

11. H. J. Berman (1983) *Law and Revolution. The Formation of the Western Legal Tradition* (Cambridge, MA: Harvard University Press).

12. B. Berry (2001) *Culture and Equality. An Egalitarian Critique of Multiculturalism* (Cambridge, UK: Polity).

13. J. Bhagwati (2004) *In Defense of Globalization* (New York: Oxford University Press).

14. N. Blyth (2002) *Great Transformations. Economic Ideas and Institutional Change in the Twentieth Century* (Cambridge, UK: Cambridge University Press).

15. R. Brandt (1996) Das Titelblatt des Leviathan. In W. Kersting (Ed) *Leviathan oder Stoff, Form und Gewalt eines bürgerlichen und kirchlichen Staates* (Berlin: Akademie Verlag): 29–53.

16. H. Bredekamp (2003) *Thomas Hobbes: Der Leviathan. Das Urbild des modernen Staates und seine Gegenbilder, 1651-2001*, 2nd revised edn (Berlin: Akademie-Verlag).

17. J. A. Caporaso (2000) Changes in the Westphalian order: territory, public authority, and sovereignty. *International Studies Review*, **2**(2): 1–28.

18. J. A. Caporaso (2003) Democracy, Accountability and Rights in Supranational Governance. In M. Kahler and D. A. Lake (Eds) *Governance in a Global Economy. Political Authority in Transition* (Princeton, NJ etc.: Princeton University Press): 361–385, pp. 377ff.

19. J. Clifton, F. Cornín and D. D. Fuentes (2003) *Privatisation in the European Union: Public Enterprises and Integration* (Dordrecht, NL: Kluwer).

20. B. J. Cohen (2004) *The Future of Money* (Princeton, NJ: Princeton University Press).

21. R. A. Dahl (1994) A democratic dilemma: system effectiveness versus citizen participation. *Political Science Quarterly*, **109**(1): 23–34.

22. R. David (1985) *Major Legal Systems in the World Today. An Introduction to the Comparative Study of Law*, translated and adapted by J. E. C. Brierley (London: Stevens).

23. K. W. Deutsch (1953) The growth of nations. Some recurrent patterns of political and social integration. *World Politics*, **5**(2): 168–195.

24. U. DiFabio (1998) *Das Recht offener Staaten* (Tübingen: Mohr Siebeck), pp. 151f.

25. J. D. Donahue and J. S. Nye (Eds) (2002) *Market-Based Governance. Supply Side, Demand Side, Upside, and Downside* (Washington, DC: Brookings).

26. W. Eberlei and C. Weller (2001) *Deutsche Ministerien als Akteure von Global Governance: Eine Bestandsaufnahme der auswärtigen Beziehungen der Bundesministerien* (Duisburg: Institut für Entwicklung und Frieden an der Gerhard-Mercator-Universität): 53.

27. N. Elias (2000) *The Civilizing Process: Sociogenetic and Psychogenetic Investigations*, translated by E. Jephcott with some notes and corrections by the author and edited by E. Dunning, J. Goudsblom, and S. Mennell (Oxford, UK; Malden, MA: Blackwell Publishers).

28. G. Esping-Andersen (1990) *The Three Worlds of Welfare Capitalism* (Cambridge, UK; Princeton, NJ: Polity Press, Princeton University Press).

29. G. Esping-Andersen (1996) *Welfare States in Transition. National Adaptations in Global Economies* (London: Sage).

30. P. B. Evans, D. Rueschemeyer and T. Skocpol (Eds) (2004) *Bringing the State Back In* (Cambridge, UK: Cambridge University Press).

31. H. Feigenbaum, J. Henig and C. Hamnett (1998) *Shrinking the State. The Political Underpinnings of Privatization* (Cambridge, UK: Cambridge University Press).

32. P. Flora and A. J. Heidenheimer (Eds) (1981) *The Development of Welfare States in Europe and America* (New Brunswick, NJ: Transaction Books): 417.

33. T. M. Franck (1992) The emerging right to democratic governance. *American Journal of International Law*, **86**(1): 46–91.

34. T. Friedman (1999) *The Lexus and the Olive Tree: Understanding Globalization* (New York: Farrar Straus Giroux), title of his chapter 5, pp. 83–92.

35. G. Garrett and J. Rodden (2003) Globalization and fiscal decentralization. In M. Kahler and D. A. Lake (Eds) *Governance in a Global Economy. Political Authority in Transition* (Princeton, NJ: Princeton University Press): 87–109.

36. E. Gellner (1983) *Nations and Nationalism* (Oxford: Blackwell, last publ. 1996).

37. P. Genschel (2002) Globalization, tax competition and the welfare state. *Politics and Society*, **30**(2): 245–272.

38. P. Genschel (2002) *Steuerharmonisierung und Steuerwettbewerb in Europa. Die Steuerpolitik der EU* (Frankfurt a.M.: Campus).

39. A. Giddens (1985) *The Nation State and Violence* (Cambridge, UK: Polity Press).

40. A. Graser (2004) Sozialrecht ohne Staat? Politik und Recht unter Bedingungen der Globalisierung und Dezentralisierung. In A. Héritier, M. Stolleis and F. W. Scharpf (Eds) *European and International Regulation after the Nation State* (Baden-Baden: Nomos): 163–184.

41. D. Grimm (2003) Die Verfassung im Prozess der Entstaatlichung. In J. Allmendinger (Ed) *Entstaatlichung und soziale Sicherheit* (Opladen: Leske + Budrich): 71–93.

42. J. Habermas (2001) *The Post-national Constellation*, translated, edited and introduced by M. Pensky (Cambridge, MA: MIT Press; first published in German, 1998).

43. J. Habermas (2004) Hat die Konstitutionalisierung des Völkerrechts noch eine Chance? In J. Habermas (Ed) *Der gespaltene Westen* (Frankfurt a.M.: Suhrkamp): 113–193 (forthcoming: Cambridge, UK: Polity Press).

44. J. S. Hacker (2004) Privatizing risk without privatizing the welfare state: the hidden politics of social policy retrenchment in the United States. *American Political Science Review*, **98**(2): 243–260, see figure 1 on p. 248.

45. J. A. Hall (2003) Introduction: nation states in history. In T. V. Paul, G. J. Ikenberry and J. A. Hall (Eds) *The Nation State in Question* (Princeton, NJ: Princeton University Press): 1–26, p. 15.

46. R. B. Hall and T. J. Bierstecker (Eds) (2002) *The Emergence of Private Authority in Global Governance* (Cambridge, UK: Cambridge University Press).

47. G. W. F. Hegel (2003 [about 1800]) *Über die Reichsverfassung*, H. Maier and M. Stolleis, Eds. (München: C. H. Beck): 11.

48. D. Held (1995) *Democracy and the Global Order. From the Modern State to Cosmopolitan Governance* (Cambridge: Polity Press): 147.

49. D. Held, A. McCrew, D. Goldblatt and J. Perraton (1999) *Global Transformations: Politics, Economics and Culture* (Cambridge, UK; Stanford, CA: Polity; Stanford University Press).

50. E. P. Hennock (1997) *British Social Reform and German Precedents. The Case of Social Insurance, 1880–1914* (Oxford, UK: Clarendon Press at Oxford University Press).

51. T. Hobbes (2004 [1651]) *Leviathan, or the Matter, Forme and Power of a Commonwealth, Ecclesiastical and Civil*, edited by R. Tuck (Cambridge, UK: Cambridge University Press).

52. E. J. Hobsbawm (1990) *Nations and Nationalism since 1780. Programme, Myth, Reality* (Cambridge, UK: Cambridge University Press).

53. E. J. Hobsbawm (1994) *Age of Extremes: The Short Twentieth Century, 1914–1991* (London: Michael Joseph), section 'The Golden Age' – contrasted to the preceding section on 'The Age of Catastrophe'.

54. H. Hofmann (2004) Zur Entstehung, Entwicklung und Krise des Verfassungsbegriffs. In A. Blankenagel, I. Pernice and H. Schulze-Fielitz (Eds) *Verfassung im Diskurs der Welt. Liber Amicorum für Peter Häberle zum siebzigsten Geburtstag* (Tübingen: Mohr Siebeck): 163, 165.

55. J. Holzgrefe and R. O. Keohane (Eds) (2003) *Humanitarian Intervention: Principles, Institutions and Change* (Cambridge, UK: Cambridge University Press).

56. S. P. Huntington (2004) *Who Are We? America's Great Debate* (New York, London: Simon & Schuster, The Free Press).

57. G. J. Ikenberry (2001) *After Victory. Institutions, Strategic Restraint, and the Rebuilding of Order after Major Wars* (Princeton, NJ: Princeton University Press): 163–214.

58. R. H. Jackson (1990) *Quasi-States: Sovereignty, International Relations, and the Third World* (Cambridge, UK: Cambridge University Press).

59. A. J. Jacobson and B. Schlink (Eds) (2000) *Weimar. A Jurisprudence in Crisis* (Berkeley, CA: University of California Press): 326f.

60. G. Jellinek (1880) *Die rechtliche Natur der Staatenverträge* (Wien: Alfred Hölder; no English translation available).

61. M. Kaase and K. Newton (1995) *Beliefs in Government* (Oxford: Oxford University Press; Series *Beliefs in Government*, edited by M. Kaase, vol. 5).

62. R. A. Kagan (2001) *Adversarial Legalism. The American Way of Law* (Cambridge, MA: Harvard University Press).

63. M. Kahler and D. A. Lake (2003) Globalization and changing patterns of political authority. In M. Kahler and D. A. Lake (Eds) *Governance in a Global Economy. Political Authority in Transition* (Princeton, NJ: Princeton University Press): 412–438, int. al. p. 425.

64. M. Kahler and D. A. Lake (2003) Globalization and governance. In M. Kahler and D. A. Lake (Eds) *Governance in a Global Economy. Political Authority in Transition* (Princeton, NJ: Princeton University Press): 1–30, pp. 1ff.

65. M. Kahler and D. A. Lake (Eds) (2003) *Governance in a Global Economy. Political Authority in Transition* (Princeton, NJ: Princeton University Press).

66. I. Katznelson and H. V. Milner (2002) American political science: the discipline's state and the state of the discipline. In I. Katznelson and H. V. Milner (Eds) *Political Science. State of the Discipline* (New York: Norton): 1–32.

67. F.-X. Kaufmann (2001) Towards a theory of the welfare state. In S. Leibfried (Ed) *Welfare State Futures* (Cambridge, UK: Cambridge University Press): 15–36.

68. F.-X. Kaufmann (2003) *Varianten des Wohlfahrtsstaates: Der deutsche Sozialstaat im internationalen Vergleich* (Frankfurt a.M.: Suhrkamp).

69. R. O. Keohane (2002) *Power and Governance in a Partially Globalized World* (London: Routledge): 115–189.

70. R. O. Keohane and J. S. Nye Jr. (2000) Introduction. In J. S. Nye and J. D. Donahue (Eds) *Governance in a Globalizing World* (Washington, DC: Brookings): 1–41.

71. T. Kingreen (2003) *Das Sozialstaatsprinzip im europäischen Verfassungsverbund. Gemeinschaftsrechtliche Einflüsse auf das Recht der deutschen Krankenversicherung* (Tübingen: Mohr Siebeck).

72. S. Krasner (2004) Shared sovereignty: new institutions for collapsed and failing states. *International Security*, **29**(1) (forthcoming).

73. W. Kymlicka (1995) *Multicultural Citizenship* (Oxford, UK: The Clarendon Press at Oxford University Press).

74. G. T. di Lampedusa (1960 [1958]) *The Leopard*, translated by A. Colquhoun (London: Collins; first Italian publication 1958 with Feltrinelli Editore, Milan). The citation can be found on p. 21 of the last edition (London: The Harvill Press 1996).

75. A. Lijphart (1969) Consociational democracy. *World Politics*, **21**(2): 207–225.

76. A. Lijphart (1999) *Patterns of Democracy. Government Forms and Performance in Thirty-Six Countries* (Princeton, NJ: Princeton University Press).

77. P. H. Lindert (2004) *Growing Public*, vol. 1: *Social Spending and Economic Growth Since the 18th Century*, vol. 2: *Further Evidence. Social Spending and Economic Growth Since the 18th Century* (Cambridge, UK: Cambridge University Press).

78. C. S. Maier (2000) Consigning the twentieth century to history: alternative narratives for the modern era. *American Historical Review*, **105**(3): 807–831.

79. H. Maier (1966) *Die ältere deutsche Staats- und Verwaltungslehre (Polizeiwissenschaft). Ein Beitrag zur Geschichte der politischen Wissenschaft in Deutschland* (Neuwied: Luchterhand; last edn Munich: Deutscher Taschenbuch-Verlag 1986).

80. N. Malcolm (2002) *Aspects of Hobbes* (Oxford, UK: Oxford University Press): 200.

81. T. H. Marshall (1950) *Class, Citizenship and Social Development* (Cambridge, UK: Cambridge University Press).

82. R. Mayntz and F. W. Scharpf (1995) *Gesellschaftliche Selbstregelung und politische Steuerung* (Frankfurt a.M.: Campus).

83. W. Merkel (1999) *Systemtransformation: Eine Einführung in die Theorie und Empirie der Transformationsforschung* (Opladen: Leske + Budrich): 368.

84. H. J. Morgenthau (1973) *Politics among Nations: The Struggle for Power and Peace*, 5th edn (New York: Knopf): 600.

85. P. Nanz and J. Steffek (2004) Global governance, participation and the public sphere. *Government and Opposition*, **39**(2): 314–335.

86. J. Newman (2001) *Modernising Governance. New Labour, Policy, and Society* (London: Sage).

87. D. C. North (1990) *Institutions, Institutional Change and Economic Performance* (Cambridge, UK: Cambridge University Press).

88. J. S. Nye (2002) *The Paradox of American Power: Why the World's Only Superpower Can't Go it Alone* (New York: Oxford University Press).

89. J. S. Nye and J. D. Donahue (Eds) (2000) *Governance in a Globalizing World* (Washington, DC: Brookings).

90. H. Obinger and R. Zohlnhöfer (2005) Selling off the 'Family Silver': The Politics of Privatization in the OECD 1990–2000 (Cambridge, MA: Center for European Studies; Bremen: TranState Research Center, WP 15/2005).

91. C. Offe (2003) Demokratie und Wohlfahrtsstaat. Eine europäische Regimeform unter dem Streß der europäischen Integration. In C. Offe (Ed) *Herausforderungen der Demokratie. Zur Integrations- und Leistungsfähigkeit politischer Institutionen* (Frankfurt a.M.: Campus): 239–273, pp 251f.; abridged English version: The democratic welfare state in an integrating Europe. In M. Th. Greven and L. W. Pauly (Eds) *Democracy Beyond the State? The European Dilemma and the Emerging Global Order* (Lanham, MD: Rowman and Littlefield 2000): 63–89.

92. T. V. Paul, G. J. Ikenberry and J. A. Hall (Eeds) (2003) *The Nation State in Question* (Princeton, NJ: Princeton University Press).

93. J.-C. Pielow (2001) *Grundstrukturen öffentlicher Versorgung. Vorgaben des europäischen Gemeinschaftsrechts sowie des französischen und deutschen Rechts unter besonderer Berücksichtigung der Elektrizitätswirtschaft* (Tübingen: Mohr Siebeck).

94. G. Poggi (1990) *The State: Its Nature, Development and Prospects* (Cambridge, UK: Polity Press).

95. M. A. Pollack (2003) *The Engines of European Integration. Delegation, Agency, and Agenda Setting in the EU* (Oxford, UK: Oxford University Press).

96. W. Reinhard (1996) Power elites, state servants, ruling classes and the growth of state power. In W. Reinhard (Ed) *Power Elites and State Building* (Oxford, UK: Oxford University Press): 1–18.

97. W. Reinhard (2002) *Geschichte der Staatsgewalt. Eine vergleichende Verfassungsgeschichte von den Anfängen bis zur Gegenwart* (München: C. H. Beck, 1999).

98. W. Reinhard (2002) Man nehme den modernen Staat, haue das morsche Innere heraus. Und fertig ist die klassische Republik unserer Väter noch lange nicht: Die Geschichte der Macht zwischen Nostalgie und Aufklärung. *Frankfurter Allgemeine Zeitung*, 25 June, p. 49.

99. E. Rieger and S. Leibfried (1998) Welfare state limits to globalization. *Politics & Society*, **26**(4): 363–390.

100. E. Rieger and S. Leibfried (2003) *Limits to Globalization. Welfare States and the World Economy* (Cambridge, UK: Polity).

101. T. Risse (2004) *Transnational Governance and Legitimacy* (Berlin: Free University, unpublished manuscript): 3ff. (to appear in a volume edited by A. Benz and I. Papandopoulos with Routledge).

102. D. T. Rodgers (1998) *Atlantic Crossings. Social Politics in a Progressive Age* (Cambridge, MA: Harvard University Press).

103. S. Rokkan (1975) Dimensions of state formation and nation-building. A possible paradigm for research on variations within Europe. In C. Tilly (Ed) *The Formation of National States in Western Europe* (Princeton, NJ: Princeton University Press): 562–600.

104. C. P. R. Romano (1999) The proliferation of international judicial bodies. The pieces of a puzzle. *New York University Journal of International Law and Politics*, **31**(4): 709–751.

105. R. I. Rotberg (Ed) (2003) *State Failure and State Weakness in a Time of Terror* (Cambridge, MA; Washington, DC: World Peace Foundation; Brookings).

106. R. I. Rotberg (Ed) (2004) *When States Fail. Causes and Consequences* (Princeton, NJ: Princeton University Press).

107. F. W. Scharpf (1997) *Games Real Actors Play: Actor-centered Institutionalism in Policy Research* (Boulder, CO: Westview Press): 200–205.

108. M. G. Schmidt (2000) *Demokratietheorien. Eine Einführung*, 3rd edn (Opladen: Leske + Budrich).

109. C. Schmitt (1950) *Der Nomos der Erde im Völkerrecht des Jus Publicum Europaeum* (Köln: Greven Verlag): see 112ff. [117], 155f.; on p. 143 Schmitt notes in contrast to the oceans 'Das feste Land ist durch klare lineare Grenzen in Staatsgebiete und Herrschaftsräume aufgeteilt.' ('Solid ground is divided by clear and precise demarcations into state territories and spheres of power.') This volume is now available as *The Nomos of the Earth in the International Law of the Jus Publicum Europaeum* (New York: Telos Press 2003).

110. C. Schmitt (1985) *Political Theology. Four Chapters on the Concept of Sovereignty*, translated by G. Schwab (Cambridge, MA: MIT Press 1985; first published in German, 1922).

111. P. W. Schroeder (2004) What would Kant say? Iraq: the case against preemptive war, *The American Conservative* http://www.amconmag.com/10_21/iraq.html (accessed 19 September 2004).

112. F. G. Schupppert (2003) *Staatswissenschaft* (Baden-Baden: Nomos).

113. A. M. Slaughter (2004) *A New World Order* (Princeton, NJ: Princeton University Press).

114. H. Spruyt (1994) Institutional selection in international relations: state anarchy as order. *International Organization*, **48**(4): 527–557.

115. M. Stolleis (2004) Was kommt nach dem souveränen Nationalstaat? Und was kann die Rechtsgeschichte dazu sagen? In A. Héritier, M. Stolleis and F. W. Scharpf (Eds) *European and International Regulation after the Nation State* (Baden-Baden: Nomos): 17–30.

116. W. Streeck (1995) From market making to state building? Reflections on the political economy of European social policy. In S. Leibfried and P. Pierson (Eds) *European Social Policy: Between Fragmentation and Integration* (Washington, DC: Brookings): 389–431.

117. W. Streeck and K. Thelen (2004) Introduction. In W. Streeck and K. Thelen (Eds) *Institutional Change in Advanced Political Economies* (Cambridge, UK: Cambridge University Press): 1–39.

118. E. Suleiman (2003) *Dismantling Democratic States* (Princeton, NJ: Princeton University Press).

119. P. Taylor-Gooby (2002) The silver age of the welfare state: perspectives on resilience. *Journal of Social Policy*, **31**(4): 597–621.

120. C. Tilly (1985) War making and state making as organized crime. In P. B. Evans, D. Rueschemeyer and T. Skocpol (Eds) *Bringing the State Back In* (Cambridge, UK: Cambridge University Press): 169–191.

121. P. A. Toninelli (Ed) (2000) *The Rise and Fall of State-Owned Enterprises in the Western World* (Cambridge, UK: Cambridge University Press).

122. J. Vickers and V. Wright (Eds) (1989) *The Politics of Privatisation in Western Europe* (London: Frank Cass).

123. H. Wallace, W. Wallace and M. Pollack (Eds) (2005) *Policy-Making in the European Union* (Oxford, UK: Oxford University Press, 5th edn (forthcoming)).

124. M. Weber (1978) *Economy and Society*, 2 vols, edited by G. Roth and C. Wittlich, translated by E. Fischoff (Berkeley, CA: University of California Press; first published in German, 1921): 54–55.

125. M. Weber (1994) The profession and the vocation of politics. In M. Weber *Political Writings* (Eds P. Lassman and R. Speirs) (Cambridge, UK: Cambridge University Press; first published in German 1919): 309–369, p. 369.

126. L. Weiss (2003) Is the state being transformed by globalization? In L. Weiss (Ed) *States in the Global Economy. Bringing Democratic Institutions Back In* (Cambridge, UK: Cambridge University Press): 293–317, p. 316.

127. L. Weiss (Ed) (2003) *States in the Global Economy. Bringing Democratic Institutions Back In* (Cambridge, UK: Cambridge University Press).

128. B. Zangl and M. Zürn (2003) *Frieden und Krieg. Sicherheit in der nationalen und post-nationalen Konstellation* (Frankfurt a.M.: Suhrkamp): 250.

129. M. Zürn (1998) *Regieren jenseits des Nationalstaates. Denationalisierung und Globalisierung als Chance* (Frankfurt a.M.: Suhrkamp): 395.

130. M. Zürn (2002) From interdependence to globalisation. In W. Carlsnaes, T. Risse and B. A. Simmons (Eds) *Handbook of International Relations* (London: Sage): 235–254.

131. M. Zürn (2004) Global governance and legitimacy problems. *Government and Opposition*, **39**(2): 260–287.

132. M. Zürn and B. Zangl (Eds) (2004) *Verrechtlichung – Baustein für Global Governance?* (Bonn: Dietz Verlag).

About the Authors

Michael Zürn was Professor of Political Science at the University of Bremen, where he was one of the four founders of the 'Transformations of the State' (TranState) national Research Centre in 2003, serving as its Director until June 2004. Currently, he is the Founding Dean of the Hertie School of Governance, and Research Director of the Division for International and Transnational Relations at the Science Centre Berlin (WZB). His main areas of research are global governance and theories of international relations. Recent English language publications are: with Christian Joerges (Eds) *Law and Governance in Post-National Europe* (Cambridge, UK: Cambridge University Press, 2005); (Ed) *Globalizing Interests. Pressure Groups and Denationalization* (Albany, NY: SUNY Press, 2005).

Stephan Leibfried is Professor of Political Science at the University of Bremen, where he founded and now co-directs the Center for Social Policy Research (CeS) and the Bremen Graduate School for the Social Sciences (GSSS). He was a founder and is current Director of the TranState national Research Centre, and is, with **Herbert Obinger**, the principal investigator in its 'Welfare States in Small Open Economies' project. His main research interest is the comparative study of states and their transformation through globalization and supranationalization, with particular emphasis on the welfare state dimension. Recent English language publications are: with Herbert Obinger and Frank Castles (Eds) *Federalism and the Welfare State. New World and European Experiences* (Cambridge, UK: Cambridge University Press, 2005); with Elmar Rieger *Limits to Globalization. Welfare States and the World Economy* (Cambridge, UK: Polity, 2003); with Paul Pierson (Eds) *European Social Policy: Between Fragmentation and Integration* (Washington, DC: Brookings, 1995).

European Review, Vol. 13, Supp. No. 1, 37–52 (2005) © Academia Europaea, Printed in the United Kingdom

THE MODERN TERRITORIAL STATE: LIMITS TO INTERNATIONALIZATION OF THE STATE'S RESOURCES

2 The monopoly of legitimate force: denationalization, or business as usual?

MARKUS JACHTENFUCHS

As Max Weber and many others in his tradition have argued, the monopoly of the legitimate use of physical force is the core of the modern state. What counts here is not the frequency of the actual use of force but the fact that only the state has the legitimate right to use such force. The military and the police are the most concrete expressions of this monopoly. In recent decades, the use of the military and the police has been subject to external challenges – 'globalization' – and new ideas about police and military intervention. Although at an operational level the state retains full control over the actions of the police and military, the conditions for their use are increasingly shaped by institutionalized legitimating ideas.

The monopoly of the use of physical force – functions and form

For Max Weber,[20:54-55] the monopoly of the legitimate use of physical force – henceforth 'monopoly of force' – was the feature that distinguished the modern state from all other forms of political organization. It has two elements – the monopoly of the use of force and the legitimacy of its use. The monopolization of the means of force by a single centre is the result of a long evolution. It took centuries for the state successfully to centralise control over the means of coercion against all major rival groups. This monopolization has now become a generalized expectation. A state that is unable to uphold this monopoly is considered a 'failed state'. With respect to the legitimacy of the use of physical force, this means that only the state has a generally accepted right to use force against its citizens or against other states. Other groups or individuals may use force in exceptional cases, but their use of force is not generally considered legitimate. Except under narrowly defined circumstances, the use of force by actors other than the state is considered a crime. What is more, the criteria for the use of force are defined by the state itself. During the stages of their development, the state's criteria for the use of force became increasingly defined by legal rules and controlled by democratic processes. As a result, legitimating criteria for the use of force are not set at will by executives but are linked to the state's *demos*. The *demos*, in turn, is bound by universal human rights norms. These norms, however, are of a very general nature. Specific rules on the use of the means of force by the state vary greatly over time and across countries. But the basic idea that in the Western world the state has exclusive control over the means of force and that the legitimating criteria for its use are developed domestically has remained stable for a long time.

The use of the monopoly of force is not a field of state activity like any other. It penetrates the core of human existence even more than does taxation, since it has the potential to take away people's life and freedom. Historically, it is the first attribute of modern statehood to have emerged in a competitive process against rival forms of political organization.[17] The key function of the monopoly of force is protection against external and internal threats. This takes place in a Hobbesian world of the (potential) war of all against all. In this view, the monopoly of force is most important domestically. It pacifies domestic society and prevents civil wars or high levels of force within society. Whereas, in Hobbes' vision, the price for pacification was authoritarian rule, this price does not have to be paid after the Leviathan has been bound by constitutional rules and controlled by democratic procedures. The monopoly of force is a precondition for the emergence of complex social interactions that rely on interpersonal and intertemporal trust. Many of the institutions and organizations that make modern society so attractive for people living outside the OECD – such as health, transportation and educational systems and modern markets – require the absence of force as a standard prerequisite for action by individuals or organizations.

There is a monopoly of force within the state but not above it. Many observers believe that the world of states is not very far from the Hobbesian state of nature. Although the various schools of thought in international relations arrive at different assessments of its specific extent,[4] it is clear that the actual use of force as a means of policy is much more common in international than in domestic politics in the OECD world, and that it is much less constrained by legal norms or democratic constituencies.

The monopoly of force has developed into two distinct organizational forms: the military and the police. What is important here is not the difference in organizational structure between the two forms but the fact that both operate in different institutional contexts and are generally perceived to be separate policy fields. Research typically focuses on either the military and security policies *or* on police affairs plus internal or home affairs. But in terms of understanding the nature of the state and potential changes in it, both are two sides of the same coin.

In both cases, the normal and legitimate state of affairs is total state control. A state that is unable to uphold its monopoly of control over the army or the police, and has to accept rival private 'armies' or private 'police forces' on its territory, is considered a failed state. The same is true of complete internationalization or regionalization. A Bavarian, Scottish or Basque army would be as revolutionary as a European army. These kinds of radical changes are not likely to happen in the foreseeable future. But can we therefore conclude that, in the field of the monopoly of force, everything remains as it was? If we distinguish between the *actual use* of the means of force and the *legitimation* of such means, important changes become apparent. They become even clearer when we distinguish between 'classical interstate wars' and 'new wars' in the field of military affairs and 'terrorism' and 'organized crime' in the field of police affairs. These concepts will be explained below.

Challenges to the monopoly

In the core states of Western Europe, the prime direction of change is towards internationalization. Privatization, the only realistic alternative, is much more important outside the OECD world than inside it.[14] In order to understand the significance of potential changes, their direction and their impact on the state, it is important to have analytical categories that can accommodate the huge variety of particular processes and events taking place in the field of military and police affairs.

In order to arrive at such an analytical framework, we may distinguish between problem structure and ideas. The underlying theoretical model argues that state actors are responsive to the changing nature of problems, but that the perception of the nature of these problems and the measures to be taken very much depend on systems of ideas. To put it more formally: ideas are intervening variables between problem structure and action.

Problem structure

We can assume that the monopoly of force is a means to solve functional problems, in other words, a means of governance. Narrowly defined, the problem to be solved is internal and external pacification. Over the last 30 years or so, the two most important causal factors appear to be internationalization and the stronger involvement of societal actors, i.e. privatization.

For many authors, the end of the Cold War represents a watershed in the field of *military affairs*. Before this point, the balance-of-power logic between the superpowers dominated the logic of international conflict. The wars that took place in the decades preceding the end of the Cold War, or, more importantly, the wars that could potentially have taken place but were prevented, were classical interstate wars and in many cases heavily influenced by the underlying rivalry between East and West. Classical interstate wars are wars fought by regular armies under the tight control of a unified political leadership. They presuppose a functioning monopoly of force. After the end of the Cold War, the nature of conflict changed. Ethnic and nationalist mobilization seemed to replace the rivalry between capitalist democracies and communist systems. In addition, the nature of the actors changed. Regular armies under state control were increasingly replaced by private armies, mercenaries, guerrilla groups and the like. These groups were sometimes ideologically motivated and under the strict control of an undisputed leadership, but more often their internal coherence was rather low. In general, they cannot be considered instruments of a leadership acting strategically in the pursuit of certain goals.

Those bold statements are clearly idealised abstractions from a much more complex reality. However, the trend is clear. Since the end of the Cold War, policy-makers in the OECD world have been faced with, in Mary Kaldor's words, 'new wars',[12] which are characterized by shifting and fluid conflict lines, varying degrees of participation and low degrees of strategic action. Now, there is typically no functioning monopoly of force.

In the field of *police affairs*, organized crime has entered the scene. The very concept of organized crime is rather recent. Although there are still doubts as to whether it describes a clearly defined phenomenon, the concept has come to be widely accepted and used.[6] The new challenge on the agenda is not only that crime is organized, it is also its transnational reach. Criminal organizations increasingly operate across state borders in an attempt to escape state control. One major field of activity is drug trafficking. The second major field of transnational criminal organizations is terrorism. Simply put, in the 1970s, German terrorists attacked German politicians and industrialists in order to change the German political system and appeal to the German public. The same applies to French and Italian terrorists. Contacts between the national groups existed, and West European terrorists went to training camps in the Near East. However, this is very different from the current situation in which the composition of terrorist groups is much more multinational and their operational base almost global.

A further characteristic of the current problem structure is the blurring of the boundaries between the different fields of activity. Terrorists participate in large-scale drug trafficking in order to finance their operations. They are also players in the new wars and use war-torn countries as bases of operations, as do transnational criminal organizations. Based on the outcomes of terrorist actions, large-scale transnational terrorism is now considered an issue of international security and not just of criminal and police affairs. This development, while widely known since 9/11, began even earlier.[21] The strict division between the competencies of the military and the police is becoming more fluid because the current problem structure does not seem to follow this neat distinction.

Finally, states are losing control over their borders independently of the development of transnational crime, conflict, and terrorism. The most important cause of the loss of border control is European integration and the related attempt to create an area without internal borders. Whereas the literature on globalization often considers a state's loss of control over its borders and over what is happening within its territory, a result of social processes beyond state control, or at best an unintended consequence of state policies, the case is different in the EU. Here, the abolition of border controls is an explicit policy goal intended to increase transborder interactions. Conflicts over the desirability of this goal, and over its potential consequences, have led to the formation of the so-called Schengen Group, a sub-system within the EU named after the small city in Luxembourg where the initial agreement was reached. Over the years, the Schengen countries have gradually abolished border controls. By doing so, they have explicitly given away border controls as a traditional means to fight crime, or at least to contain it within a state's borders.

However, the general trend of an increased mobility of persons applies to members as well as to non-members of the Schengen Group within the EU. The best illustration of this is the UK, which has consistently refused to participate in the Schengen Group on the grounds that its island location constitutes a natural border that is easy to control. However, with 90 million people entering the country each year (or almost 250,000 every day), the idea of effective border controls appears to be more of a symbolic reference in political discourse than an empirical reality.[16]

Ideas

However, hard facts do not directly influence the behaviour of political actors. Facts do not speak for themselves. They are not even perceived by everybody to the same degree: most of us (happily) do not directly perceive transnational crime or new wars, and many of us are not even indirectly affected by these phenomena. Individual and corporate actors are faced with a complex reality; with an overload of constantly changing factual information. They use systems of ideas in order to sort and interpret this information, to make sense of it and to decide on appropriate strategies. These systems of ideas contain empirical, normative, and symbolic elements.[10]

In the field of *military affairs*, the post-Second World War consensus on state sovereignty and its twin concept of non-intervention is eroding. Although the concept of sovereignty has always been much more a normative concept than an empirical one, or at least more a Weberian ideal type than an inductively generated description of reality, the present debate goes well beyond the usual mismatch of reality with an ideal type. The UN Security Council, the only body that is entitled by the UN Charter to authorize the use of force against a state, has repeatedly agreed to military interventions by groups of states into the domestic affairs of another state. In a strict reading of the UN Charter, this is clearly prohibited. For this reason, the Security Council has always legitimated such interventions with reference to a reasoning that is acceptable on the basis of the UN Charter, arguing that the conflict at stake constitutes a threat to international peace and security. But were the events in, for example, Somalia, terrible as they were, really a threat to anybody outside the country, as suggested by the reference to *international* peace and security?

The idea which helps both to interpret the significance of many of these new wars and to direct and justify action is the concept of humanitarian intervention.[9] According to this concept, state sovereignty does not have to be respected at any price. Human rights are rising in importance and moving towards equal footing with the norm of state sovereignty. In this view, large-scale violations of human rights justify a violation of the territorial integrity of a state. The concept of humanitarian intervention faces a number of difficulties that were avoided by the older concept of absolute state sovereignty: what is the threshold for an intervention? How can one avoid the abuse of humanitarian intervention for the material or power interests of some states?

Closely linked to the idea of humanitarian intervention is the idea of 'failed states'. As in the case of humanitarian intervention, the concept is still evolving and clear operational definitions that would allow one to establish beyond reasonable doubt that a state is a failed state are still lacking. Basically, failed states are characterized by a lack of governmental authority. A failed state may not even have an operational government. Hence, it can neither enforce internal peace nor assume its international responsibilities. As it is not a sovereign state, humanitarian intervention cannot violate the norm of sovereignty. In the field of military affairs, we are thus witnessing a slow shift from one set of ideas, the sovereignty of intact states and non-intervention in them, to another set, graduated sovereignty of failed states and limited humanitarian intervention in them.

The situation is much less clear in the field of *police affairs*. The development of the police was closely linked to the emergence and development of modern states.[2,13] As a result, police organization and the basic norms governing its operation have taken very different development paths in different countries. Since a low degree of denationalization of the problem structure prevailed most of the time, police systems in Western states developed in parallel but without much interaction. Only with the beginning of denationalization after the Second World War, and its increase since the 1970s, have concepts developed at the international level that started to have an impact on national police systems.

The strongest pressure, in terms of norms governing police action, has had to do with problem definitions. Each country has developed highly particular conceptions of what constitutes a crime and a criminal. The differences among countries are strongest with regard to terrorism – a person might be considered a celebrated freedom fighter in one country and a ruthless criminal in another. Effective international cooperation in combating terrorism does, however, require a definition of terrorism. September 11 constitutes a strong push in that direction and makes it more difficult for individual countries to resist emerging ideas about what is a terrorist or a terrorist attack. The situation is similar in the field of organized crime. As in the field of terrorism, international institutions have constantly worked on more narrowly defining particular types of organized crime, such as drug trafficking. In contrast to the field of military affairs, where one can observe a large-scale move away from a strict interpretation of sovereignty and non-intervention that goes beyond the narrow realm of state executives, conceptual thinking about terrorism and organized crime is largely restricted to civil servants and police experts. As a consequence, the ideas currently discussed are much more tightly coupled to concrete problems and much less bold in the field of police affairs than in the field of military affairs.

Changes of the monopoly

Military

In order to analyse potential changes in the monopoly of force in the field of military affairs, it is useful to distinguish between classical interstate wars and new wars, including civil wars. Interstate wars are characterized by the predominance of state-controlled military forces. For the realist school of international relations, represented here by Kenneth N. Waltz,[19] interstate war is an existential challenge to the state because its physical survival is at stake. In such a situation, realists claim, states do everything they can in order to assure their survival. The only external influence they respect is superior power. International norms will only be followed as long as states do not perceive them to be against their interests. This is the Hobbesian vision of the war of all against all with no restrictions on the use of force.

The liberal school of international relations acknowledges that norms at the international level are weak when compared with domestic norms, and that they are frequently broken during wartime. However, liberal theorists see the development of the international law of war during the last few centuries as an evolutionary process, in which rights and obligations in the field of warfare have been defined in an increasingly precise and constraining manner. Despite the many breaches of international law, this process of legalization is, on the whole, matched by actual behaviour. If this assessment is true, the use of the monopoly of force is subject to a very slow process of restriction by the international law of war.

As in most other fields of international politics, there has been a strong increase in the institutionalization and legalization of classical warfare since the Second World War. The UN Charter prohibits the use of force except for self-defence. Everybody knows that this norm is often violated. But the effectiveness of a norm cannot be measured exclusively by the degree of compliance with it. The impact of a norm is more usefully measured by the effect it has on behaviour in a broader sense and on the justification discourse. Many states have violated the provisions of the UN Charter. In an era in which information is quickly available at a small cost for citizens, organizations and governments, these violations of generally accepted norms require a particular effort for legitimation. Norm violations may be taken up by social movements, NGOs and domestic opposition groups. It is true that strong states can ignore all this, and it is also true that they have frequently done so in the past. All other things being equal, however, the use of the monopoly of force for interstate war requires greater efforts for legitimation today than a century ago.

This becomes even clearer when we look at more specific aspects of the use of the monopoly of force, namely the use of particular weapons. The non-proliferation regime, the convention on chemical weapons and the ban on landmines, for example, delegitimate the production, possession, or use of certain types of weapons. States are thus no longer free to use the weapons of their choice. Again, states can produce, possess or even use delegitimated weapons, but at a higher cost.

In Europe, the system of norms and institutions regulating the use of the means of force is more concrete and more demanding than the general and universal UN-based system. Article 5 of the NATO treaty stipulates the obligation of all members to help in case of an attack against any one of them, and includes the use of force as a means for doing so. This falls short of the plan for an integrated European army, which failed in 1954, but goes considerably beyond a purely defensive alliance in which members participate on a strictly voluntary basis and are entirely free to determine their policies.

Since the end of the Cold War, security institutions in Europe have changed profoundly. This is true for NATO as well as for the EU. Apart from its traditional function as an organization for collective defence, NATO has developed into a security management institution,[18] an institution that is directed inward. Its main purpose is to ensure that member states will not use force against each other. This is achieved by creating institutionalized ties among the member states at all levels, from broad political statements to exchanges in terms of military strategy and equipment, and to common manoeuvres. As a result, the anarchical international system in the North Atlantic area is slowly being transformed into a much more institutionalized system, where trust and information about other states' capabilities and intentions, and the credibility of their commitments to joint policies and rules of behaviour is high. States retain ultimate control over the use of their military machinery, but they credibly communicate, both to other states and to their domestic constituencies, that they will not use it against NATO partners.

In addition, NATO has specified the terms and conditions for the use of military forces in cases that do not fall under the category of defence proper. This development is a response to the denationalization of problems such as new wars and failed states, the proliferation of weapons of mass destruction, and transnational terrorism. Although NATO members are free to use their military in cases not covered by these types of 'out-of-area' operations, this is unlikely to happen, especially for member states without a tradition of military intervention. In areas where they believe unilateral action to be ineffective, member states have formally pooled their sovereignty in the field of military power. A pooling of a part of the monopoly of force is synonymous with the joint exercise of these powers within an institutional framework. It is not to be confused with delegation. In the case of delegation, states temporarily or permanently surrender certain powers to an independent institution. In the case of the monopoly of force, this would amount to the creation of a supranational European army under a single command and political leadership. Such a situation is far away, if at all realistic. But in order to ascertain changes in the legitimation, control and exercise of the monopoly of force, it is useful to think in terms of a continuum instead of clearly defined alternatives.

The EU is moving in the same direction by restricting its activity to the field of new security issues.[8] Its justification for this follows the standard pattern in international cooperation: states cooperate when they are unable to solve perceived problems alone. However, this cooperation is not ad hoc but strictly rule-based. The conditions and forms of the use of the means of force are precisely defined. EU member states thus have jointly defined criteria for the use of the means of force in some areas. These norms legitimate the use of force by referring to specific circumstances and suggesting concrete measures while delegitimating others. The institutions that the EU has developed in order to deal with military affairs only pool sovereignty, they do not delegate it. Nevertheless, they release the use of force from complete state control.

Two unresolved issues remain with respect to legitimating the use of force on the international level. The first is the debate between those who prefer it to be regulated on a case-by-case basis, either by decisions of the UN Security Council or with reference to specific international treaties, and those who advocate a universal law compelling intervention (*jus cogens*), which specifies the rights, or even the duty, of states to intervene in particular cases irrespective of Security Council decisions or explicit treaties. Those who argue for a decisionist approach and for a strong role for the UN Security Council advocate a precautionary principle against the misuse of force for anything other than humanitarian purposes. If a resolution authorizing the use of force finds a majority in the Security Council, including the five veto powers, it is unlikely to be motivated by particularistic national interests. The proponents of a *jus cogens* of intervention share this concern about the misuse of force, but do not believe the solution to this problem lies in making decisions dependent upon the interests of Security Council members alone.

The second issue is the question of universal versus regional legitimation. Universal legitimation means legitimation by the UN Security Council. The advantage of this solution is its universal acceptance and the strong bias against misuse. The disadvantage is the danger of non-decision. China's reluctance towards intervention in Kosovo may have been motivated by a simple calculation of egoistic interest – avoiding a precedent for Tibet – with no relationship to the issue at hand. Regional organizations, such as NATO, are more homogeneous and closer to the events. They may be better informed and more efficient in decision-making. They may also be able to express a regional normative consensus. However, the development of regional subsystems of legitimate intervention creates the danger of this subsystem being dominated by the interests of one or a few powerful states.

Police

In the field of police affairs, important changes have occurred since the 1970s. These changes relate both to changes in the real world and to changes in the realm of ideas. Both factors have led to substantial changes in the way states use the police. This must be viewed in a broader context. Functional incentives for cooperation have existed for many decades. Criminals have tended to escape prosecution by using the exit option and hiding in other states. Criminals who have been both able and willing to organize such an escape, and to shoulder the high costs associated with it, have usually been of a different type than local thieves. Transnational crime is a costly activity. It only pays off if the rewards are considerable and the costs acceptable. This is the case, for example, with terrorism and with activities yielding very high profits, such as the drug trade. Without wanting to push an economic explanation of transnational crime too far, it is clear that transnational crime is comparatively hard to situate and difficult to classify. It is, in any case, not a broad phenomenon but by and large restricted to certain types of activities, which have not dramatically changed over the decades.

Formalized cooperation in the field of police affairs has rather a long history. Interpol was founded as early as 1923.[1] It is a prototype of the organization one would expect in a situation where states want to retain as much freedom of action as possible without foregoing the advantages of international cooperation. Interpol was and is an organization with a low profile, dominated by technical expertise and devoted mainly to the exchange of information. It does not restrict the rights or the ability of states to act unilaterally or through channels other than Interpol. From the perspective of Western states, its universality – most of the world's states are members – is not only an asset but also severely restricts the potential for more intensive cooperation. This is because cooperation in a field that is closely linked to civic liberties and constitutional issues seems inconceivable in an organization in which a large part of the members do not even meet basic democratic standards. In addition, the heterogeneity of membership and the ensuing diversity of preferences have made cooperation difficult.

Terrorism has proved to be a particularly difficult case. On the one hand, terrorism has long been regarded as a phenomenon that concerns more than one state. Politically motivated assassinations of politicians have affected states in their roles as states. The goal of terrorists is the destruction of the prevailing political order in a given state. Hence, they are the incarnation of the public enemy. Given the high stakes involved, terrorists have tended to move across state boundaries, and in recent years we have seen a quantitative and qualitative increase in the degree of transnationalization. The fact that terrorists have often been supported directly or indirectly by other states that shared their hostility towards the political systems of the target state has made international cooperation particularly difficult.

From the perspective of the individual states that are victims of terrorist activities, international cooperation is necessary in order to fight terrorism effectively. First and foremost, this requires agreement among cooperating states on a definition of terrorism. Joint action against terrorism can only be effective and legitimate on the basis of such a commonly agreed problem definition. However, arriving at such a universally agreed general definition has proved to be extremely difficult. The story begins with an effort undertaken by the League of Nations in the 1930s[5] and continues to the present day. The heterogeneity of state preferences has often led to irreconcilable positions, particularly in the 1970s, when – in addition to the East–West conflict – the Third World had a strong political role and tended to object to proposals by Western states. As a result, cooperation has proceeded in an ad hoc manner, often in the aftermath of a major terrorist attack. This ad hoc cooperation has not resulted in an incremental emergence of a more general definition of terrorism, but in finding majorities for the endorsement of international action against terrorism on a case-by-case basis.

The situation is different in the field of drugs. Consensus about the nature of the precise definition of the threat has been easier to achieve. As a result, there now exists quite a comprehensive drug control regime under the auspices of the United Nations.[3] This regime not only defines the nature of the problem, and thus legitimizes police action, it also delegates authority over monitoring and control to UN bodies. As in the case of terrorism, there is no general definition of drugs. Unlike the terrorism case, however, this lack of a universally agreed upon general definition does not lead to deadlock because cooperation can proceed on the basis of a list of incriminating substances that can easily be amended.

The relative weakness of universal international cooperation in the field of police affairs and the widely shared perception of an increase in transnational criminal activity in the broadest sense, have led to the emergence of regional cooperation within Europe. Here, the trend is one of rapidly increasing scope and depth of international cooperation. More permanent patterns of cooperation started in the 1970s on a purely intergovernmental basis, explicitly outside the framework of the European Union treaties. The groups established – TREVI, the Pompidou group, and others – started off as arenas for information exchange and informal policy coordination among police experts. The nature of their proceedings was so confidential that little serious empirical research is available. Often, these groups were considered police conspiracies against citizens' rights.

The situation changed with the Maastricht Treaty, which came into force in 1993. Police affairs were now part of the formal Treaty structure and an officially acknowledged agenda of the EU. As a matter of fact, this area has proved to be one of the growth areas of European policy-making since the 1990s. It became further institutionalized in subsequent intergovernmental agreements. In several steps, the European Police Office (Europol) became operational.[15] This institutional growth has started to affect the exercise of the monopoly of force in the member states in important ways.

At first glance, Europol is not much different from Interpol. Both organizations are mainly concerned with information exchange. However, the intensity of cooperation within Europol is much higher than within Interpol. The amount of information exchanged and the quality of the information is much higher. Europol, which cooperates in justice and home affairs in general, is faced with the same problems as Interpol regarding cooperation in a broader international framework: its member states differ greatly in terms of the definition of crimes, the principles and content of penal law, the patterns of police organization, and the rights of citizens in relation to the police. A centralized monopoly of force at the EU level is not even on the horizon. Europol is not equivalent to the US FBI in that it has no executive power. Only the police forces of a member state can arrest citizens of that state. What, then, is the significance of the enormous amount of legislative and policy-making activity in this area in the last decade? How can it be explained?

In order to understand the changes happening to the monopoly of force in the field of police affairs in the EU member states, it is important to avoid a zero-sum logic between the EU level and its member states. Powers and competencies acquired by European institutions are not necessarily lost to the same degree by the member states. In the EU, the state monopoly of force is becoming embedded within an increasingly dense set of institutions.

These institutions legitimate state action in practically all relevant fields of transnational crime, including terrorism and drugs. This has led to a convergence of views on what the crimes in question are actually about and may, over time, lead to a convergence of approaches towards these issues within member states. Concrete action has also been undertaken. With the creation of 'joint investigation teams', EU member states have an instrument that allows intensive cooperation among two or more member states, even at the operative level, but falls short of allowing 'foreign' police forces to act autonomously on a given member state's soil. The European Arrest Warrant is in the process of being implemented in a number of member states. Like joint investigation teams, the European Arrest Warrant falls short of an automatic permission for courts or police forces in one member state to act in another. The significance of the European Arrest Warrant lies in the fact that in the decision about whether or not somebody is to be arrested and sent to another signatory country, political discretion is much reduced in favour of a legal examination of the case. The scope of the European Arrest Warrant is defined by a list of offences and, as in the case of the UN drugs regime, this list can be amended rather easily. As a result, member states are finding their discretionary powers gradually reduced.

In sum, cooperation in the field of police affairs is much more intensive in the EU than within the UN. This may not be surprising, as the former is much more homogeneous than the latter. But why do we find cooperation at all in an area that touches the core of the democratic constitutional state and reduces state autonomy in this field?

The first reason is the classical explanation for international cooperation. Faced with increasing problems of border control and policy externalities, states choose to cooperate. They pool sovereignty, or delegate it to independent institutions, in order to increase policy efficiency. In the case of the EU, the rise in transboundary criminal activity is not only an external factor beyond the control of EU member states, it is to a large extent the result of the explicit decision to eliminate borders within the EU. Thus, cooperation in police affairs looks like a classical case of spillover: integrationist steps in one policy field create externalities and pressures for integration in other areas.

Second, this spillover logic may have been supplemented by prevailing ideas about how to construct a European political order.[11] The German government in particular has for some time argued that, in its view, the EU should not be restricted to market-making institutions, but also possess competencies in the field of military and police affairs. The British and French governments have been much less enthusiastic about European cooperation in the field of police affairs. However, the Commission's concept of creating an area of freedom, security and justice, as part of a larger strategy to supplement the internal market with something closer to citizens' concerns, was acceptable to them. The Commission thus served as a facilitator of potential agreement by providing concepts that made a solution acceptable to all participants.

Without entering into too much speculation about the future of police cooperation in the EU, it seems safe to state that the present trend is towards increased institutionalization and increased legalization, propelled by concerns about democratic accountability and the protection of fundamental rights.

Conclusion

Within the OECD world, there is no alternative institution to the state as the holder of the monopoly of force. Internationalization – and privatization, which has not been covered here – have an impact on the state's monopoly of force, but do not fundamentally challenge it. Are we thus still living in the ideal-typical Weberian state, with globalization changing everything but the monopoly of force? Such a conclusion would be premature. Instead, a number of summary observations may be made.

First, the monopoly of force is not *transferred* to international institutions but increasingly *embedded* within such institutions. What is new, with respect to earlier periods, is both the scope and the depth of this embeddedness.

Second, as a consequence of this process of embedding, the conditions for the use of the monopoly of force and the legitimating reasons for its use are increasingly *determined* by *international* institutions. States are slowly losing their autonomy for justifying the use of the monopoly of force.

Third, the loss of autonomy with respect to legitimating the use of the monopoly of force must not be confused with a loss of autonomy in its actual use. Within the OECD world, the police and military are *still under the tight control of the state*.

Fourth, the *actual use* of the police and military is increasingly characterized by the search for efficient and, simultaneously, autonomy-preserving *forms of intergovernmental cooperation*. When compared with supranational institutions of market integration in the EU, the level of cooperation in the field of police affairs – and to a lesser degree in military affairs – seems weak. When compared with the ideal of exclusive control over the police and the military, it is quite far advanced. The concerns of some groups and political parties about democratic control and the protection of fundamental rights are an indication that this assessment is also shared in political discourse.

In the long run, we might, relying on Norbert Elias, interpret this process as a part of the grand civilizing process.[7] In this view, the increasing embeddedness of the state into an institutional framework it cannot exclusively control would be a sign of progress. But this discussion is beyond the scope of this article.

Acknowledgement

Comments and suggestions by Stephan Leibfried are greatfully acknowledged.

References

1. M. Anderson (1989) *Policing the World. Interpol and the Politics of International Police Co-operation* (Oxford: The Clarendon Press at Oxford University Press).
2. D. H. Bayley (1975) The police and political development in Europe. In C. Tilly (Ed) *The Formation of National States in Western Europe* (Princeton, NJ: Princeton University Press): 328–379.
3. H. Busch (1999) *Polizeiliche Drogenbekämpfung – eine internationale Verstrickung* (Münster: Westfälisches Dampfboot).
4. M. W. Doyle (1997) *Ways of War and Peace. Realism, Liberalism, and Socialism* (New York: Norton).
5. M. D. Dubin (1991) *International Terrorism. Two League of Nation Conventions, 1934–1937* (Millwood: Kraus International Publications).
6. A. Edwards and P. Gill (Eds) (2003) *Transnational Organized Crime. Perspectives on Global Security* (London: Routledge).
7. N. Elias (2000) *The Civilizing Process. Sociogenetic and Psychogenetic Investigations* (Oxford: Blackwell).
8. A. Forster and W. Wallace (2000) Common foreign and security policy. From shadow to substance? In H. Wallace and W. Wallace (Eds) *Policy-Making in the European Union*, 4th edn (Oxford: Oxford University Press): 461–491.
9. J. L. Holzgrefe and R. O. Keohane (Eds) (2003) *Humanitarian Intervention. Ethical, Legal, and Political Dilemmas* (Cambridge: Cambridge University Press).
10. M. Jachtenfuchs (1996) *International Policy-Making as a Learning Process? The European Union and the Greenhouse Effect* (Aldershot: Avebury).
11. M. Jachtenfuchs, T. Diez and S. Jung (1998) Which Europe? Conflicting models of a legitimate European political order. *European Journal of International Relations*, **4**(4): 409–445.
12. M. Kaldor (2001) *New and Old Wars. Organized Violence in a Global Era* (Cambridge: Polity Press).
13. W. Knöbl (1998) *Polizei und Herrschaft im Modernisierungsprozeß. Staatsbildung und innere Sicherheit in Preußen, England und Amerika 1700–1914* (Frankfurt a.M.: Campus).
14. A. Leander (2002) Global ungovernance. mercenaries and the control over violence, COPRI Working Paper 4/2002 (Copenhagen: Copenhagen Peace Research Institute).

15. J. D. Occhipinti (2003) *The Politics of EU Police Cooperation. Toward a European FBI?* (Boulder, CO: Lynne Rienner).
16. The United Kingdom Parliament (retrieved 14 July 2004), http://www.publications.parliament.uk/pa/cm200102/cmhansrd/vo011211/text/11211w13.htm.
17. C. Tilly (Ed) (1975) *The Formation of National States in Western Europe* (Princeton, NJ: Princeton University Press).
18. C. A. Wallander and R. O. Keohane (1999) Risk, threat, and security institutions. In H. Haftendorn, R. O. Keohane and C. A. Wallander (Eds) *Imperfect Unions. Security Institutions over Time and Space* (Oxford: Oxford University Press): 21–47.
19. K. N. Waltz (1979) *Theory of International Politics* (New York: McGraw-Hill).
20. M. Weber (1978) *Economy and Society. An Outline of Interpretive Sociology* (Berkeley, CA and London: University of California Press).
21. P. Williams (1994) Transnational criminal organizations and international security. *Survival*, **36**(1): 96–113.

About the Author

Markus Jachtenfuchs is Professor of Political Science at the International University Bremen. His main fields of research are international governance and European integration. In his research project on 'The internationalisation of the monopoly on the legitimate use of force', that is part of the Research Centre 'Transformations of the State' (TranState), he works with the researchers **Jörg Friedrichs**, **Eva Herchinger** and **Holger Stritzel**. Recent English-language publications include Governance and institutional development, in: A. Wiener and T. Diez (Eds) *European Integration Theory* (Oxford: Oxford University Press, 2004): 97–115 (with Beate Kohler-Koch); The governance approach to European integration. *Journal of Common Market Studies*, **39**(2) (2001): 221–240.

European Review, Vol. 13, Supp. No. 1, 53–71 (2005) © Academia Europaea, Printed in the United Kingdom

3 Globalization and the transformation of the tax state

PHILIPP GENSCHEL

How does globalization affect taxation? The academic wisdom is split on this question. Some argue that globalization spells the beginning of the end of the national tax state, while others maintain that it hardly constrains tax policy choices at all. This paper comes down in the middle. It finds no indication that globalization will fatally undermine the national tax state, but still maintains that national tax policy is affected in a major way. The effect is not so much to force change upon the tax state as to reduce its freedom for change. Comparing the first three decades of the 20th century to the last three decades, it is remarkable how much change and innovation there was then and how much incrementalism and stasis there is today.

National taxes and global markets

Taxes are monetary levies imposed by governments on persons or other entities. They are compulsory and unrequited: taxpayers are legally obliged to pay taxes and cannot expect to receive any specific benefit in return, such as, for example, a piece of public property or a particular health care treatment in a public hospital. Taxes are not fees. While taxes are presumably collected for the sake of the public good, the liability of the individual taxpayer is independent of the personal utility she derives from that good. This is what makes taxes such a nuisance for the taxpayer and such a versatile source of finance for the state.

Over past few centuries, taxes have become the main basis of governmental revenue. The modern state is, in Joseph A. Schumpeter's words, a 'tax state'.[27] It is sovereign because (and to the extent that) it disposes of tax revenue. The availability of tax revenue determines what the state can and cannot do, how many civil servants it can hire, how many services it can deliver, how modestly or ambitiously it can define its goals, and how effectively it can impose its authority domestically and internationally. In a very real sense, therefore, 'the revenue of a state is the state',[3] which in turn implies that public finance is 'the key'[11] to understanding what the state is and how it changes.

As even a cursory look confirms, the history of public finance is one of misery and drama. Rare are the moments of fiscal abundance and ease. Most of the time, finance ministers feel strapped for cash and are barely able to make public ends meet. Fiscal stress is nothing unusual; it is the normal state of affairs in public finance. What varies over time, however, is the interpretation of where the stress is coming from. During the 1990s, a lot of the blame went to globalization. The opening of national economies was feared to undermine the ability of national governments to subject their economies to tax. Tax sovereignty seemed to evaporate in global markets.

The crisis has been long in coming. The liberalization of the world economy has been going on for almost 50 years now, and for almost equally as long there has been unease and concern about its negative implications for tax policy. The purpose of this essay is to trace the evolution of these concerns, and to analyse how national tax states have coped with them. The following section briefly summarizes the characteristics of national taxation systems before the onset of deep globalization in the 1980s and 1990s. The next section analyses how these characteristics were challenged by globalization, and a subsequent section looks at tax policy reactions to these challenges. The paper concludes with a brief consideration of the future of the tax state in a global economy.

Taxes in national containment

The tax systems of OECD countries are products and symptoms of economic closure. Their main components – taxes on private and corporate income, consumption taxes on goods and services, and social security contributions – were conceived between 1910 and 1970 when national borders were relatively closed to economic transactions. The progressive income tax made its breakthrough in the huge fiscal expansion during the First World War. Taxes on general consumption were introduced on a broad front during the interwar years, when first inflation and then the depression cut into income tax revenues. Corporate income taxes made their debut at around the same time and, after the Second World War, developed into a standard tool of economic policy in OECD countries. The post-war period also saw a massive expansion of social security contributions to finance the build-up of the welfare state.[14,29]

All these taxes were introduced in a context of clearly separated national markets. Trade barriers restricted international trade, and capital controls limited the international movement of capital. Tax policy was a purely national affair. There was no international spillover because all effects were limited to the national market, and there was little escape from the national market. Tax policy was all voice and little exit. In those unusual cases where taxpayers had a viable chance to exit, the sentiment was not to adjust taxes in order to reduce the incentive for exit, but to increase the road blocks on the escape route in order to make exit impossible. The two main protagonists of the Bretton Woods negotiations, Harry

Dexter White and John Maynard Keynes, were united on this point: states need the freedom to increase capital controls when necessary to prevent capital flight. According to Eric Helleiner, they were motivated by a desire to prevent the evasion of taxes and 'the burdens of social legislation'.[12]

Behind the wall of capital controls and trade barriers, the tax state had a notably 'good 20th century'.[13] It grew vigorously: in the major industrial countries, the tax take as a share of Gross Domestic Product (GDP) rose from an average of around 10% or less before the First World War to around 30% fifty years later, and almost 40% at century's end. This expansion was made possible by radical innovation and modernization. While, in the late 19th century, most government revenues derived from customs, excises and property taxes, by the middle of the 20th century personal income taxes, corporation taxes, social security contributions, and general consumption taxes were already the main revenue raisers by far. Within 50 years, the tax state was put on an entirely new basis. In addition, the tax state, during the period of national containment, enjoyed the liberty to develop in specifically national ways. The total tax take and the tax mix varied widely. Some countries relied heavily on indirect taxes, while others leaned mainly on direct taxes. Ireland, for example, derived more than 50% of its total tax revenues in 1970 from taxes on consumption while the same share in Luxembourg stood at less than 15%. Taxes that were popular in some countries were hardly used in others. For example, while social security contributions amounted to more than 13% of Dutch GDP in 1970, they raised barely 1.5% of GDP in Denmark. The level of total taxation also varied widely. In 1970, total tax revenue amounted to more than 40% of GDP in Denmark and less than 20% in Japan.

The challenges of globalization

The size and heterogeneity of national tax systems were no cause for concern so long as the fences separating national markets were up. When these fences began to come down, however, cross-national differences in taxation started to give politicians headaches. There were four problems in particular that governments worried about: competitiveness, tax evasion and avoidance, tax competition, and the transnationalization of the tax base. Of course, these problems are not independent of one another; rather, they embody different aspects of the same syndrome – national taxation in a context of international markets. However, since they developed at different times and at different speeds, and triggered different political reactions, it is useful to consider them separately.

Competitiveness

The 1950s witnessed the first cautious reductions of trade barriers. At this time it was the implications of national taxes for the international competitiveness of national industries that most concerned tax policy makers. The reasoning was simple: if domestic taxes imposed a higher tax burden on domestic producers than foreign taxes imposed on foreign competitors, then, in the absence of offsetting customs regulations or quotas, domestic producers were at a competitive disadvantage. Their costs of production were higher with potentially negative consequences for profitability, output, and employment, and, indirectly, for tax revenues.

The history of the European Coal and Steel Community provides a showcase example of these concerns. Shortly after the Community had, with much fanfare, opened its Common Market for Coal and Steel, a fierce dispute erupted between Germany and France over trade and taxation. Germany charged high company but low turnover taxes, while France charged low company and high turnover taxes. The German government suspected that this difference in taxation worked to the disadvantage of German industry, because exports were routinely relieved of domestic turnover taxes but not of company taxes.[a] As a consequence, French exports entered the German market free of high French turnover taxes, while German exports, in turn, entered the French market without compensation for high German company taxes. This disadvantage had been offset by tariffs and export subsidies in the past, and it was feared that the elimination of these protections in the Coal and Steel Community would leave Germany defenceless, ultimately resulting in 'an extended "marché français" rather than a true "marché commun"'.[26]

An expert panel under the economist Jan Tinbergen was hurriedly formed to settle the matter. It ruled that the German argument was wrong because any tax-induced competitive disadvantage for German exporters would be offset by automatic exchange rate adjustments.[37] This so-called equivalence theorem was a striking academic achievement. Its practical value, however, was limited because exchange rates were fixed by the Bretton Woods system – and nobody wanted them to be flexible. There simply was no room for compensatory exchange rate adjustments. The tax conflict eventually died down because the French Franc was, for political reasons, fixed at such a high level that whatever advantage French producers might have had from their tax treatment was more than offset by the unfavourable exchange rate. The fear that high taxes might undermine national competitiveness remained, however, and continues to be a top concern of policy makers.

---

[a] This, of course, had practical reasons. While it is relatively straightforward to compute the turnover tax burden of goods, it is very difficult to estimate the company tax burden falling on goods.

Tax evasion and avoidance

The erosion of the fences separating national markets accelerated during the 1960s. Not only did the Kennedy round of GATT negotiations and the EEC Customs Union result in further reductions of trade barriers, but the divisions between national capital markets were also breaking down. In part, this was the states' own doing. By 1958 most European countries had made their currencies fully convertible, and during the early 1960s they cautiously eased off capital controls. In part, however, it followed from processes beyond state control, namely the emergence of offshore capital markets and the rise of multinational companies. The resulting increase in the cross-border movements of capital raised a new set of problems for tax authorities: international tax avoidance and evasion, i.e. the reduction of tax liabilities by legal (avoidance) and illegal (evasion) means.

Of course, there had always been an incentive for private investors to hold financial assets abroad in order to evade domestic taxes. For most intents and purposes, however, this incentive had been neutralized by the costs of escaping from or overcoming capital controls. The partial reduction of capital controls in the EEC reduced these costs, and thus increased the attractiveness of tax evasion. Hence, when – in the mid-1960s – Belgium, Italy and Germany imposed new source taxes on capital income, the result was an 'anti-economical capital flight of the largest magnitude'.[36] The emergence of offshore capital markets further added to the appeal of international tax evasion by reducing the attendant currency risk. If a capital owner residing in country A invested in country B in order to evade domestic capital income taxes, she ran the risk that country B's currency would depreciate, and thus reduce the value of her assets in terms of her home country's currency. Offshore markets took care of this risk by allowing for foreign investments in domestic currency. For example, an offshore market physically located in country B would trade assets and liabilities denominated in the currency of country A. This allowed tax evaders from country A to hold their capital in B, and thus beyond the reach of A's tax collectors, but in A's currency, i.e. without any currency risk. This advantage, according to some observers, was a key factor behind the rapid growth of offshore or Euro-markets during the 1960s and 1970s: 'Half of all Eurobonds are held by individuals, whose motives are a combination of the security offered by a hard-currency investment in a high-rated borrower, as well as tax evasion'.[22]

While offshore markets were a new phenomenon, multinational companies were not. Many major industrial and raw material enterprises were already established on a global level by the end of the 19th century. However, for a variety of reasons – the European recovery, the improved military position of Europe after Stalin's death, convertibility of most European currencies, the creation of the EEC – transnational corporate activity rose sharply only from the late 1950s. The ascendancy of the multinational corporation increased concerns about tax avoidance for two reasons. First, the real investments of multinational companies are likely to be more tax sensitive than the investments of purely national companies. While it is improbable that a purely German company would terminate its operation in Germany and move to, say, Ireland, to take advantage of lower corporate taxes there, it appears much more probable that an American multinational company that wants to set up shop in the Common Market would be attracted by low Irish taxes and locate its European headquarters there rather than in Germany. Second, and potentially more importantly, the simultaneous presence of multinational companies in various countries allows them to optimize their tax liabilities between these countries (international tax planning). They can, for example, manipulate the prices used in internal exchanges in order to artificially shift profits from high tax to low tax countries. For this purpose, company subsidiaries in low-tax locations will charge inflated prices for deliveries to subsidiaries in high-tax countries, and, in turn, pay deflated prices for deliveries from them (*transfer pricing*). Other techniques can also reduce the tax bill of the multinational corporation as a whole. The specifics are complicated but the basic concept is simple: taxable profit is rerouted from parts of the company located in high-tax countries to parts located in low-tax countries, and is then stored there. The company saves taxes, high-tax countries lose revenue.

Tax competition

Tax avoidance and evasion brought formerly separate tax systems into contact. How much money the tax authorities raised no longer depended on national tax levels alone but also on foreign tax levels. Low foreign tax levels threatened to depress domestic revenues by causing an outflow of mobile tax base. High foreign tax levels, in turn, promised to boost domestic revenues by attracting a mobile tax base in from abroad. One country's revenue became dependent on other countries' tax policies. This interdependence created not only constraints for national tax policy but also opportunities. Governments could exploit it to their advantage by undercutting the tax rates of other countries. Tax-sensitive business activities could be lured away from foreign markets and into the home economy, bringing in their wake not only additional revenues but also growth, employment, and wealth. This was a particularly attractive option for small countries. Small countries have little domestic tax base to lose but a lot of foreign tax base to win. Hence, the chance that lower tax rates will be overcompensated for by an enlargement of the tax base is rather high. This is why tax havens are always relatively small countries, and why it is always large countries that feel victimized by them.[4]

Already in the 1960s, the US was incensed by what it saw as the blatant abuse of Swiss holding companies for the purpose of reducing the tax bills of American multinationals in the US. In reaction, Congress passed a first piece of 'anti-avoidance' legislation in 1962, intended to limit the tax advantages that US-based enterprises could derive from holding companies in foreign tax havens. Other (large) countries also began to look into the problem. In 1973, for example, France and Germany formally requested the EC Commission to investigate the fiscal treatment of holding companies in Luxembourg. They suspected that these companies were being misused by multinational enterprises for the purpose of reducing French and German tax liabilities. Luxembourg, they insisted, should not be allowed to take a fiscal free ride at their expense.[10]

To Luxembourg, of course, the issue decidedly did not look like free-riding. In a debate on the Commission's holding report, a socialist Member of the European Parliament from Luxembourg asked the Commission 'whether it felt that it ought to organize the capital movement of holding companies towards Liechtenstein or the Swiss canton of Glaraus [sic!], rather than allowing these companies to establish themselves in a Community financial centre where, apart from anything else, they provided employment for young professional people' (*Bulletin of the EC* 6–1973:83). From Luxembourg's point of view, the holding law was part of a national development strategy. Luxembourg's old industrial base in coal and steel was in decline, and the financial service industry looked like a promising substitute. Helping this industry through appropriate (low-)tax legislation would, it was believed, eventually also benefit France and Germany through better access to capital and more efficient financial intermediation. Other countries followed Luxembourg's example. In 1983, for example, Belgium established a preferential tax regime for so-called coordination centres that provided overhead functions, such as financing, accounting, or captive insurance for multinational companies. Shortly thereafter, Ireland established the so-called *International Financial Services Center* in Dublin – a regime that awards a special, reduced corporate tax rate of only 10% to companies providing financial services to non-residents. Outside Europe the number of tax havens also increased, as small states such as the Seychelles, the Netherlands Antilles, and Barbados entered the business of providing individuals and corporations with a low-tax basis for international tax planning activities. The selling point of these locations was that they provided protection from foreign taxation without the need to physically relocate there, i.e. people and companies did not actually work and operate in the tax havens, they just let themselves be taxed there. Tax havens offer '*juridical* rather than *de facto* abodes'.[20:163]

Tax competition, however, is not limited to a contest for attracting virtual activity. Governments also use low tax strategies to attract real economic activity, i.e. real investment in 'real' production. When Ireland entered the EC in 1973, for example, it insisted on the right to apply a reduced corporate tax rate to all manufacturing operations, with a view to increasing inward investment. This strategy is generally seen as quite successful and as a major ingredient in the long Irish boom of the 1990s. It is hardly surprising, therefore, that Ireland has become a role model for the new EU Member States from Eastern Europe. The Baltic States and Slovakia in particular have made low or no corporation taxes[b] a selling point of their economic policies, and have thereby attracted the wrath of some of the old member states. The German government has been particularly outspoken in its criticism of fiscal free-riding. The emerging conflict shows the same normative ambiguities as the conflict with Luxembourg some 30 years ago. On the one hand, it is true that the large countries are taken advantage of: after all, a small country's low tax strategy only pays off if another high tax country loses tax base. On the other hand, it is unclear on what normative and legal grounds the large Member States can deny their smaller peers the freedom to structure their national tax systems to national advantage.

The transnationalization of the tax base

The twin problems of tax avoidance/evasion and tax competition are exacerbated by a third one: the transnationalization of the tax base. The traditional architecture of the tax state was based on the assumption that all taxable events have a clearly identifiable place in space: either they fall within a national tax jurisdiction, and are therefore liable to national tax, or they fall within the jurisdiction of some other state, and are therefore liable to tax there.[34] Of course, this notion of a 'natural nexus' between tax base and a particular territory has always been a fiction. Some taxable events, such as inheritance, always posed problems for separate national taxation. If somebody died in country A while the heir resided in country B, in which state did the inheritance take place and become liable to tax? These exceptions were of little practical importance, however, and did not significantly reduce the workability of the 'natural nexus' assumption. The process of globalization threatens to make transnational tax bases less of an exception, thereby raising the difficulties of establishing nexus.[2] Two developments in particular contribute to this: the ascendancy of multinational corporations and the emergence of electronic commerce.

The problem with multinational corporations is that their organizational reality is not adequately reflected in law. At the organizational level, they constitute a transnational whole. At the legal level, however, they are fragmented into a multitude of national parts. Formally, each national subsidiary of a multinational company is an independent business firm of its own. This legal fragmentation is supposed, inter alia, to allow each state to tax its part of the profits of the

---

[b] Estonia charges no corporation tax on retained profits.

multinational company independently. However, it tends to thwart this purpose by opening up options for international tax planning that multinational corporations can use in order to reduce their tax liabilities in high tax countries: only because subsidiaries in low tax jurisdictions are independent legal entities can they serve as tax shelters for profits generated in high tax jurisdictions.[20:172] Tax planning was comparatively easy for governments to check and control as long as the organizational structure of multinational corporations resembled a loose confederation of largely self-contained national companies, i.e. as long as the gap between the organizational and the legal concept of a multinational enterprise was still fairly narrow. However, as most multinational companies went from a confederative structure towards integrated transnational production in the course of globalization, it became much harder to find meaningful criteria for the division of overall profits. Consider a recent quarrel between GlaxoSmithKline, a big multinational drugs company, and the US tax authorities. At issue was how much of the profits of Zantac, Glaxo's hugely successful ulcer drug, derived from advertising and marketing in the US, and how much from research and development in Britain.[1] The problem is, of course, that there is no simple answer to this question because the profits reflect synergies from transnationally integrated production. It is impossible, therefore, to allocate them unambiguously to any particular location. This implies, on the one hand, that Glaxo potentially enjoys very large degrees of freedom in allocating profits between Britain and the US in the most tax efficient way. The mistrust of US authorities is thus well founded. On the other hand, it also implies that any national claim to a particular share of Glaxo's profits is hard to justify on the basis of principle.

The problem with electronic commerce is often viewed as structurally similar to that of integrated transnational production. Established tax rules assume that the generation of income presupposes a physical presence, i.e. a 'permanent establishment'. The new information technologies challenge this assumption. Internet addresses are relational constructs that often do not reflect physical location. Servers routinely shift clients from location to location to balance loads. Buyers can log on to any server remotely. Service suppliers such as architects, software writers or lawyers may collaborate just as easily from offices in Tokyo, Palo Alto and Bremen, as they do within the same office building. Enterprises may conduct substantial business in countries where they have no 'permanent establishment'. Territoriality-based tax claims are hard to justify, and hard to enforce.[19,21] Since the burst of the new economy bubble, however, concern over the tax implications of electronic commerce has abated. As it turns out, it has proved quite difficult to effect electronic transactions in high tax jurisdictions without establishing any physical presence there. And even in cases where physical presence can be avoided, it seems relatively easy to adjust international tax law concepts to establish a territorial nexus – for example, by defining a minimum threshold of sales as constituting presence in a jurisdiction for tax purposes.

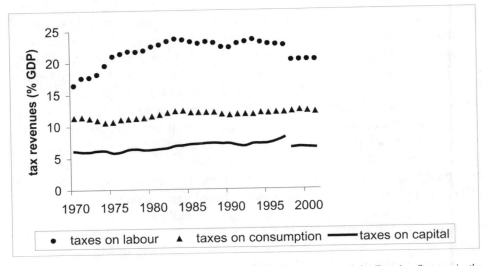

Notes: Data are unweighted averages from Eurostat *Structures of the Taxation Systems in the European Union* 2001 and 2003. Countries included are Belgium, Denmark, Germany, France, Ireland, Italy, Luxembourg, Netherlands and United Kingdom. Data for periods 1970–1997 and 1998–2002 are based on different national account systems (ESA 79 and ESA 95) and not fully comparable.

Figure 1. Tax revenues according to macroeconomic tax base in nine EU member states, 1970–2002.

Coping strategies

Looking at aggregate revenue levels, there can be little doubt that the tax state copes rather well with the onslaught of globalization. Figure 1 presents data for the EU, arguably the most economically integrated area of the world economy. It shows, first, that the total tax take of the average EU state is holding firm at about 40% of GDP. This is high by historical standards, and definitely much higher than during the years of relative economic closure in the 1950s and 1960s. The figure also shows that the tax base that is potentially the most mobile, most susceptible to tax avoidance and evasion, most endangered by tax competition, and most transnational in character, namely capital, contributes least to total tax revenues. Therefore, even if globalization were to undermine the ability of the state to derive revenue from this basis, its impact on the state's fiscal viability would be modest. Finally, there is no evidence of a decline in capital tax revenues; to the contrary, Figure 1 suggests a slight increase since the mid-1980s. If tax revenues have declined at all, then it is in labour taxation and not in capital taxation.

Some observers conclude from this rather innocuous picture that globalization has not really changed much for the tax state. It retains considerable taxing power: governments 'wishing to expand the public economy for political reasons may do so (including increasing taxes on capital to pay for new spending)'.[8:823,23,32] This conclusion, however, is not completely warranted. First, it overlooks the fact that globalization was not the only challenge that the tax state had to meet during the 1980s and 1990s; there were also slow growth and massive unemployment, and there were high spending requirements, especially in social policy. Given these internal challenges, globalization did not trap the tax state in a race to the bottom in taxation so much as box it in between external pressures to reduce the tax burden on capital, on the one hand, and internal pressures to maintain revenue levels and relieve the tax burden on labour, on the other. Tax aggregates did not change much, not because globalization was business as usual for the tax state but because the tax state was left with very little room to manoeuvre.[6,9,33] Second, the continuity in aggregate indicators masks underlying structural changes. Precisely because they had so little freedom to adjust tax levels in reaction to globalization, governments looked for revenue-neutral ways to make their national tax systems more globalization-proof. To this end they introduced an increasingly complex body of anti-avoidance and evasion legislation; they intensified international cooperation in tax matters, and, most importantly, they fundamentally reformed their income tax systems.

Anti-avoidance and evasion legislation

Since the 1960s, practically all OECD states have developed anti-avoidance rules to rein in international tax planning. The basic purpose of these rules is to limit the tax advantages that multinational companies can derive from their legal fragmentation.[6:623] Transfer pricing and thin capitalization regulations limit the extent to which multinational companies can use commercial or financial transactions between subsidiaries to optimize their overall tax load. 'Controlled Foreign Company' legislation restricts their freedom to evacuate profits to subsidiaries in tax havens. By attributing part of the income of the tax haven subsidiary to the parent company at home, this legislation reduces the benefits of offshore deferral and, hence, the leeway for international tax planning. Some governments, including those of the US, Australia and Great Britain, have also introduced advance information requirements obliging tax advisers to reveal to national tax authorities the tax avoidance schemes they sell to corporate customers. This reduces the information gap between tax authorities and tax planners. The problem with anti-avoidance rules is that they tend to be exceedingly complex. Compliance and administration costs are high for tax payers and tax authorities alike, and must be balanced against any potential revenue gain.[c] In

---

[c] It is hard to come by data on the exact magnitude of the compliance and administrative costs connected to anti-avoidance rules. It is interesting to note, however, that in a country such as the United Kingdom, the total administrative compliance costs of the tax system are estimated to be 1.5% of GDP, which implies that tax administration is an industry as large as agriculture, forestry and fishing.[18]

addition, to the extent that anti-avoidance rules are successful in effectively reducing opportunities for artificial cross-border shifts of profits, they may increase the incentives to shift the underlying profit generating assets. An out-migration of production facilities, however, is much more painful than the out-migration of the mobile tax base because it harms not only tax revenues but also growth and employment.

Anti-evasion measures focus mostly on personal capital income from interest and dividends. Unlike corporations, individuals are not subject to elaborate bookkeeping requirements. If individual capital owners hold their assets abroad, national tax authorities will usually not know. Some observers, like Jeffrey Owens, the head of OECD's Centre for Tax Policy and Administration, conclude that taxes on private capital income are now 'almost a voluntary tax': they can be evaded at liberty.[17] Anecdotal evidence suggests, however, that anti-evasion measures can be effective at deterring capital tax evasion. During the 1990s, German tax authorities conducted a series of well-publicized country-wide investigations of German banks, prosecuting bank managers for aiding and abetting international tax evasion.[6:624] Of course, they uncovered only a fraction of total German capital tax evasion, but they sent a powerful signal to potential tax evaders and their helpers about the unpleasant consequences if detected. The cost–benefit balance of tax evasion was thus somewhat tilted towards the cost side.

International cooperation

Tax policy experts like Vito Tanzi, an economist associated with the International Monetary Fund for decades, often lament the lack of international cooperation in taxation,[35] but it does exist, and it has a fairly long history. As early as the 19th Century, states began to conclude bilateral tax treaties, codifying common rules for sharing transnational tax bases. These helped the contracting parties to keep their tax systems separate even in cases where they participated in the same tax base. As long as transnational tax bases were few in number and fiscally unimportant, the number of tax treaties remained low: by the mid-1950s only about 100 treaties had been concluded worldwide. With the advent of globalization, however, the treaty network began to expand. Today, it connects virtually all OECD member states to each other and extends to almost all other countries worldwide, with the total number of treaties approaching 2300. Why the tax treaty regime is still organized bilaterally although, as many argue, a multilateral regime would be much more efficient and effective is, in itself, an interesting question.[25] Still, there can be no doubt that the spread of this regime is a reaction to the increased coordination needs of national tax administrations in a globalized economy.

Recently, international institutions such as the OECD and the EU have also become active in the struggle against international tax evasion and avoidance. In 1998, the OECD started a project on so-called 'harmful tax practices'.[16,24] One purpose was to coax tax havens outside the OECD into agreement on common standards on information exchange in civil and criminal tax matters. Only a handful of tax havens, including Andorra, Liechtenstein, and the Marshall Islands, still refuse to accept this international infringement on their sovereign right to 'commercialize'[20] their state sovereignty. In contrast to the OECD project, which aims only at forcing tax havens to provide relevant tax information upon request, the recent EU directive on the taxation of interest income provides for an automatic exchange of all tax relevant information between the member states.[5] If a financial institution in member state A pays out interest to a resident of member state B, it will automatically inform B's tax authorities about this. The scope for international capital tax evasion in the Internal Market is thus substantially reduced while the national tax sovereignty of the member states is buttressed.

International institutions have been less successful in fighting international tax competition. The problem is that, unlike cooperation against tax evasion and avoidance, international cooperation against tax competition tends to limit rather than buttress national tax sovereignty. Since tax competition is driven by incentives to undercut other countries' (effective) tax rates, the way to stop it is to agree on some harmonized level of tax rates. Some countries, such as the UK, object to such harmonization for reasons of principle. They insist that the national parliament and not an international body should have the final say on tax levels. Other states, especially small and relatively poor ones, object to the idea of tax rate harmonization for reasons of national interest; for them, tax competition is not a threat but a promising strategy for national development. This is why Ireland, for example, has always opposed attempts to harmonize corporate tax rates in the EU.[4]

Tax reform

The most important tax policy response to globalization has been tax reform. Practically all OECD countries revamped their tax systems during the 1980s and 1990s with a view to making them more competitive and globalization-proof. The most visible result of this was a significant drop in the corporate tax rate: in the average OECD country it fell from about 50% in 1983 to about 30% in 2003, and looks set to fall even further.[7] Since the tax cuts were paralleled by measures to broaden the tax base, they did not usually result in substantial tax revenue losses. This did not mean, however, that they were painless.

The problem is that corporate income tax is intimately linked with personal income tax. The distinction between corporate profits and personal income is one of legal form rather than material difference. Hence, if corporate income is taxed at significantly lower rates than (top) personal income, (rich) taxpayers can potentially save tax by reclassifying their personal labour and/or capital income as corporate income.[28] As a consequence, most OECD countries have tended in the past to treat the corporate and the individual income tax as a more or less integrated block (with more or less aligned tax rates and tax base definitions) rather than as two completely separate taxes.

Tax competition forced governments to slice up this block. There were basically two options for doing this.[7] One option was to slice up the block vertically so as to separate the taxation of mobile income, which is susceptible to tax competition (mostly corporate profits and personal capital income), from the taxation of immobile income, which is not (mostly wage income). This option was taken, for example, by the Swedish government in 1991, when it introduced its so-called dual income tax system. The essence of the dual income tax is to remove capital income from the scope of the progressive individual income tax and to tax it separately at low proportional rates. Personal capital income is now taxed at a uniform rate of 30%, which is closely aligned with the corporate tax rate of 28%. Labour income, by contrast, continues to be taxed at fairly steep progressive rates. The top individual income rate stands at 57%. The advantage of the dual income tax system is that it increases competitiveness at minimal fiscal cost. It targets tax cuts where they matter most in terms of tax competition and are most easily made up through tax base broadening, thus avoiding unnecessary revenue losses. However, there is a price to be paid in terms of efficiency and equity. In terms of efficiency, the problem is that the gap between the top personal income tax rate and the proportional rate on capital income weakens the backstop function of the corporate tax. Given the gap, there is an incentive to reclassify labour income as capital income. This makes taxation difficult wherever labour and capital income accrue jointly, as, for example, in unincorporated businesses or closely held corporations. The equity problem is that one Swedish Crown in capital income is no longer liable to the same amount of income tax as one Swedish Crown of labour income. True, there are good economic arguments for taxing capital income at lower rates – or not at all. However, it is hard to sell these arguments politically: after all, why should (rich) heirs contribute less to the common good than (poor) wage earners? The efficiency and the equity problems of the dual income tax increase with the size of the tax rate gap between capital and labour income. The higher the tax rate on labour and the lower the tax rate on capital, the more difficult it becomes to police the border between them, and to explain to an electorate of mostly wage earners why this tax system is in their interest. Stabilizing the tax rate gap, or even increasing it in the face of increased tax competition, are, therefore, major problems of a dual income tax.

The alternative reform option avoids these problems by cutting tax rates across all types of income. This is basically what the Red–Green coalition government in Germany tried to accomplish with its tax reform of 2001. In order to increase competitiveness without sacrificing the formally equal tax treatment of capital and wage income, it reduced corporate and top individual income taxes to roughly the same rate: they are set to fall to 42% (income tax) and 38% (corporate tax including local business tax) by 2005. The major drawback of this reform option is, of course, that it multiplies the fiscal costs of adjustment to tax competition. By de-taxing (immobile) labour income in order to make taxes on (mobile) capital and corporate income more competitive, it causes huge revenue losses where it does not matter in terms of tax competition (since labour is mostly immobile there is hardly any inter-jurisdictional competition in labour taxation), and which are very difficult to make up for by base broadening. Despite all attempts at base broadening, it is estimated that the German reform will reduce total income tax revenues by 1.3% of GDP. Such a revenue loss will be very difficult to accommodate, especially if low growth and high unemployment continue. This approach, too, suffers from a serious equity problem. While it defends horizontal equity – different types of income are taxed equally – it reduces vertical equity. The reduction of top personal income tax rates decreases progressivity at the high end of the income spectrum; the concomitant revenue losses have to be compensated for by spending cuts or by more regressive taxes such as VAT, both of which are likely to burden low to medium income earners more than high income earners.

The transformation of the tax state

Ten or fifteen years ago it was fashionable in academic circles to make dire predictions about what globalization would do to the nation state. Nothing less than the very survival of the state seemed to be in question. Today, probably in embarrassment at this former misjudgement, it is fashionable to doubt that globalization is of any consequence to the nation state. Governing in the globalized world is now portrayed as more or less business as usual; nothing much has changed for the state. The truth, of course, lies somewhere between the two extremes. Globalization is neither fatal nor irrelevant for the nation state; it is one important factor in its continuous transformation. This study has analysed how globalization contributes to the transformation of the state by affecting the state's main source of revenue, taxation.

There is no doubt that taxation will remain the main revenue source of the modern state. Globalization has not visibly undermined tax revenue. There has been no perceptible drop in the tax levels of OECD countries. To the contrary, globalization has been accompanied, over the past 20 years, by historically high levels of taxation. Also, globalization has not undermined taxation as the organizing principle of public finance. There simply is no alternative conception of public income generation that could potentially raise more revenue at less opportunity cost. There seems to be no substitute for taxes: taxation's erstwhile rival, state socialism,[11] is passé. The idea that the state should live off its own economic activities rather than participate 'parasitically' via taxation in the private economic activities of its citizens, has lost much of the appeal that it enjoyed during important periods of the 20th century. There also seems to be no substitute for the state as the taxing unit. The 'globalization of taxation', as Roland Paris recently put it,[21] that is, the idea that taxation could be lifted from the level of the nation state to the supranational level of international institutions, has so far failed to gain any support. Even in the EU, where economic integration is deeper and tax coordination further developed than anywhere else in the world, the proposal of a Euro-tax has, so far, been a non-starter. Comparing today's utopian visions for the EU's future[31] with expert reports from the 1960s,[15] it appears that the Europeanization of taxation was considered back then a much more realistic option than it is now.

Even if globalization does not threaten the organizing principle or overall size of the tax state, it is, nevertheless, a challenge. By increasing the interdependencies between national economies, it increases the interdependencies between national tax regimes. These interdependencies present governments with a new set of tax policy problems: industrial competitiveness, international tax avoidance and evasion, tax competition, and transnational tax bases. Governments have reacted to these challenges in two ways. First, they have adopted measures to increase their boundary control. Such measures include unilateral acts of new or strengthened anti-avoidance and evasion legislation to stop a mobile tax base from leaking out of the national domain. They also include international cooperation to reinforce national control – for example, through cross-border information exchange or common sharing rules for transnational tax bases. The tax treaty regime and OECD and EU activities against tax evasion and 'harmful tax practices' are the most visible outcomes of this cooperation.

Secondly, governments have reformed their national tax systems in order to make them more competitive and less costly to the owners of mobile tax bases. To be sure, large cross-national differences remain in terms of tax level and tax mix. Yet there has been a strong convergence with respect to policy priorities and reform patterns.[30] Efficiency and neutrality have replaced equity and redistribution as key criteria of a 'good' tax policy. Tax reforms invariably aim to cut top personal and corporate income tax rates while at the same time broadening the tax bases, and to finance any attendant revenue loss – or additional revenue needs – through other more regressive taxes, such as VAT and social security contributions.

In conclusion, globalization has triggered important changes in the tax state. However, the significance of these changes pales in comparison to the changes the tax state experienced during the period of 'national containment', i.e. roughly the time between the First World War and 1970, when the introduction of a set of new taxes – the personal income tax, the corporate tax, general consumption taxes, and social security contributions – completely revolutionized the tax state's revenue base and architecture. In fact, the most striking contrast between then and now is how much volatility and change there was then and how much stability and incrementalism there is now. Hence, globalization's most important consequence may not be so much to force change upon the tax state but to limit its freedom to change. The status quo is not fundamentally threatened. But it has become harder for any one government to change that status quo unilaterally. Globalization, rather than undermining the tax state, freezes it in its current form.

Acknowledgements

Comments by Berit Dencker, Markus Jachtenfuchs, Stefan Leibfried, Thomas Rixen, and Ingo Rohlfing are gratefully acknowledged.

References

1. *The Economist* (2004) A taxing battle, *The Economist*, 31 January, p. 60.
2. R. M. Bird and J. S. Wilkie (2000) Source- vs. residence-based taxation in the European Union: the wrong question? In S. Cnossen (Ed) *Taxing Capital Income in the European Union: Issues and Options for Reform* (Oxford: Oxford University Press): 78–109.
3. E. Burke ([1790] 1999) *Reflections on the Revolution in France* (Oxford: Oxford University Press).
4. V. H. Dehejia and P. Genschel (1999) Tax competition in the European Union. *Politics & Society*, **27**(3): 403–430.
5. European Community (2003) Council Directive 2003/48/EC of 3 June on taxation of savings income in the form of interest payments. *Official Journal*, **L** (157): 38–48.
6. S. Ganghof (2000) Adjusting national tax policy to economic internationalisation: strategies and outcomes. In: F. W. Scharpf and V. A. Schmidt (Eds) *Welfare and Work in the Open Economy*. Vol. II: *Diverse Responses to Common Challenges* (Oxford: Oxford University Press): 597–645.
7. S. Ganghof (2004) *Wer regiert in der Steuerpolitik? Einkommensteuerreform in Deutschland zwischen internationalem Wettbewerb und nationalen Verteilungskonflikten* (Frankfurt a.M.: Campus).
8. G. Garrett (1998) Global markets and national politics: collision course or virtuous circle? *International Organization*, **52**(4): 787–824.

9. P. Genschel (2002) Globalization, tax competition and the welfare state. *Politics & Society*, **30**(2): 244–274.

10. P. Genschel (2002) *Steuerharmonisierung und Steuerwettbewerb in der Europäischen Union* (Frankfurt a.M.: Campus): 172–174.

11. R. Goldscheid (1917) *Staatssozialismus oder Staatskapitalismus* (Wien: Anzengruber Verlag): VII–33, esp. p. 3.

12. E. Helleiner (1994) *States and the Reemergence of Global Finance: From Bretton Woods to the 1990s* (Ithaca/London: Cornell University Press): 33, 34.

13. C. Hood (2003) The tax state in the information age. In J. A. Hall (Ed) *The Nation-State in Question* (Princeton, NJ: Princeton University Press): 213–233, esp. p. 213.

14. K. Messere (2000) 20th century taxes and their future. *Bulletin for International Fiscal Documentation*, **54**(1): 2–29.

15. Neumark Report (1963) *The EEC Reports on Tax Harmonization. The Report of the Fiscal and Financial Committee and the Reports of the Sub-Groups A, B and C* (Amsterdam: International Bureau for Fiscal Documentation).

16. OECD (2004) *The OECD's Project on Harmful Tax Practices: The 2004 Progress Report* (Paris: OECD).

17. J. Owens (1993) Globalization: the implications for tax policies. *Fiscal Studies*, **14**(3): 21–44, esp. p. 33.

18. J. Owens (1997) Emerging issues in taxing business in a global economy. In: R. Vann (Ed) *Taxing International Business. Emerging Trends in APEC and OECD Economies* (Paris: OECD): 25–66.

19. J. Owens (1998) Taxation within a context of economic globalization. *Bulletin for International Fiscal Documentation*, **52**(7): 290–296.

20. R. Palan (2002) Tax havens and the commercialization of state sovereignty. *International Organization*, **56**(1): 151–176.

21. R. Paris (2002) The globalization of taxation? Electronic commerce and the transformation of the state. *International Studies Quarterly*, **47**(2): 153–182.

22. S. Picciotto: (1992) *International Business Taxation. A Study in the Internationalization of Business Regulation* (New York: Quorum): 123.

23. D. Quinn (1997) The correlates of change in international financial regulation. *American Political Science Review*, **91**(3): 531–551.

24. C. M. Radaelli (2001) The new politics of corporate taxation in the European Union. In: M. Gammie (Ed) *EU Corporate Tax Reform* (Brussels: Center for European Policy Studies): 10–29, esp. p. 10–18.

25. T. Rixen and I. Rohlfing (2004) Bilateralism and multilaterlism: institutional choice in international cooperation. Paper presented at the American Political Science Association Meeting, Chicago, 3–7 September 2004.

26. G. Schmölders (1953) Der Steuerstreit in der Montanunion. *Archiv des öffentlichen Rechts*, **79**: 91–106, esp. p. 101.

27. J. Schumpeter (1918) *Die Krise des Steuerstaats* (Graz: Leuschner & Lubensky).

28. J. Slemrod (2004) Are corporate tax rates, or countries, converging? *Journal of Public Economics*, **88**(6): 1169–1186, esp. p. 1171.

29. S. Steinmo (1993) *Taxation and Democracy. Swedish, British and American Approaches to Financing the Modern State* (New Haven: Yale University Press).

30. S. Steinmo (2003) The evolution of policy ideas: tax policy in the 20th century. *British Journal of Politics and International Relations*, **5**(2): 206–236.

31. D. Strauss-Kahn (2004) *Building a Political Europe. 50 Proposals for Tomorrow's Europe* (Brussels: European Commission).

32. D. Swank (2002) *Global Capital, Political Institutions, and Policy Change in Developed Welfare States* (Cambridge: Cambridge University Press).

33. D. Swank and S. Steinmo (2002) The new political economy of taxation in advanced capitalist democracies. *American Journal of Political Science*, **46**(3): 642–655.

34. V. Tanzi (1995) *Taxation in an Integrating World* (Washington, DC: Brookings Institution): 67–69.

35. V. Tanzi (1999) Is there a need for a World Tax Organization? In E. Sadka (Ed) *The Economics of Globalization. Policy Perspectives from Public Economics* (Cambridge: Cambridge University Press): 173–186.

36. Tinbergen Report (1953) *Report on the Problems Raised by the Different Turnover Tax Systems applied within the Common Market* (Paris: European Coal and Steel Community).

37. P. VerLoren van Themaat (1966) Die Steuerharmonisierung in der EWG. *Der Betrieb*, **19**(22): 834–840, p. 838.

About the Author

Philipp Genschel is Associate Professor of Political Science at the International University Bremen. His main field of research is international political economy and European integration. In his research project on 'The tax state and international tax politics', which is part of the Research Center 'Transformations of the State' (TranState), he works with **Ingo Rohlfing**, **Thomas Rixen**, and **Susanne Uhl** as investigators. Recent English language publications include: Globalization, tax competition and the welfare state. *Politics & Society*, **30**(2): 244–274 (2002), and Globalization and the welfare state: a retrospective. *Journal of European Public Policy*, **11**(4): 621–644 (2004).

European Review, Vol. 13, Supp. No. 1, 73–91 (2005) © Academia Europaea, Printed in the United Kingdom

THE RULE OF LAW: INTERNATIONALIZATION AND PRIVATIZATION

4 Is there an emerging international rule of law?

BERNHARD ZANGL

An international rule of law complementing modern states' domestic rule of law seems to be emerging. At least in the four issue areas of international law considered here – international trade, security, labour, and environmental law – empirical evidence suggests that relevant dispute settlement procedures have been judicialized and their use by complainants as well as their acceptance by defendants have increased in practice. Albeit still far from what we are used to from the domestic rule of law, the emergence of an international rule of law can be regarded as indicative of a fundamental transformation of modern states.

Introduction

Since the 17th century, the rule of law has emerged as the dominant legal principle *within* modern states, while *between* modern states sovereignty has become the central legal principle. The former principle reflects the domestic hierarchy of the state over its society, while the latter institutionalizes the anarchy within the international society of states. Legally, both principles are fundamental to modern states' identity. As principles, however, rule of law and sovereignty could hardly be more contradictory. While the rule of law requires that states respect domestic law, sovereignty gives states the justification to act arbitrarily at their discretion beyond international law. If, therefore, a substantial international rule of law were to emerge that complements the domestic rule of law, this would amount to a fundamental transformation of the modern state.

To trace this transformation, I will discuss whether issue-area-specific international judiciaries constitute, similar to domestic judiciaries, the institutional backbone of an emerging international rule of law. After all, internationally, there are more and more judicial procedures designed to adjudicate in disputes over breaches of international law.[11,18] The diplomatic dispute settlement procedures under GATT, for instance, have been replaced by a judicial dispute settlement mechanism under the WTO, which is authorized to convict, and if necessary punish, states that do not fulfil their commitments. Recently, an International Criminal Court was created to sentence war criminals, and the UN

Security Council now regularly criticizes those states threatening international peace and authorizes or mandates sanctions against them. The rulings of the European Court of Justice enjoy both direct effect and supremacy in domestic legal orders. International environmental regimes such as the ozone and the climate regime have various built-in, quasi-judicial procedures designed to cope with non-compliance, and an International Tribunal for the Law of the Sea has also been established.[26]

For many idealists, the judicialization of adjudication procedures leads almost automatically to better compliance with international law and also to a comparable treatment of breaches of international law. They consider the emergence of an international rule of law as mainly a matter of good – i.e. judicial rather than diplomatic – institutional design for adjudication procedures.[5] By contrast, for so-called realists it is not a matter of institutional design of adjudication procedures whether states comply with international law and whether comparable breaches of international law will be treated comparably. They assume that, due to the anarchical structures in international relations, powerful states in both judicial and traditional diplomatic adjudication procedures can and will act as they please, while less powerful states have to suffer what they must.[15]

However, the question whether – and if so where and when – judicialized adjudication procedures coincide with a corresponding practice of dispute settlement is an entirely empirical one, and cannot be answered with theoretical assumptions, idealist or realist. Idealist assumptions are clearly undermined by the fact that the existence of the International Court of Justice (ICJ), with a judicialized adjudication procedure, has hardly transformed international practices of dispute settlement. Since it has rarely been invoked and its rulings were often ignored, it could hardly institutionalize an international rule of law. But realist assumptions are also dampened, here by the fact that the European Court of Justice (ECJ), marked by a heavily judicialized process of adjudication, has transformed European dispute settlement. In contrast to the ICJ, the ECJ is regularly invoked and its rulings are usually followed, thereby establishing an international rule of law in Europe.[1]

The judicialization of adjudication procedures can be regarded as a first necessary condition for an emergent international rule of law. In contrast to traditional diplomatic adjudication, judicialized procedures offer at least the chance for a comparable treatment of comparable breaches of international law.[11,18] For a fully-fledged international rule of law, however, at least two further conditions have to be met. First, complainants should generally be prepared to make use of these adjudication procedures when others do not comply with their international commitments. Second, defendants should be prepared to accept these adjudication procedures when faced with complaints about their non-compliance with international commitments. Hence, the judicial dispute settlement system within the GATT/WTO context only points to an emergent international rule of law on trade if settlement procedures are both generally used by complainants and accepted by defendants.

Preliminary evidence suggests that all the conditions for an international rule of law are met to a larger degree today than they were two decades ago. To substantiate this, three areas of international law that are structurally similar to three major areas of domestic law need to be scrutinized:

(1) **Private goods law**. In one area that is structurally similar to domestic private law, international law is designed to protect private goods of state or non-state actors. In this area, disputes usually imply that a state or non-state actor files a complaint with an international institution about another state or non-state actor's violation of international legal obligations. An example for this area of international law, to which almost all international regimes dealing with economic issues belong, is the World Trade Organization (WTO).

(2) **Public goods law I.** There are two other areas of international law, in both of which international public goods are legally protected. In the first of these areas – which can be regarded as the structural equivalent to domestic criminal law – disputes typically position international institutions against single state or non-state actors that allegedly violate their international obligations. Most international regimes concerning security issues are located in this area of international law. The regime of the UN Security Council (SC) is an example.

(3) **Public goods law II.** The second area in which international law is meant to protect public goods has some structural similarities to domestic public law. Here, disputes typically imply that non-state actors file a complaint – for example with an international institution – about state actors' violations of their international legal obligations. Various international environmental regimes (IERs) and the International Labour Organization (ILO), for example, belong to this area.

This essay investigates whether an international rule of law is emerging in each of these areas: First, I outline the *judicialization* of issue-area-specific adjudication procedures over the last two decades. Second, I present preliminary evidence that the procedures in these issue areas are generally *used* by complainants in order to defend their rights. Third, I give some evidence indicating that adjudication procedures in these issue areas are generally *accepted* by defendants. The paper concludes with an assessment on the emergence of an international rule of law.

Judicialization as a procedural precondition of an international rule of law

Although it is in practice an important dimension of the modern state, the rule of law is hard to define. Many different definitions have been given;[23] however, I conceive of an international rule of law as a legal order based on the principle that all actors are equal before the law and, hence, no actor is above the law. Within this order, all actors, no matter how powerful, are equally bound by legal rules and, regardless of their power position, violations of these legal rules by these actors are treated equally. In other words, within a legal order based on the rule of law like cases must be treated alike.

In most issue areas with traditional diplomatic adjudication procedures, the conditions for a comparable treatment of comparable cases do not hold;[15] more powerful states are more likely to get away with violations of their legal obligations, while less powerful states are more likely to have to face consequences when committing similar violations.[27] For example, although China and North Korea might have a similar human rights record, owing to the diplomatic procedures of the United Nations Human Rights Commission (UNHRC), China has much less cause to worry about United Nations resolutions condemning its human rights violations than North Korea.

With the establishment of judicial adjudication procedures in some issue areas of today's international relations, however, at least a procedural framework has been established for treating like cases alike. Under such procedures, based on independent courts, the likelihood of powerful actors having to face consequences when they violate their legal obligations should be similar to that of a less powerful actor committing a similar violation. For instance, before the European Court of Human Rights (ECHR), comparable human rights practices of, say, Germany and Luxembourg are likely to lead to comparable legal consequences.[a]

While it is true that neither diplomatic adjudication procedures, like those of the UNHRC, have become the exception, nor are judicial adjudication procedures, like those of ECHR, the rule,[14,18] over the last two decades many adjudication procedures in international relations have gradually become judicialized, i.e. they have departed from the negotiation and mediation mode and have become more court-like. The key developments in this respect are that adjudication procedures have become increasingly politically independent, rely increasingly on compulsory jurisdiction and have become more access-ible.[11,24]

---

[a] However, even with respect to the European Court of Justice the degree to which power can affect rulings is a matter of debate, as can be gathered from the works of Garret[7] and Mattli and Slaughter.[13]

Independence

The political independence of adjudication procedures is a crucial precondition for the equitable treatment of comparable violations of international legal rules.[11:459–462] Up until the early 1980s there were only a few independent international adjudication procedures for deciding whether or not legal rules have been violated. In most issue areas of international relations, adjudication systems, if they existed at all, were dominated by panels, bodies, committees or commissions like the UNHRC, made up of politically dependent state representatives. Today, however, there are more than 40, mostly independent international courts or court-like bodies, most of which were established during the 1990s.[14,18:723–728]

One prominent example is the GATT/WTO.[10:107–137] In the 1950s, decisions on disputes over alleged violations of GATT obligations were undertaken by so-called panels, composed of three legal experts acting in their individual capacities.[9] Their independence was compromised, however, by the fact that those states involved in a dispute themselves selected the panellists on a case-by-case basis. Frequently, representatives from neutral states rather than truly independent legal experts were selected as panellists.[17:66–91] However, in the late 1980s and early 1990s, especially after the WTO had replaced the old GATT, the adjudication procedure became more politically independent. While the composition of the panels did not change, a remarkably independent Appellate Body was established to revise panel reports in appeal cases. In contrast to the panels, the Appellate Body is composed of legal experts who are as independent as judges of ordinary courts. Rather than being selected by the states involved on a case-by-case basis, the seven members of the Appellate Body are now elected to deal with all disputes that might arise during their four-year term. This gives them a significant degree of political independence.[17:177–198]

By contrast, the independence of the Security Council is still limited. The SC has to be considered as an adjudication authority because its main task is to determine whether states' violations of international legal obligations constitute threats to international peace, breaches of international peace, or acts of aggression. Its independence, however, is compromised, because, as stipulated in the United Nations Charter of 1945, its decisions are made by 15 state representatives comprising representatives of the five permanent members – i.e. France, Great Britain, China, Russia and the US – and ten non-permanent members elected by the United Nations General Assembly. These representatives are committed to follow instructions they receive from the foreign ministries of their respective states. Decisions made by the Council can therefore hardly be conceived of as being free of political motivations.[12]

In numerous IERs, as well as in the ILO, it has been possible to enhance the independence of adjudication procedures.[2,21] Generally speaking, until the early 1980s hardly any IER contained provisions for independent authorities to adjudicate on violations of legal obligations. In the International Whaling Commission, states had to settle disputes over the violation of their legal obligations amongst themselves. By contrast, most IERs established since the 1980s do have adjudication procedures, albeit with a limited degree of political independence.[16] The international regime for the protection of the ozone layer was probably the first IER in which a committee of experts was given the task of adjudicating disputes over alleged breaches of international obligations. Since then, however, expert committees have to some extent become standard for most IERs. Most of these committees enjoy remarkable political independence, as the experts who act in their individual capacities, once elected, cannot be removed for their entire term. In most of today's IERs, the political independence of these committees is only compromised by the financial dependence of their experts on the states from which they come.[16]

Jurisdiction

Another, equally important, precondition for an international rule of law is that adjudication procedures can exercise compulsory jurisdiction.[15] Only when those allegedly in breach of their legal obligations have no means of preventing the procedure from being implemented does a comparable treatment of comparable offences seem viable.[27] Traditionally, in most international issue areas, adjudication procedures could not exercise compulsory jurisdiction. This is the case for the ICJ, whose jurisdiction largely depends on its recognition by the states involved in a legal dispute. Since the 1980s, however, adjudication procedures in a growing number of issue areas have been given the authority to give a ruling without the consent of the defending state.

The GATT/WTO is an example of an institution in which jurisdiction of adjudication procedures has become compulsory.[17:182] Throughout the 1970s and 1980s, jurisdiction of GATT panels was not obligatory.[9] The establishment of a panel, as well as the adoption of its report, required the decision of the GATT Council. These decisions, however, were dependent on the consensus of all states, which meant that even the defending state could always block the procedure.[17:66–91] This changed in the mid 1990s, when the WTO came into existence. Since then, neither the establishment of panels nor the adoption of panel reports requires a unanimous decision. On the contrary, the newly established Dispute Settlement Body can reject panel reports only by consensus.[10:107–137] The only possibility remaining for defending states now is to invoke the Appellate Body. Again, however, its reports can only be rejected by a unanimous decision of the Dispute

Settlement Body. Therefore, the defendant can no longer block the adoption of reports.[17:177–198]

The jurisdiction of the Security Council also seems to be compulsory: all states that threaten international peace are subject to SC resolutions. And since these resolutions can be passed with 9 out of 15 votes it would, at first glance, seem difficult for any state to prevent the SC from denouncing any threat to peace it might have committed. However, as permanent members, Great Britain, France, China, Russia and the US can use their veto power to block any SC resolution that is directed against them, and they can, moreover, protect their allies from censure by SC resolutions. Although less accepted since the end of the Cold War, this nevertheless substantially restricts the SC's compulsory jurisdiction.

By contrast, jurisdiction of adjudication procedures has become quasi-compulsory in many IERs as well as in the ILO. In most IERs, committees of experts are given the authority to decide independently whether information they receive on violations of environmental rules merits further investigation. Although, in most IERs, the reports of expert committees have to be approved by the relevant conference of states, in practice they are always adopted without further revision.[16] Similar to other expert committees within the ILO, the Committee on Freedom of Association has acquired quasi-compulsory jurisdiction. It may decide on complaints about violations of the freedom of association without the accused state having any chance of blocking the transfer of its report to the ILO Governing Body.[b]

Access

A further precondition for the comparable treatment of comparable violations of international legal rules is that adjudication procedures cannot only be invoked by states.[11:462–466,24:57] For reasons of diplomacy, states tend to refrain from complaining about other states violating international legal rules, which means that only some violations, those of less powerful states, lead to legal proceedings, while others, especially those of powerful states, do not. To rectify this, non-state actors should be given access to international adjudication procedures. Traditionally, however, international adjudication procedures can only be instigated by states, the ICJ being a typical example here. Adjudication procedures in which non-state actors had standing were traditionally rare, an early exception being the ECHR. However, today's international adjudication systems increasingly provide access for non-state actors such as individuals, private groups, and supranational agencies.

---

[b] The political independence of other ILO committees remains limited, however.[20:290]

Table 1. Judicialization of international adjudication procedures

	GATT/WTO	SC	ILO/IER
Degree of independence	high (independent court)	low (political body)	medium (committee of experts)
Degree of compulsory jurisdiction	high (compulsory)	medium (limited)	medium (quasi compulsory)
Degree of accessibility	low (states only)	low (states only)	high (also private actors)
Overall degree of judicialization	high (increasing)	low (almost unaltered)	medium (increasing)

Nevertheless, the adjudication procedure within the trade regime of the WTO still only provides access for states, and, as in the GATT, only states may call for a panel. Beyond the access already given to them under the GATT, private actors can only 'participate' in the WTO dispute settlement proceedings by means of so-called *amicus briefs* in which they provide information that should be taken into consideration by the Appellate Body.[22]

Similarly, access to the adjudication procedures of the SC is largely limited to states. Although the Secretary General of the UN can bring to the attention of the SC any matter that may threaten international peace, he cannot bring in draft resolutions to force the Council to decide on such matters. The SC is free to use or ignore information brought to its attention by the Secretary General. Ultimately, only states can bring in draft resolutions the Council can be forced to vote on, and thus only states have standing before the SC.

Access to the adjudication procedures of IERs, in contrast, has increasingly been opened up to include complaints from non-state actors. In most of today's IERs, such as the regime for the protection of the ozone layer and the regime to combat climate change, adjudication procedures can be initiated 'ex officio'.[16] Expert committees entrusted with adjudication can act upon information on potential violations they either acquired themselves or received from the regime's secretariat. This indirectly gives environmental groups such as Greenpeace access to the adjudication procedures. Although formally, such groups' complaints do not have to be heard, IERs' committees of experts have so far never refused to act upon credible information about potential violations of legal obligations by states. Moreover, in accordance with its principle of tripartism, the ILO provides access for labour unions as well as employers' organizations to its adjudication procedures (Table 1).[20:284–300]

Overall, in terms of their changing accessibility as well as their growing political independence and increasing compulsory jurisdiction, adjudication procedures have become more judicial than they used to be. This certainly holds true for the WTO, but also, albeit to a lesser extent, for most IERs and the ILO; only the SC is lagging behind. A greater degree of judicialization, however, does not lead to uniform adjudication procedures but, depending on the issue area in question, it does give rise to adjudication procedures with a specific profile. The adjudication procedures of the WTO, for instance, are more judicialized in terms of their political independence and their compulsory jurisdiction, but not with respect to their accessibility. By contrast, most IERs and the ILO are more judicialized in terms of access to the relevant adjudication procedures, but their political independence and their compulsory jurisdiction are still compromised. Judicialization of the SC is not only less advanced, but also quite contained in terms of its jurisdiction, since its independence as well as its accessibility are still restricted.

What is, however, the driving force behind this process of judicialization? It seems at least plausible that it is to some degree a consequence of accelerated processes of globalization in certain issue areas during the 1970s and 1980s, which would also explain why judicialization is far more advanced within the GATT/WTO than within the SC. By the same token, the medium level of globalization in the field of environment politics might explain why the judicialization of adjudication in IERs is less advanced than in the GATT/WTO but more so than in the SC.

Globalization has become the driving force behind judicialization because states have had to respond to its challenges with new international rules. Since, in the context of globalization, national borders are increasingly penetrated, states have increasingly agreed on behind-the-border rules, which are particularly difficult to implement. In contrast to at-the-border rules they not only regulate how states have to act towards other states, but also how they should regulate their own societies, as in the case of WTO rules on consumer safety, SC rules on terrorism and ILO rules on child labour, for example. In response to the complexities of globalization, the rules themselves have become increasingly complex, and their application particularly difficult, requiring the weighing of conflicting legal principles. For example, the application of many WTO rules rests on balancing free trade against consumer safety. These 'new' rules encouraged states gradually to accept judicialized adjudication, as it became apparent that judicial adjudication is better suited to the reliable implementation and application of such rules than diplomatic adjudication.

The use of procedures by complainants

For an international rule of law, judicialization is, however, just one requirement; if adjudication procedures are judicialized, but hardly used in practice, one cannot, at least not meaningfully, speak of an international rule of law. It is, of course, a common feature of all legal orders that complainants seek settlement out of court. Consequently, complainants do not have to invoke the relevant adjudication procedures in each and every instance of a breach of international law. However, for the rule of law within a legal order to be effective, complainants must not take the law into their own hands. Hence, for the emergence of an international rule of law it seems to be imperative that complainants use the relevant adjudication procedures.

There are, in fact, a number of indications that international adjudication procedures are increasingly being used. One indicator is that they are invoked more frequently today than they were two decades ago. The dispute settlement proceedings of the GATT/WTO are an interesting case in point. After an impressive start in the 1950s, when GATT dispute settlement proceedings were invoked in 53 instances, the use of the dispute settlement system dropped to about seven instances in the 1960s, but rose again in the 1970s and the 1980s, to 32 and 115 cases respectively.[9:287] But after the introduction of judicialized dispute settlement proceedings under the WTO, figures jumped in the 1990s to 311 cases in less than a decade (http://www.wto.org).[c] Furthermore, not only small, and therefore less powerful, but also large and powerful states became targets of WTO dispute settlement proceedings. Indeed, the US and the EU – the most powerful members – have been the targets of almost half of all complaints registered with the WTO. Even less powerful states regularly invoke WTO dispute settlement proceedings against US and EU trade policies.[d] Moreover, not only small and therefore less powerful states, but also large, and powerful states, which could easily take the law into their own hands, rely on the WTO dispute settlement procedures. Taken together, the US and the EU are indeed responsible for about half the complaints submitted to the WTO since the mid-1990s. And they invoke the WTO dispute settlement procedures even when they complain about violations of less powerful states.[e]

The Security Council developed in a similar fashion. In the 1950s the SC passed only 54 resolutions. Since then, its use has increased to more than 140 resolutions in the 1960s and over 180 in the 1970s and 1980s, but in the 1990s it increased dramatically to 700 resolutions over that decade (http://www.un.org). Notably, the majority of SC resolutions concern alleged violations of fundamental legal

---

[c] Although this is partly due to intensified trade relations as well as a growth in internationally agreed trade rules and the rising number of member states of the GATT/WTO,[3,4] the frequent use of the dispute settlement proceedings remains quite remarkable. Some even suspect that the judicialization of the dispute settlement procedures has exacerbated GATT/WTO dispute settlement.[1]

[d] From 1995 to 2003, developing countries initiated more than 20 dispute settlement proceedings against the EU and more than 30 against the US (see http://www.wto.org). However, more than half the developing country members of the WTO have never participated in dispute settlement proceedings.

[e] From 1995 to 2003 the US and the EU each invoked WTO dispute settlement proceedings against developing countries in around 30 cases respectively (see http://www.wto.org).

rules by less powerful states such as Somalia, Haiti, Rwanda, Yugoslavia etc. Due to their power of veto, it is impossible to enforce resolutions against the most powerful states such as the US. But other powerful states such as India and Pakistan, which have no power of veto, have also seldom been the subject of SC resolutions. Nowadays, however, even the most powerful states tend to invoke the SC to deal with situations they conceive of as threats to peace, as in the case of the US in the 1990s, for example, with respect to the civil wars in Somalia, Bosnia, Haiti and Kosovo.[25:224–245] Moreover, the US not only engaged the Council in 1991 before the first Iraq war, but also in 2003 before the second Iraq war, and in both cases the Council ascertained that Iraq was in violation of its international commitments. The problem of the SC is not so much that powerful actors are not prepared to use it, but rather that without being invoked by powerful states the SC remains inactive. The SC can only be activated if powerful states such as the US are affected, as in the cases of Haiti or Bosnia, but if no powerful state is interested, as was the case with respect to Sudan or Nigeria, the SC cannot act.

The use of the ILO adjudication system is quite remarkable. Since its introduction in the 1950s, proceedings of the Committee on Freedom of Association were invoked in more than 2,300 instances (http://www.ilo.org). In particular, trade unions use that procedure to protest about states' interventions in their right to freedom of association. Since the mid-1970s, an increasing number of unions have also taken the opportunity to add critical comments to their governments' annual reports.[20:288] Other procedures under the ILO, such as the Representation Procedure and the Complaints Procedure, are invoked less often, but their use has also increased. The Representation Procedure, for instance, was initiated in 45 instances in the 1980s and early 1990s, as compared to only 14 instances from the 1940s to the 1970s.[19] Moreover, the committees of experts in numerous IERs are quite frequently invoked. Environmental organizations, such as Greenpeace, regularly report violations of international environmental obligations to the relevant secretariats and expert committees, which then initiate investigations. For example, within the Convention on the International Trade in Endangered Species (CITES), TRAFFIC – an organization set up by environmental groups – is the main source of information on potential violations for the secretariat and the standing committee. TRAFFIC's complaints are not only directed against small and relatively powerless states, but also against powerful states such as Russia, China, Japan, Great Britain, France and Germany. Similarly, the committee of experts for the protection of the ozone layer investigated alleged violations of rules concerning the reduction of CFCs by Russia.

The increasing use of international adjudication procedures is not only indicated by their increasing invocation, but also by the increasing propensity of complainants to stick to the procedures if defendants do not respond constructively.

The GATT/WTO trade regime provides a useful example here. In contrast to the GATT, the WTO dispute settlement system provides complainants with effective means to deal with defendants who are not prepared to comply with WTO rulings. Today therefore, complainants rarely take the law into their own hands, but rather abide by the rules of procedure for dispute settlement. This can be illustrated by comparing how the US reacted when the EU violated rulings of the old GATT and the WTO respectively. For example, in the hormones dispute between 1985 and 1994, the US employed non-authorized sanctions because the EU did not comply with a GATT panel report criticizing its ban on beef treated with certain growth hormones.[9] By contrast, when the same dispute arose again in the WTO between 1995 and 2003, the US refrained from taking unauthorized sanctions. Although the EU did not comply with the WTO ruling, criticizing again its ban on hormone-treated beef, the US applied sanctions only after having been authorized to do so. At least within the WTO context the propensity to take the law into one's own hands has clearly changed.

The same can be said with respect to the SC. A comparison of the 1980s and the 1990s indicates that the propensity of the US to ask the SC for approval before using military force against states threatening international peace has grown. The US intervened, for instance, in Grenada in 1983 and in Panama in 1989 without any prior involvement of the SC. In the 1990s, by contrast, in almost every case the US not only sought SC resolutions that criticized the states in question, but also resolutions that approved military interventions in those states. This certainly holds true for the interventions authorized by the UN in Somalia in 1992, Haiti in 1994 and Bosnia in 1995. One can even argue that these interventions would not have taken place without SC authorization. But this also holds true for the interventions in Kosovo in 1999 and Iraq in 2003, when the SC could not agree on authorizing resolutions. Admittedly, when Russia and France blocked these resolutions the US nevertheless took the law into its own hands, which only underlines that the use of SC procedures remains precarious. But the fact that the US had at least sought the authorization of the SC sets these interventions clearly apart from earlier, similar measures in Panama and Grenada, and demonstrates that the use of the SC procedures has been transformed.[25:275–277]

With respect to the ILO and IERs, incentives for complainants to single-handedly take sanctions against states that do not respect their international commitments are almost non-existent. Therefore, even when violators ignore the 'rulings' of the relevant expert committees within the ILO or IERs, complaining states hardly ever take the law into their own hands, but prefer to use the relevant procedures in order to persuade others to join authorized sanctions. It should be pointed out, however, that in most IERs, as well as the ILO, the scope for imposing sanctions is limited,[16] so it is hard to say whether complainants' reluctance to take the law into their own hands has changed.

The acceptance of procedures by defendants

Within the issue areas analysed here, the propensity of states to use relevant adjudication procedures against non-compliant states has increased. For the emergence of an international rule of law, however, not only the use but also the acceptance of judicialized adjudication procedures by those accused of violating their legal obligations must be considered imperative. It goes without saying that it is a common feature of legal orders under any rule of law that defendants seek to avoid being tried and convicted in court. Consequently, the unconditional acceptance by defendants of the rulings of international adjudication committees cannot be considered a criterion for an international rule of law. In a legal order based on the rule of law, however, defendants must not put themselves above the law by preventing, with single-handed measures, relevant adjudication procedures dealing with their alleged violations. For the emergence of an international rule of law it seems to be imperative that defendants generally accept the adjudication procedures as well as their rulings.

Indeed, evidence suggests that states allegedly in breach of legal obligations are increasingly willing to accept international adjudication rulings, and one indicator of this is that fewer states today try to prevent adjudication procedures from being initiated.

Under the terms of the old GATT, defendants often used their right to block the establishment of dispute settlement panels. In the hormones dispute with the US, for example, the EU prevented a GATT panel from being established.[9:225–226,229–230] Additionally, as with the US in its dispute with the EU about Domestic International Sales Corporations, defendants sometimes threatened to file counter-complaints if complainants asked for the establishment of a GATT panel. Today, however, under the dispute settlement system of the WTO, defendants are no longer able to prevent panels from being established. Consequently, there has been an increase in attempts to prevent complainants from requesting WTO panels with threats of counter-complaints. The US threat to file a counter-complaint against European tax systems in its dispute with the EU about Foreign Sales Corporations is one example. However, defendants now strictly refrain from threatening with illegal counter-measures to block the establishment of panels.

The same cannot be said of the Security Council. What is remarkable though, is the sharp drop in the use of veto. On average, from the 1950s to the late 1980s, France, Great Britain, Russia, China and the US vetoed more than 50 resolutions per decade. Within the context of the Cold War they either blocked resolutions criticizing their own use of force or protected their allies from being criticized by the SC. By contrast, during the 1990s, fewer than ten resolutions were vetoed (http://www.un.org). While the five permanent members continue to protect themselves from SC resolutions, their propensity to protect their allies has decreased. Instances like the repeated veto by the US in order to prevent Israel from being denounced for its use of force in the Middle East, have become less frequent. This even holds true despite the fact that today the threat of a permanent SC member using its veto – such as Russia's threat in 1999 to veto a resolution authorizing the use of force against Yugoslavia – often leads to the withdrawal of the respective resolution by its sponsors.

Within most IERs and the ILO, defendants are increasingly prepared to accept that potential violations of international legal obligations are subject to investigations of relevant expert committees, and by and large they refrain from attempting to block such investigations. In fact, in many IERs, expert committees have through customary practice acquired the right to conduct these investigations.[16] The CITES standing committee entrusted with investigating violations of restrictions on the trade in endangered species is a case in point. However, also in regimes where this task was formally introduced, defendants usually desist from obstructing relevant expert committees from becoming involved. This even holds for investigations of child labour by the relevant ILO committee. Instead of criticizing its investigations for interfering into their domestic affairs, most states collaborate with the ILO in order to curb child labour. Moreover, the sustained willingness of most states to submit annual reports, despite the fact that these often lead to criticisms about the unsatisfactory implementation of social standards, seems to indicate a widespread acceptance of ILO procedures.[20:288]

Another indication of the growing acceptance of international adjudication procedures by states accused of violating international legal obligations is that the states generally comply with rulings. For instance, the compliance record of the WTO, although far from perfect, is more satisfactory than that of the GATT, and complaints about violations of WTO rulings are comparatively rare. In particular, small and therefore less powerful states tend to comply.[4] Also, the compliance records of large and powerful states have at least improved.[4] A comparison between transatlantic disputes from the early 1960s to the mid-1990s under the old GATT and in the late 1990s and early 2000s under the WTO reveals increasing rates of compliance by the US and the EU. When convicted under the GATT, these states complied fully in only 21 out of 53 disputes, but under the WTO they complied fully in 21 out of 32 disputes. The non-compliance rate also dropped from 18 out of 53 to 8 out of 32 [3] disputes.[f] More remarkably, these powerful states not only comply when WTO rulings are backed by equally powerful states, but also when less powerful states complain about their trade practices. The US, for example, complied with a ruling that was the result of a complaint filed by Costa Rica. The fact that a small state like Costa Rica was able to win a dispute under the WTO against a state like the US and induce its compliance with the ruling shows the remarkable acceptance the WTO dispute settlement system enjoys.

---

[f] The compliance record of powerful states deteriorates when stakes become higher, however. In high-stakes disputes between the US and the EU under the WTO, the losing party made full concessions in only two out of seven disputes.[3]

Security Council resolutions are frequently ignored, however. In the 1990s, for instance, Libya, Sudan and Afghanistan were found responsible for backing terrorist organizations and the SC resolved that they should renounce their support for terrorists. As they did not respond constructively, the Council imposed sanctions. However, only Sudan – and later also Libya – gave up supporting terrorists, while Afghanistan persisted in giving support to terrorist organizations throughout the early 2000s.[6:107–134] More prominently, although hard hit by SC sanctions, Iraq under the leadership of Saddam Hussein ignored numerous SC resolutions throughout the 1990s. Moreover, in almost every civil war of the 1990s, the SC passed resolutions requiring the warring parties to refrain from force, but many of the resolutions, dealing for instance with Bosnia, Somalia and Kosovo, were ignored. In some instances, however, the SC was able to authorize sanctions that forced the warring parties to respect at least parts of its resolutions. For example, the sanctions against the Khmer Rouge in Cambodia proved to be an important factor leading to its dissolution.[6:135–145]

Moreover, compliance records with expert committees' rulings made in IERs as well as the ILO seem to be satisfactory. The ILO expert committee, for example, reported in 1994 that in at least 2034 cases it had investigated during the previous 30 years, progress towards compliance had been made.[20:288] More specifically, the ILO Committee on Freedom of Association documented that in the 180 cases it had to deal with between 1971 and 2000, progress towards compliance had been made, with a rapid improvement in compliance rates in the 1990s.[8] For 1996 alone, the Committee registered more cases of progress towards compliance than in the period between 1971 and 1977. Similarly, most IER expert committees are able to elicit respect for their deliberations. For example, an expert committee of the international regime for the protection of the ozone layer managed to bring Eastern European countries back in line with their obligations to reduce CFCs.

The rule of law in international relations

All in all, at least in the issue areas analysed here, the three preconditions for an international rule of law seem to be emerging gradually. International adjudication procedures have not only become more judicialized, but their use and acceptance by states has increased as well (Table 2). The three preconditions are not uniformly fulfilled across issue areas; however, the rule of law is considerably well-advanced with regard to trade issues (GATT/WTO), on a remarkable, albeit lower level with respect to environmental and labour issues (IERs, ILO) and on a much lower level as regards security issues (SC).[g]

---

[g] Moreover, the use of adjudication procedures is more advanced than their acceptance. Under the WTO as well as within the SC, the propensity of defendants to comply with adverse rulings does not match the complainants' propensity to invoke the relevant adjudication procedures. In the long run this imbalance could endanger the whole project of an international rule of law.

Table 2. Transformation of international dispute settlement procedures

	GATT/WTO	SC	ILO/IER
Judicialization of procedures	high (increasing)	low (unaltered)	medium (increasing)
Use of procedures	high (increasing)	medium (increasing)	medium (increasing)
Acceptance of procedures	medium (increasing)	low (unaltered)	medium (increasing)
Overall	high	low	medium

The judicial nature of adjudication procedures seems to be at least one of the driving forces behind their generally increasing use and acceptance. The reasons why the judicialization of adjudication procedures has strengthened their use and acceptance are twofold:

(1) Their judicialization gives adjudication procedures stronger teeth as instruments for coping with violations of international law. Judicialized procedures are stronger because it is more difficult to prevent their invocation and their rulings. Complainants therefore know in advance that using the procedures might help them to protect their rights, and defendants are aware that not respecting the procedures might have consequences. As the example of the WTO demonstrates, this gives complainants additional incentives to use these procedures while also creating additional incentives for defendants to accept them.

(2) In addition, the judicialization of adjudication procedures has strengthened their use and acceptance because they convey more dignity. Therefore, both complainants and defendants know in advance that not using these procedures and not accepting their rulings is more difficult to justify in public. And this in turn, as the case of the WTO has shown, supports the propensity of complainants to use these procedures while at the same time supporting defendants' propensity to accept them.

However, the emergence of an international rule of law is not a one-way street to progress; there are certainly pitfalls along the way, among which the continuing US hegemony might be the deepest. Although in many issue areas the emergence of an international rule of law took place in tandem with a growing US hegemony, there are indications now that US hegemony might endanger the international rule of law. Notably, the judicialization of procedures as well as their use and acceptance have come under severe pressure in areas where US dominance is particularly strong. This is particularly obvious in the Security Council, where the US has repeatedly flouted the pertinent adjudication procedures. By contrast, in issue areas in which US dominance is not as pronounced, the judicialization of adjudication procedures, their use and their acceptance continues uninterrupted. This holds true in the WTO, for instance, where the US generally respects the relevant adjudication procedures.

However, even in these issue areas, the emergent rule of law is still far from what we are used to from the domestic rule of law of modern states in the OECD world in terms of the adjudication procedures, their use and their acceptance. It does not seem likely that within the foreseeable future the international rule of law will be as binding on states as the domestic rule of law, not even in the OECD world. Moreover, in contrast to the domestic rule of law, the emergent international rule of law is not integrated. There is not one rule of law which extends across all issue areas, but rather a variety of rules of law differing from one issue area to the next. And so far there are no indications that such an integrated rule of law might come about. The international rule of law remains issue-area-specific and, therefore, of a different kind than the domestic rule of law.

Nevertheless, the emergent international rule of law certainly indicates a fundamental transformation of the sovereignty of modern states. It significantly limits states' discretion to arbitrarily act outside of international law and, given that sovereignty was one of the characteristics that have defined modern states for centuries, the emergence of an international rule of law must be considered as one of the most fundamental transformations of modern states within the last century.

Acknowledgements

This article presents preliminary results of the research project 'Judicialization of international dispute settlement' which is part of the Research Centre 'Transformations of the State' (TranState) funded by the German Research Foundation (DFG). For helpful comments on an earlier version of this article I would like to thank Achim Helmedach, Stephan Leibfried, Aletta Mondré and Gerald Neubauer.

References

1. K. Alter (2003) Resolving or exacerbating disputes? The WTO's new dispute resolution system. *International Affairs*, **79**(4): 783–800.
2. E. Brown Weiss and H. K. Jacobson (Eds) (1998) *Engaging Countries. Strengthening Compliance with International Environmental Accords* (Cambridge, MA: MIT Press).

3. M. L. Busch and E. Reinhardt (2002) Testing international trade law. empirical studies of GATT/WTO dispute settlement. In: D. L. M. Kennedy and J. D. Southwick (Eds) *The Political Economy of International Trade Law. Essays in Honor of Robert E. Hudec* (New York: Cambridge University Press): 457–481.

4. M. L. Busch and E. Reinhardt (2002) Transatlantic trade conflicts and GATT/WTO dispute settlement, Paper presented at the Conference on Dispute Prevention and Dispute Settlement in the Transatlantic Partnership at the European University Institute, Florence, Italy, 3–4 May 2002.

5. G. Clark and L. Sohn (1960) *Introduction to World Peace Through World Law* (Cambridge, MA: Harvard University Press).

6. D. Cortright and G. A. Lopez (2000) *The Sanctions Decade. Assessing UN Strategies in the 1990s* (Boulder, CO: Lynne Rienner).

7. G. Garrett (1995) The politics of legal integration in the European Union. *International Organization*, **49**(1): 171–181.

8. E. Gravel, I. Duplessis and B. Gernigon (2002) *The Committee on Freedom of Association: Its Impact over 50 years* (Geneva: International Labour Office): 22–24, 74–75.

9. R. E. Hudec (1993) *Enforcing International Trade Law. The Evolution of the Modern GATT Legal System* (Salem, NH: Butterworth Legal Publishers).

10. J. H. Jackson (1997) *The World Trading System. Law and Policy of International Economic Relations* (Cambridge, MA: MIT Press).

11. R. O. Keohane, A. Moravcsik and A. Slaughter (2000) Legalized dispute resolution: interstate and transnational. *International Organization*, **54**(3): 457–488.

12. M. Koskenniemi (1998) The place of law in collective security: reflections on the recent activity of the security council. In: A. J. Paolini, A. P. Jarvis and C. Reus-Smit (Eds) *Between Sovereignty and Global Governance. The United Nations, the State, and Civil Society* (Basingstoke: Macmillan): 35–59.

13. W. Mattli and A. Slaughter (1995) Law and politics in the European Union: a reply to Garrett. *International Organization*, **49**(1): 183–190.

14. J. G. Merrills (1998) *International Dispute Settlement* (Cambridge, UK: Cambridge University Press).

15. H. J. Morgenthau (1948) *Politics among Nations. The Struggle for Power and Peace* (New York: A. Knopf).

16. S. Oberthür (2004) Auf dem Weg zum Weltumweltrecht? Tendenzen und Wirkungen der Verrechtlichung der internationalen Umweltpolitik. In: M. Zürn and B. Zangl (Eds) *Verrechtlichung – Baustein für Global Governance?* (Bonn: Dietz-Verlag): 119–139.

17. E. U. Petersmann (1997) *The GATT/WTO Dispute Settlement System. International Law, International Organizations and Dispute Settlement* (Den Haag: Kluwer Law International).

18. C. P. R. Romano (1999) The proliferation of international judicial bodies. The pieces of a puzzle. *New York University Journal of International Law and Politics*, **31**(4): 709–751.

19. E. Senghaas-Knobloch (2004) Zwischen Überzeugen und Erbringen – Nachhaltiger Druck für Geltung und Wirksamkeit internationaler Arbeits- und Sozialstandards. In M. Zürn and B. Zangl (Eds) *Verrechtlichung – Baustein für Global Governance?* (Bonn: Dietz-Verlag): 140–158.
20. N. Valticos and G. von Potobsky (1995) *International Labour Law* (Deventer: Kluwer Law and Taxation Publishers).
21. D. Victor, K. Raustiala and E. B. Skolnikoff (Eds) (1998) *The Implementation and Effectiveness of International Environmental Commitments. Theory and Practice* (Cambridge, MA: MIT Press).
22. J. Waincymer (2002) *WTO Litigation. Procedural Aspects of Formal Dispute Settlement* (London: Cameron May): 328–331.
23. A. Watts (1993) The international rule of law. *German Yearbook of International Law* **36**: 15–45.
24. B. Zangl (2001) Bringing courts back in. Normdurchsetzung im GATT, in der WTO und der EG. *Schweizerische Zeitschrift für Politikwissenschaft*, **7**(2): 49–80.
25. B. Zangl and M. Zürn (2003) *Frieden und Krieg. Sicherheit in der nationalen und postnationalen Konstellation* (Frankfurt a.M.: Suhrkamp).
26. B. Zangl and M. Zürn (2004) Verrechtlichung jenseits des Staates – Zwischen Hegemonie und Globalisierung. In M. Zürn and B. Zangl (Eds) *Verrechtlichung – Baustein für Global Governance?* (Bonn: Dietz Verlag, series *EINE Welt-Band der Stiftung Entwicklung und Frieden*): 239–262.
27. B. Zangl and M. Zürn (2004) Make law, not war: Internationale und transnationale Verrechtlichung als Baustein für Global Governance. In M. Zürn and B. Zangl (Eds) *Verrechtlichung – Baustein für Global Governance?* (Bonn: Dietz-Verlag): 12–45.

About the Author

Bernhard Zangl is Professor at the University of Bremen/Germany where he is a member of the Research Centre on Transformations of the State (TranState) as well as a Codirector of the Institute for Intercultural and International Studies (InISS). Currently he is a Jean Monnet Fellow at the European University Institute (EUI) in Florence/Italy. He heads the TranState Research Centre group 'Judicialization of international dispute settlement' for which **Achim Helmedach**, **Gerald Neubauer** and **Aletta Mondré** work as researchers. His major publications related to this research are: Bernhard Zangl and Michael Zürn *Frieden und Krieg* (Frankfurt a.M.: Suhrkamp, 2003); Bernhard Zangl and Michael Zürn (Eds) *Verrechtlichung – Baustein für Global Governance?* (Bonn: Dietz Verlag, 2004); Bernhard Zangl, Bringing courts back in – Normdurchsetzung im GATT, in der WTO und der EG. *Schweizerische Zeitschrift für Politikwissenschaft*, **7**(2) (2001): 49–80.

European Review, Vol. 13, Supp. No. 1, 93–117 (2005) © Academia Europaea, Printed in the United Kingdom

5 Free trade: the erosion of national, and the birth of transnational governance

CHRISTIAN JOERGES and CHRISTINE GODT

Free Trade has always been highly contested, but both the arguments about it and the treaties that regulate it have changed dramatically since the Second World War. Under the 1947 General Agreement on Tariffs and Trade (GATT) regime, objections to free trade were essentially economic, and tariffs were a nation state's primary means of protecting its interests. However, by the early 1970s, tariffs had been substantially reduced, and the imposition and removal of non-tariff barriers that reflected a wide range of domestic concerns about the protection of health, safety, and the environment have since come to dominate trade agreements and their implementation. The expanding scope of these international treaties, and their effect on domestic regulatory objectives, has created new challenges for the nation-state, and for the international trade system as a whole. Domestic regulatory objectives that are generally embedded in a nation state's legal system or even in its constitution, are now negotiable and are susceptible to adjudication at the international level where they may, or may not, be used to camouflage unrelated economic interests. The international trade system adapted to this situation in 1994 by transforming the GATT into the World Trade Organization (WTO), which has more effective means for dispute resolution and includes a number of special agreements – such as the Agreement on the Application of Sanitary and Phytosanitary Measures (SPS) and the Agreement on Technical Barriers to Trade (TBT) – with rules for balancing the economic concerns of free trade with the social concerns of regulatory objectives. These developments have generated legal queries about the general legitimacy of transnational governance arrangements and their 'constitutionalization', i.e. the quest for transnational governance that is mediated by law and not only accepted *de facto* but considered deserving of acceptance.

Introduction

When the European Commission launched its legendary programme on the 'Completion of the Internal Market'[7] in the mid-eighties, both proponents and critics expected broad deregulation and a 'race to the bottom', wherein EC Member States sought to defend or strengthen their economic competitiveness by loosening the regulatory grip. Regulation was considered a cost, and deregulation a gain in efficiency. These expectations were thoroughly disappointed. Instead, we witnessed intense re-regulation and the emergence of new forms of cooperation among governmental and non-governmental actors. To use the terminology of the first essay in this work: the post-national constellation which Europeanization has generated has led to an erosion of the regulatory powers of TRUDI and of its capability to weigh autonomously the costs and benefits of opening the national economy. But Europeanization has also led to the establishment of sophisticated transnational governance arrangements which nation states could not have accomplished on their own.

Are there lessons to be learnt from the European experience for the organization of free trade at the international level? To what degree do we have to attribute the 'regulatory re-embedding' of free trade in Europe to specific supranational institutional features and interest configurations? To what degree should these developments simply be understood as responses to internationally salient concerns? To what degree has workable social regulation become a precondition for the functioning of international markets? If free international trade can only be realized in conjunction with the establishment of transnational governance arrangements, how can the 'reasonableness' of transnational governance be assessed and ensured? Does the nation state have to accept the loss of regulatory autonomy because this is what the functioning of international markets requires? Do the emerging transnational governance arrangements, to take up the formula of Jürgen Habermas[14], 'deserve recognition'?

This essay is going to explore this bundle of questions in three steps.

The first step will be concerned with the European experience. We will place special emphasis on Europe's institutional ingenuity in embedding its market-building efforts in the construction of sophisticated regulatory machinery as a key part of the European multi-level system of governance.

The second part will explore the regulatory choices open to the international trade system. Its institutional centre, the World Trade Organization (WTO), simply does not have the kind of regulatory powers on which Europe can rely. Nevertheless, it does have to deal with non-tariff barriers to trade, i.e. with precisely the type of regulatory concerns to which Europe has responded in its regulatory policies since the mid 1980s. We would like to underline here that the shift from the old GATT to the new WTO regime needs to be understood as a twofold process in which the regulatory autonomy of nation states is eroded while their regulatory concerns are built into the new transnational governance arrangements.

The third and concluding section takes up what has just been alluded to as Jürgen Habermas' concern for legitimacy. It will underline the parallels in the organization of responses to regulatory concerns at all 'levels of governance'. The emergence of novel forms of governance, it is submitted, is a response to the *impasses* of traditional regulatory techniques, which cannot be refuted. This development is, by the same token, a challenge to the notions of legitimacy that we have learned to appreciate within our national constitutional democracies. The legitimacy *problematique* is particularly precarious at the international level, and thus it is important to become aware of the prospects for law-mediated legitimacy in transnational constellations – and also for the limits of 'juridification' strategies.

A note on terminology may be in order here. 'Juridification' is just one of the concepts that we cannot avoid because they have come into use in pertinent academic circles. Other examples of what has been called 'Euro-speak' will follow. These terms are sometimes well defined; often, however, they are contested. We will try to explain the most important key concepts briefly either in the text or in notes.[a]

Non-tariff barriers in the European Community: free trade as an instigator of regulatory innovation

The re-regulatory and modernizing side-effects of the 'completion' of the European Internal Market remain puzzling but are so well documented, for example by Volker Eichener,[6] that we can refrain from reporting them in any detail. What we will instead focus on are the governance patterns that Europe has developed in its search for integration strategies that ensure the compatibility of the logic of market-building with the market-correcting logic of social regulation.

The Cassis jurisprudence under Article 28 EC Treaty: a conflict-of-laws approach

The most important of Europe's institutional innovations is hardly mentioned any longer in the debates on the so-called 'new modes of governance'. Back in 1979, the *Cassis de Dijon* case[8] saw the European Court of Justice (ECJ) declare that a German ban on the marketing of a French liqueur – the alcohol content of which

---

[a] 'Juridification' is a particularly tricky case. The term was introduced into the parlance of law and society studies as a translation of the notion of '*Verrechtlichung*' first used in the Weimar Republic by labour lawyers from the Left in their critique of the use of law to domesticate class conflicts, as Gunther Teubner[33;9] has shown. It hence carries with it a perception of the ambivalent effects of the use of law, which were characterized first as depoliticization, and later, and most famously, as a destruction of social relations, a 'colonialization of the life-world' in the view of Jürgen Habermas.[12] 'Legalization' analysis, as presented by Kenneth W. Abbott *et al.*,[1] is not linked to these traditions and their critical normative agenda. Pertinent studies explore parallels and differences between the subjection of political processes to rule of law requirements within states, and the causes and consequences of rule-bound governance beyond the nation states. But there is no consensus among political scientists and legal sociologists and theorists on the proper use of both terms.

was lower than its German counterpart – was incompatible with the principle of free movement of goods (Art. 30 EC Treaty, now 28 EC). The ECJ's response to the conflicts between French and German policies was as convincing as it was trifling: confusion of German consumers could be avoided and a reasonable degree of protection against erroneous decisions by German consumers could be achieved by disclosing the low alcohol content of the French liqueur. With this observation, the Court, on its own initiative, adopted the constitutional competence to review the legitimacy of national legislation that presented a non-tariff barrier to free intra-Community trade. This move was of principled theoretical importance and had far-reaching practical impact, as Miguel Poiares Maduro[23] has shown.

In a comparison of European and international responses to non-tariff barriers to trade, it is important to underline that the ECJ's celebrated argument can be translated into the language of a much older discipline, namely, that of conflict of laws. What the ECJ did in substance was to identify a 'meta-norm' which both France and Germany, as parties to the conflict, could accept. Since both countries were committed to the free trade objective, they could be expected to accept that restrictions of free trade must be based on credible regulatory concerns. The general importance of this type of conflict resolution becomes immediately apparent once we take into account the fact that market-creating and market-correcting regulatory policies are nothing exceptional and that they are the cause of the non-tariff barriers to trade with which the WTO regime seeks to cope. Without going into the theoretical underpinnings of this argument in any depth here, we simply submit that trade with increasingly sophisticated products 'requires' the development of regulatory machinery to ensure the 'trustworthiness' of such products to both traders and consumers.[3]

The new approach to technical harmonization and standards: towards 'private transnationalism'

In the presentation of its White Paper on Completion of the Internal Market, the European Commission[7] prudently underlined the basis of its new integration strategy in the jurisprudence of the ECJ in general and its *Cassis* judgment in particular. The White Paper's proposals were, however, much more radical than the Court's jurisprudence. What the Commission suggested was a twofold move: from mediation between conflicting regulatory policies, to the establishment of transnational governance patterns *and* from public to private transnationalism. The so-called new approach to technical harmonization and standards was the most significant contribution to this new orientation.

The story of the new approach has often been told, most recently and brilliantly by Harm Schepel[31:243–279]. In its efforts to build a common market, the EC found itself in a profound dilemma: market integration depended upon the 'positive' harmonization of countless regulatory provisions. Harmonization was difficult to achieve even after the old unanimity rule of Art. 100 EC Treaty was replaced in 1987 by qualified-majority voting (Art. 100a EC Treaty). Similarly, the implementation of new duties to recognize 'foreign' legislation, which the *Cassis de Dijon* decision of 1979 had arguably imposed, posed complex problems. Somewhat paradoxically, self-regulation, a technique very widely used in Germany in particular, was by no means easier to live with. Voluntary product standards were 'private' obstacles to trade, which the Community legislature could not overcome by legislative fiat. How could the EU get out of this *impasse*? The new approach achieved exactly that through a bundle of interrelated measures: European legislation was confined to laying down 'essential safety requirements', whereas the task of detailing the general requirements was delegated to the experts of the European and national standardization organizations. The involvement of non-governmental actors involved a *de facto* 'delegation' of law-making powers, which could not be openly admitted. Harm Schepel[31:70] cites a leading representative of the standardization community:

> The new method 'makes it possible better to distinguish between those aspects of Community harmonisation activities which fall within the province of the law, and those which fall within the province of technology, and to differentiate between matters which fall within the competence of public authorities and those which are the responsibility of manufacturers and importers'.[26]

The language covers and hides the political dimensions of standardization. This is small wonder, because the advocates of the new approach had to present their project in legally acceptable clothes. They were perfectly aware of the limited guidance that 'essential safety requirements' can offer in the standardization process. But they had good reasons to trust in the responsibility of the standardization process – and in the readiness of national and European public authorities to intervene should that trust be misplaced.

Administering the Internal Market: European committees and European agencies

Two more European institutional innovations need to be mentioned, the European committee system and European agencies. Both operate at the crossroads of market building and social regulation.

The European committee system is particularly interesting and contested. In it, the Commission organizes, in cooperation with experts and administrators appointed by the Member States, the implementation of Community legislation – technically speaking of 'comitology committees' – and the work on new regulatory projects for policy areas such as food safety, occupational health and safety. The Committee system was established to compensate for the lack of genuine Community administrative powers and the scarcity of its resources. It also fosters the acceptance of European prerogatives through the involvement of national bodies. These committees embody the functional and structural tensions, which characterize internal market regulation. They hover between 'technical' and 'political' considerations, between the functional needs and the ethical/social criteria, that inform European regulation. Their often very fluid composition not only reflects upon the regulatory endeavour to balance the rationalization of technical criteria against broader political concerns, but also forcefully highlights the schisms that exist among the political interests of those engaged in the process of internal market regulation. Even where they are explicitly established to support and oversee the implementing powers delegated to the Commission, committees are deeply involved in political processes and often resemble 'mini-councils', in that they are the forum in which the balancing of a European market-integrationist logic against a Member State interest – in terms of the substance and the costs of consumer protection and cohesive national economic development – has to be achieved. Their activities can be characterized as 'political administration', an oxymoron, which reflects their hybrid nature, as is shown in detail by Christian Joerges,[19] also with reference to earlier work.

Independent agencies were the core institutions advocated by Giandomenico Majone[24] in his design of a European regulatory state. Majone's suggestions attracted a great deal of attention but were never implemented. Europe has, however, adopted his term and established an impressive number of bodies, which are called agencies. What these bodies are, or will become, is indeterminate. This much is uncontested: agencies are certainly not self-sufficient bureaucratic entities. Charged with the regulation of market entry and exit, or with more general informal, and policy-informing, information-gathering duties, these new European entities meet a technical demand for market-corrective and sector-specific regulation. In their public presentation, it is often submitted that their functions are primarily technocratic. This is what they may accomplish best, and such a function seems well compatible with their semi-autonomous status, and the expectation that they should also give voice to private market interests. It is equally compatible with the thesis that 'administering' the Internal Market has more to do with the 'neutral' sustenance of individual economic enterprises than with the imposition of (collective) political/social values. The placement of the new entities under the Commission's institutional umbrella, and the presence of national representatives within their management structures notwithstanding, agencies seem, in the main, to be shielded from explicitly political processes by their founding statutes (Council directives and regulations), permanent staff, organizational independence, varying degrees of budgetary autonomy, and direct networking with national administrators. Their autonomy and independence is also limited for a second reason: they must cooperate with a web of national authorities in accomplishing the tasks laid down in European legislation. The transnational governance arrangements, through which the new approach, comitology, and even the new European agencies operate, cannot be equated with some Weberian type of administrative machinery. They all leave room for, and even build upon, the institutionalization of political (deliberative) processes.[19,25]

Non-tariff barriers and the World Trade Organization: a survey of conflict-resolving and policy-integrating mechanisms

European law and WTO law represent different legal worlds. So obvious and significant are the institutional discrepancies that comparisons between them which seek to draw upon the experiences of both institutions are often considered as being all too risky. And yet, some obvious functional equivalents seem to merit closer scrutiny, as Jacqueline Peel[27] shows in detail: both institutions have to balance free trade objectives and regulatory concerns, or as the Appellate Body in the *Hormones* case put it: 'the shared, but sometimes competing, interests of promoting international trade and of protecting ... life and health'.[2:para 177] The non-tariff barriers to trade to which the proponents of international free trade had to pay ever more attention in the last decades are requirements which the EC tends to recognize as legitimate restrictions to the freedom of intra-Community trade. The SPS and the TBT Agreements are institutionalized responses to health and safety concerns and the legitimacy of trade restrictions resulting from environmental policies is explicitly recognized in the preamble of the WTO Agreement. Our exploration of these parallels in this section will deal with conflict resolutions under these agreements. We will, on the one hand, contrast juridified and 'judicialized' resolution,[b] as opposed to political conflict resolution. We will focus here on 'product' as opposed to 'process' regulation and the governance patterns in this area. Both of these distinctions refer to separate debates but are nevertheless interdependent. Product regulation is obviously more closely linked to the realization of free trade than process regulation, because product-related mandatory requirements can hinder the importation of goods directly, whereas process regulation need not affect the quality of the output of production. It seems therefore plausible to assume that the juridification of transnational product regulation will be more intense than transnational standardization in the field of safety at work and environmental protection.

---

[b] Dirk De Bièvre[5:3] defines 'judicialized' as 'the presence of binding third party enforcement. This is a workable, albeit undercomplex, definition for two interdependent reasons: first, because the process of 'enforcement' of WTO reports cannot be equated with the enforcement of court judgments, as De Bièvre[5:7] himself underlines; second, because the authority of international bodies to decide about political differences and their economic implications poses thorny normative problems.

Alternatives to substantive transnationalism: proceduralized policy coordination through conflict-of-laws methodologies

As underlined in the previous section, the celebrated jurisprudence of the ECJ on Article 28 EC which seeks to 'harmonize' the principle of freedom of intra-Community trade with the respect for the legitimate regulatory concerns of EC Member States can be understood as a modernization of conflicts law because this jurisprudence seeks to identify meta-norms which the jurisdictions involved can accept as a supra-nationally valid yardstick for evaluating and correcting their legislation. The same holds true for the reports of the WTO Appellate Body assessing the compatibility of health and safety related non-tariff barriers to trade with the SPS Agreement. To generalize this observation: the SPS Agreement does not invoke some supranational legislative authority. It provides a framework within which WTO Members are to seek a resolution of conflicts arising from the extra-territorial impact of their regulatory policies. To become aware of these parallels is not just doctrinally interesting, but also practically relevant because a conflict-of-laws approach is politically much 'softer' than the imposition of a supranational substantive rule – Robert Howse and Kalypso Nicolaïdis[17] could hardly call 'constitutionalization' through a conflict-of-laws approach 'a step too far'.

To assign to conflict of laws a constitutional function in the sense that it has to deal with the competing validity claims of legitimate legal systems is an unavoidable consequence of the developments that led to the transformation of the GATT of 1947 into the WTO in 1994. These developments challenged the traditional understanding of the various legal disciplines dealing with the international system for decades.[20:345-348]

The disciplines of international private economic and administrative law have all, albeit often hesitantly, become aware of the regulatory dimensions of modern legal systems. They have to be taken into account in determining the law that should apply in international or transnational constellations in the choice-of-law process. The core difficulty, which conflict scholars are struggling with, stems from the 'fact' that there is no comprehensive super law available that can guide this process. To rephrase the problem in more technical terminology, their difficulty lies in getting beyond 'unilateral' or 'one-sided' definitions of the international sphere of application of domestic law (the *lex fori*), and conceptualizing cooperative legal responses for all concerned jurisdictions. This hesitancy to subject their own legal system to the commands of a foreign sovereign is often expressed in the language of traditional notions of sovereignty, but it can also be based on good 'constitutional' reasons; namely, on objections to the legitimacy of validity claims of law that is not generated in democratic processes. Furthermore, where courts are expected to handle transnational matters and/or to mediate between autonomous state orders, they move beyond their constitutionally legitimated functions. Thus, a 'judicialized' solution of international conflicts is a challenge to legal theory. The reasons have already been outlined in the explanatory note[a] to this term: the courts of national states are neither legitimated nor well equipped to take substantive decisions upon competing validity claims and their economic implications, or to hand down solutions to the challenges of transnational governance.

Once one has become aware of these difficulties, the virtues of the conflict-of-laws alternative to 'substantive' supranationalism become apparent. The search for a conflict norm can be understood as a 'proceduralization'[c] of the conflict between competing validity claims, namely, as a search for a meta-norm to which parties can commit themselves in a search for a solution to their conflict without betraying their loyalty to their own law. Taking up the trivial *Cassis* case again: France does not need to adapt the alcohol content of its liqueur to German legal requirements. Germany can continue to protect the expectations of its consumers. Both jurisdictions can live with a consumer information requirement. Solutions of this kind are not always as unproblematical and soft. The transatlantic conflict over hormones in beef[2] provides another instructive example. The US and (most of the Member States of) the EU are in disagreement regarding the addition of growth promoting hormones to beef-producing cattle. Can both parties agree to expose their practices to a science-based analysis of the health risks which the consumption of hormone-enhanced beef may entail? The requirement in the SPS Agreement that the measures of the WTO Members must not be 'maintained without sufficient scientific evidence' (Art. 2.2) and be 'based on' a risk assessment (Art. 5) seems to suggest exactly that. But, as the involved actors know all too well, a meta-norm referring to science as an arbitrator is not that innocent. Three reasons are sufficient to illustrate this point: firstly, science does not typically answer the questions that policy-makers and lawyers unambiguously pose; secondly, and even more importantly, it cannot resolve ethical and normative controversies; thirdly, consumer anxieties about 'scientifically speaking' marginal risks may be so considerable that policy-makers cannot neglect them.[11,28]

It is submitted that, all of these difficulties notwithstanding, a conflict-of-laws approach to regulatory differences offers an often viable alternative to a search for substantive transnational rules. This alternative is less intrusive and therefore easier to accept. Even where the meta-norms remain indeterminate, they may

---

[c] 'Proceduralization' is another term that would merit extensive explanations. In a nutshell: 'proceduralization' substitutes immediate decision-making by a search for innovative problem-solving. This implies the imposition of rules and principles which ensure a deliberative style among the parties to the conflict.

This is not, of course, to equate 'deliberation' with democracy, or to suggest that deliberation may be sufficient to generate legitimacy. The issue will be taken up in the first part of the section on governance below.

nevertheless help to structure the controversies among the parties to a conflict by re-opening political, potentially deliberative, processes. Conflicts-of-laws is, in cases of true conflicts in the last instance, a political exercise, as Brainerd Currie[4] argued. This does not, however, exclude the proposition that conflict rules may be strong enough to guide the solution of conflicts. And even where they are not, the 'shadow of the law' may be sufficient to promote international *comitas*[d] or diplomacy.[35] The borderlines are not as strict as legal formalists tend to portray them. It follows that 'judicialization', as achieved by the WTO through the Understanding on Rules and Procedures Governing the Settlement of Disputes (DSU), does not guarantee definite solutions, but may instead initiate a re-politicization of the whole process. Is this a failure, an advantage, or simply unavoidable? We will return to this question in the concluding section.

Limits of juridification: the example of product-related transnational governance arrangements

Internationally accepted product standards, so we have argued, best ensure the compatibility of free trade with concerns over safety and health. Unsurprisingly, international standardization is taking place on a great scale in the ISO, the (non-governmental) International Organization for Standardization, the IEC (International Electrotechnical Commission) and the ITU (International Telecommunication Union). The ISO is administering around 14,000 standards. Some 30,000 experts, organized in Technical Committees, Sub-committees and Working Groups, are engaged in their elaboration.[31:191–242] The CAC, the (intergovernmental) Codex Alimentarius Commission, an institution established by both the World Health Organization (WHO) and the Food and Agriculture Organization (FAO), is the relevant body in the foodstuffs sector, and Alexia Herwig[16] and Sara Poli[30] report on its operation.

Both bodies follow a harmonization philosophy, which has its basis in the pertinent WTO-related agreements, in the case of the ISO, in the TBT Agreement, in the case of the CAC, in the SPS Agreement. But on an almost global scale, any stringent harmonization is neither economically reasonable nor politically conceivable. Moreover, contrary to the situation in the EC, the WTO-ISO or WTO-CAC compound has no supranational legal competence that could trump the validity of national legislation. Anybody sufficiently familiar with the jurisprudence of the ECJ on Art. 28 EC and on the New Approach knows that

---

[d] Again, a term from the world of conflict of laws. *Comitas* is an ancient 'doctrine' with a complex history and an ambivalent heritage. Its dark side is a subordination of law under political prerogatives and the denial of legal duties to respect foreign law and interests. Its brighter side, which we recall, is commitments which do not arise out of juridified obligations, but out of friendship and trust among nations, as Jona Israël[18:129–136] reminds us.

such legal deficiencies are important – but also knows that they are not insurmountable barriers to transnational governance.

The TBT Agreement prescribes in its Article 2.2 that the technical regulations of its Members 'shall not be more trade-restrictive than necessary to fulfil a legitimate objective, taking into account the risks that non-fulfilment of these objectives would create'. The legitimate objectives include the concerns recognized by European law, in particular the protection of health, safety and the environment. Unsurprisingly, there is no equivalent to the European mutual recognition rule, but only a softer commitment to 'give positive consideration' to foreign regulations where 'these regulations adequately fulfil the objectives' of the importing Member. The same objective is served by the preference which, in Article 2.8, is only softly prescribed for performance, rather than construction or design standards. All this caution notwithstanding, the TBT Agreement is a powerful means for the promotion of reliance on international product standards, as it provides in its Article 2.2:

> Where technical regulations are required and international standards exist or their completion is imminent, members shall use them, or the relevant parts of them, as a basis for their technical regulations except when such international standards or relevant parts would be an ineffective or inappropriate means for the fulfilment of the legitimate objectives pursued, for instance, because of fundamental climatic or geographical factors or fundamental technological problems.

The SPS Agreement pursues a very similar strategy, which has proved to be quite effective. Prior to the adoption of the SPS Agreement, the impact of the CAC standards was apparently quite limited. They had no legal significance whatsoever. The SPS Agreement, which, in Article 3.1 requires that WTO Members 'base' SPS measures on international standards, guidelines and recommendations, has changed the situation quite dramatically. Legally speaking, the SPS requirement is clearly much less than a mandatory supranationally valid rule. The 'right' of WTO Members to determine the risk level that their constituency has to live with is *de jure* not at issue. Instead, the SPS Agreement has to build upon an incentive strategy that is similar to the safety 'presumption' upon which the European New Approach to harmonization and standards rests. Its Article 3.2 provides that national 'sanitary or phytosanitary measures which conform to international standards, guidelines or recommendations shall be deemed to be necessary to protect human, animal or plant life or health, and presumed to be consistent with the relevant provisions of this Agreement and of GATT 1994.' In this way, Article 3.2 SPS Agreement imports these norms into the WTO system.

As has become apparent, neither the TBT nor the SPS Agreement seek to prescribe some substantive uniform yardstick for the weighing of the costs and benefits of product standards. They remain akin to a conflict-of-laws approach in that they identify meta-norms that help to mediate the conflicting economic interests and regulatory concerns. In the case of the SPS Agreement, 'science' is the most visible guidepost. 'Science' does not, however, figure as some objective super-standard that could prescribe the contents of regulatory decisions. The function of appeals to 'science' is to discipline and rationalize regulatory debates. But even this cautious interpretation of the potential function of commitments to 'science' needs to be qualified further. The beef hormones saga, which is of exemplary importance here, did not end in any precise agreement about the kind of scientific evidence that the parties to the conflict must submit. The Report of the Appellate Body even explicitly recognized that 'the risk that is to be evaluated in a risk assessment under Article 5.1 is not only risk ascertainable in a science laboratory operating under strictly controlled conditions, but also risk in human societies as they actually exist, in other words, the actual potential for adverse effects on human health in the real world where people live and work and die'.[2:para187] The TBT Agreement and the ISO, as well as the SPS Agreement and the CAC, provide a framework for the elaboration of transnational product standards – a framework which does, however, remain embedded in, and dependent upon, political processes.

Two interim observations

Our analysis warrants two concluding observations from which the issues to be discussed in the next section follow with a compelling logic.

The first concerns the emergence of transnational 'law'. Juridification processes that respond to concerns of social regulation, so we have argued, are most likely in the field of product safety requirements. However, neither the WTO-TBT-ISO nor the WTO-SPS-CAC norm production can be equated with the processes of law-making and regulation in constitutional democracies. The coordination and norm-generating mechanisms that we observe may be more adequately, albeit somewhat vaguely, characterized as 'governance arrangements' – and 'governance' is the category which we will explore first.

The second observation concerns the relation between law and politics, i.e. the embeddedness of juridification in political processes at the transnational level. The intensity of this dependence is a matter of degree. Where conflicts can be resolved through choice-of-law approaches, the law is relatively strong, albeit 'imperfect', in that it refrains from imposing substantive rules with supranational validity claims. Where transnational governance 'needs' substantive rules, be it in the field of product or process regulation, the intensity of political supervision is stronger. Our conclusion may sound vague and daring to political or social scientists but it also seems unavoidable to lawyers. A hypothesis may suffice at this point: we assume that the tensions between law and politics need to be rephrased as the legitimacy *problematique* of transnational governance. This is the second issue covered here, to which the following section will turn.

The turn to governance and its distinct legitimacy problematique

Governance has become an extremely popular concept in Europe ever since the President of the Commission used it in a programmatic speech delivered on 15 February 2000 to the European Parliament in Strasbourg. On this occasion, with Europe in the grip of the BSE crisis, with its impact on the reputation of the European regulatory state being felt, Romano Prodi announced far-reaching and ambitious reforms. This was a message spoken in a new vocabulary, announcing a fresh agenda and a novel working method. Prodi envisaged a new division of labour between political actors and civil society, and a more democratic form of partnership between the layers of governance in Europe. It was this package of innovation, which was strategically launched into a legally undefined space somewhere between a technocratic and administrative understanding and a fresh democratization of the European Union, that attracted the attention of political scientists and lawyers.[21]

One of the insights that this debate has produced is that the 'turn to governance' is by no means a purely European invention but has international and nation-state parallels. 'Governance' is a response to interdependent phenomena: to failures of traditional regulatory law, to the erosion of nation-state governance and to the emergence of post-national constellations. The interdependence of these phenomena is the basis of our argument, which will be submitted in three steps. First, we start with a reflection on the national level. The 'turn to governance' was discovered, albeit in somewhat different terms, decades ago – and the responses developed since the 1980s remain attractive because the tribute they paid to functional necessities did not betray the law's *proprium*: its inherent links with the legitimacy *problematique* of governance practices. Then, second, at the European level, the turn to governance came about for basically the same reasons as earlier changes had occurred within the nation-state since the European Community engaged in, or got entangled in, its own 'political administration' of the Internal Market. However, even though the similarities between the turn to governance at European and national level are striking, the European legitimacy *problematique* is distinct in one important respect: it is different in that Europe has to conceptualize legitimate governance in a 'market without a state'. However, this does not imply that Europe should, or could, forget about the constitutional idea of law-mediated legitimacy. And, third, the *problematique* is again different at international level. Transnational governance at WTO level cannot duplicate the EU model. The barriers to equivalent legitimacy-enhancing strategies strengthen the political chances of technocratic legitimacy notions. These, however, are by no means the only conceivable way out of this dilemma, as our conclusion will submit.

Governance practices in constitutional states: bringing the 1980s back in

The seemingly irresistible career of the governance concept is new, although the phenomena it denotes are less so. In Germany, the inclusion of non-governmental actors into law-making processes and their participation in the political programmes that governments design to resolve social problems is as old as that country's 'organized capitalism'. What is changing and new is the deliberate use and sophisticated design of contemporary 'modes' of governance in the context of privatization and deregulation strategies and risk society issues, and of Europeanization and globalization processes. What may also be new is their international salience. To cite one particularly interesting American contributor, Jody Freeman[9] defines 'governance' as a 'set of negotiated relationships between public and private actors', which may concern 'policy-making, implementation and enforcement'. She points to a broad variety of administrative contexts, including standard-setting, health care delivery, and prison management. Some of them are clearly public responsibilities. Does this mean that any involvement of non-governmental actors is illegitimate? The reply to this query[10] is her most interesting point: the inclusion of private actors into governance arrangements 'might extend public values to private actors to reassure public law scholars that mechanisms exist for structuring public–private partnerships in democracy-enhancing ways'.

Where this is the case, the performance of such partnerships often seems superior to the achievements of governmental actors and bureaucracies. In this sense, 'governance' could be called a productive activity. Is this a type of 'output legitimacy' with which constitutional democracies should not content themselves? Such a framing of the *problematique* of the turn to governance is too simplistic. What is at stake is not just the performance, but also the capability of the political and administrative system to deliver responses which the citizens of democratic states are constitutionally entitled to receive. To rephrase this *problematique* in an older language, what is at issue here are the failures of the legal system of the modern welfare state, of TRUDI. And these failures have been on the legal theory agenda ever since lawyers became aware of implementation problems and joined the critique of political and legal interventionism that gave rise to the particularly intense debate in the 1980s.

Broad disappointment with 'purposive' legal programmes of economic management and a new degree of sensitivity towards 'intrusions into the life-world'[12] through social policy prescriptions mirrored the understanding that economic processes were embedded within societies in far more complex ways than a simple market-state dichotomy might suggest. This further triggered a search for new modes of legal rationality which were to replace interventionism and, by the same token, free themselves from the destructive myth that law might get a grip on social reality through the simple application of 'grand theories'. At the same time, however, 'proceduralization'[13] and 'reflexive law'[32] were also concerned with very mundane issues, such as the improvement of implementation and compliance. Discrepancies were clear between grand purposive legal programmes and their real-world social impact: it became a core concern of legal sociology to establish soft-law and regulatory alternatives to command and control regulation.[32,33] In other words, law, concerned with both the effectiveness of economic and social regulation and its wider social legitimacy, was, very early on, drawn into the refashioning of constitutional and administrative legal spheres. Law was developing a far more differentiated view of the constructive and legitimate synergies between markets and hierarchies.

Constitutionalizing European governance practices through deliberative processes

The most important and most successful innovations of European governance were achieved before this concept became so popular. To recall the most prominent examples mentioned in the first part of this essay: under the new approach to technical harmonization and standards, non-governmental organizations with links to administrative bodies, industry, and expert communities are all engaged in long-term cooperative relationships. Europeanization has managed to re-arrange these formerly national arrangements in such a manner that they operate across national lines and across various levels of governance. In the governance arrangements in the foodstuffs sector, the involvement of administrative bodies has been stronger – 'food safety' has, for a long time, been a concern of public administration. This is why the role of bureaucracies in the European 'administration' of food safety through the comitology system was, and still is, stronger than in the field of standardization. But it, too, has become a governance arrangement *par excellence*. Do such arrangements fit into our inherited notions of government, administration, and the separation of powers? Can such hybrids be legitimate? Is it at all conceivable that their legitimacy will be ensured by law?

These questions concern the 'nature' of the European polity, which is now widely characterized as a 'heterarchically' – as opposed to hierarchically – structured multilevel system, which must organize its political action in networks. This thesis has far-reaching implications. If the powers and resources for political action in the EU are located at various and relatively autonomous levels of governance, the coping with functionally interwoven problem-constellations will depend on the communication between the various actors who are relatively autonomous in their various domains, but who, at the same time, remain mutually dependent. Compelling normative reasons, which militate in favour of such cooperative commitments, can be derived directly from the post-national constellation in which the Member States of the EU find themselves. Their interdependence has become so intense that no state in Europe can take decisions of any political weight without causing 'extra-territorial' effects for its neighbours. Put provocatively, but nonetheless brought to its logical conclusion, the Member States of the EU have become unable to act democratically.

This is not a critique of some of the imperfections of the systems, from which we would conclude that the European democratic deficit should not be taken too seriously. Our point is more structural and principled. Individual European nation states cannot include all those non-national (European) citizens who will be affected by their decisions in their own electoral and will-formation processes. And *vice versa*: their own citizenry cannot influence 'foreign' political actors who are taking the relevant decisions for them. This is, of course, true for 'TRUDI' in general – and one of the reasons on which the legitimacy of conflict-of-law rules and transnational juridification rests. But within the EU, the interdependence of national societies is particularly significant – and can also be attributed to the integration process itself.

We conclude, that the debate on democracy in Europe is too one-sidedly concerned with the democracy deficits of the European construction. It neglects the structural democracy deficits of nation-state members. It fails to conceptualize the potential of European law to cure the democracy deficits of European nation-states. Such a vision of European law does not suggest 'democratizing' the European institutions as if they were separate bodies. It seeks to conceptualize the whole of the European multi-level construction in such a way that the European polity will not just be compatible with, but will even strengthen, democratic processes.

This is the task that has been assigned to European law under the heading of 'deliberative' – as opposed to orthodox – supranationalism.[22] These normative claims are based upon important legal principles of European law: the Member States of the Union may not enforce their interests and their laws unboundedly. They are bound to respect European freedoms. They must not discriminate. They may only pursue 'legitimate' regulatory policies approved by the Community. They must coordinate with respect to what regulatory concerns they may follow, and design their national regulatory provisions in the most Community-friendly way.

In the field of social regulation, Christian Joerges and Jürgen Neyer[19,25] have taken a further and more daring step: the EU-specific context of risk regulation, so they suggested, favours a deliberative mode of interaction. Its epistemic components are not simply technocratic but embedded in broader normative practices of reasoning. Is it conceivable for law to strengthen such qualities of social regulation in the EU? Is it conceivable to 'constitutionalize' the European committee system so that its operation becomes compatible with essentials of the democratic ideals of policy-making? The answers we found have already (implicitly) been rephrased in the distinction between conflict-of-law methodologies and transnational governance arrangements in the European Union, which we presented elsewhere at some length, and were recently summarized by Christian Joerges:[19] 'Deliberative Supranationalism Type I' should respond to the interdependence of semi-autonomous polities by identifying rules and principles that respect the autonomy of democratically legitimated units and restrict the controls to their design. 'Deliberative Supranationalism Type II' should also cope with the apparently irresistible transformation of institutionalized government into under-legalized governance arrangements. Such supranationalism must avoid two dead-end alleys: it cannot hope to destroy, in a constructive way, the turn to governance through which legal systems have, at all levels, responded to the *impasses* of traditional (administrative, interventionist) regulation. It cannot hope to achieve at the European level that which could not be accomplished at the national level; namely, a transformation of the practices of the 'political administration' of the Internal Market into a Weberian-type transnational administrative machinery for which the European Commission and the European Parliament could be held accountable. Instead, deliberative supranationalism should build three types of mechanisms by

- attracting the interests of non-governmental (in particular, of standardization) bodies to commit themselves to fair, politically and socially sensitive procedures through which they can build up public trust;
- covering the shadows of the law which cannot prescribe and control the activities of non-governmental actors and administrators in detail;
- introducing 'hard' procedural requirements to ensure that the governance of the Internal Market remains open for revision where new insights are gained or new concerns are raised by politically accountable actors.

The Internal market is a 'Market without a State'. It need not, and should not, become a 'Market without Law'.

Towards law-mediated legitimacy of ('constitutionalized') transnational governance

All the difficulties experienced by the law with respect to governance at the national and at the European level are present at the international level, albeit in even more challenging variations.

Governance phenomena, as we have defined them in the preceding paragraphs, are responses to the regulatory 'needs' that the traditional legal system could not fulfil. The reasons for these failures and the learning processes that the law underwent at the national and European level provide the basis of the following concluding observations, which will proceed in three steps. After first substantiating the specifics of the juridification of transnational market governance, we will, secondly, review three types of responses to its legitimacy *problematique*, namely, economic and technocratic rationality, transnational 'administrative' law, and societal constitutionalism; where these approaches fail, we have, thirdly, to rely on conflict of laws, *comitas* and diplomacy.

(1) 'Juridification' has intensified at the international level in many respects. The empirical indicators are so strong that all legal disciplines, as well as political and social philosophy are in the process of re-defining their premises. Juridification in the post-national constellation is broadening in scope and deepening in its reach to such an intensity that we have to take the notion of 'law without a state' seriously, as even Jürgen Habermas[15] concludes.

The governance phenomena that this essay is exploring concern just one segment of these developments. This segment may even seem quite mundane in its importance. It is, however, theoretically particularly challenging because it concerns regulatory issues and governance practices that do not fit into the traditional categories in which legal systems perceive problems, and through which they operate. This, as we have argued again and again, holds true at all levels of governance. But the difficulties of adjusting the law to the 'new modes of governance' are significantly greater at the international than at the European level.

(2) These differences become apparent because the approaches tried out at the WTO level and in the EU are very similar in their design.

(a) The formative era of the European Community is particularly instructive in this respect. Two answers to the – by now so famous – democracy deficits were developed, which have been important up to the present and have their equivalents at the international level. One was the theory of the European Economic Constitution, which legitimized – and restricted – European governance through supranationally valid commitments to economic freedoms, open borders and a system of undistorted competition. The constitutional perspectives for the law of the WTO, which, in particular, Ernst-Ulrich Petersmann[29] defends, are anchored in this tradition. They will not be discussed here because they do not deal with the type of regulatory concerns and governance arrangements that this essay focuses on. We interpret markets as social institutions and are interested in their 'infrastructure', i.e. the web of formalized and semi-formal relations through which decisions are taken, which the economic theories of the functioning of markets do not address directly.

The second approach to European 'governance' was technocratic in that its exponents sought to defend – and to restrict! – European governance activities to a non-political type of expertise. One contemporary version of this argument has been cited in the presentation of the new approach to harmonization and standards in the analysis of the European example. Its most prominent equivalent at the international level is 'science'. There are many reasons for its attractiveness. Scientific expertise tends to claim a genuine authority in regulatory decision-making, which is, by its very nature, objective (neutral) and un-political. The standards of good science are not bound to some specific legal system which endorses the binding quality of scientific findings, but they are, by their very nature, transnationally valid. By resorting to scientific expertise, legal systems subject themselves to 'external' validity criteria – and overcome their territorial parochialism precisely for this reason. If only science could be that objective and find answers to the questions that we pose! Unfortunately, the real expert will only tell us why he cannot perform such functions. This is so widely known that the objectivity myth cannot even serve as a workable fiction, as Jacqueline Peel[27] has most recently and comprehensively shown for the WTO.

(b) The standardization bodies for foodstuffs (CAC) and technical products (ISO, IEC, ITU) are both linked to the WTO, to other governmental and non-governmental actors, and also to national legal systems. Their authority in the field of product regulation depends upon the concrete contents of these links – and on the trust that they build up. 'Expertise' is crucial in this respect. However, it is not sufficient. Since standardization involves decision-making, the quality of standardization procedures is a second dimension on which the impact of these organizations depends.

Unsurprisingly, their record is contested. The technique of incorporating the CAC standards into the WTO system (Art. 3.2 SPS Agreement) has been criticized specifically in the light of the internal CAC procedures. These procedures, the critics argue, do not merit such preferential treatment. The Appellate Body in the Hormones case has been very cautious in its determination of the legal status of the CAC standards.[e] The WTO, we can conclude, has accepted the need to integrate regulatory policies into the free trade system. Although it has not pushed the case for juridification, food standardization remains closely embedded in

---

[e] 'To read Article 3.1 [of the SPS Agreement] as requiring Members to harmonize their SPS measures by conforming those measures with international standards, guidelines and recommendations, in the here and now, is in effect, to vest such international standards, guidelines and recommendations (which are by the terms of the Codex recommendatory in form and nature) with obligatory force and effect … [Such an] interpretation of Art. 3.1 would, in other words, transform those standards, guidelines and recommendations into binding norms. But … the SPS Agreement itself sets out no indication of any intent on the part of the Members to do so.'[2:para 165]

political processes. This embeddedness, however, is not of the same quality as in European governance. The form of legitimacy claimed for (constitutionalized) comitology rests upon the epistemic and political potential of deliberative processes to achieve fair compromises between conflicting interests, to integrate a plurality of expert knowledge, to make use of the management capacities at different levels of governance, and to remain open for revision where new insights are gained or new concerns are raised by politically accountable actors. Constitutionalized comitology is a legalized, proceduralized endeavour that operates in the shadow of democratically legitimated institutions.

(c) Reservations similar to those raised against the CAC are voiced with regard to the international standard setting by ISO and IEC. But these are minority opinions. The assessment of ISO and IEC is, in general, much more favourable. The most positive evaluation is Harm Schepel's. It is also the most challenging interpretation theoretically.

In Harm Schepel's[31:191–242] account, 'good' governance, as we observe it in standardization both within the EU and at the international level, is not political rule through institutions as constitutional states have developed them. Instead, it is the innovative practices of networks, horizontal forms of interaction, a method for dealing with political controversies in which actors, political and non-political, public and private, arrive at mutually acceptable decisions by deliberating and negotiating with each other. The crux of this observation is a paradoxical one within traditional democratic theory, and it is counter-intuitive: productive and legitimate synergy between market and civil society cannot be furnished within traditional democratic theory, be that theory majoritarian (working with a *demos*) or deliberative (dispensing with the *demos*, but placing a 'governing' emphasis on the primacy of the public sphere). How can this be? To cite Harm Schepel[31:241] again:

> The paradox is, of course, that the mechanism through which to achieve this is, well, politics. Due process, transparency, openness, and balanced interest representation are norms for structuring meaningful social deliberation. They are not obviously the appropriate vehicles for revealing scientific 'truth' or for allowing room for the invisible hand.

This is a message with many theoretical premises and practical provisos. To relate it back to the beginnings of this essay: the modern economy and its markets are 'politicized' in the sense that politically important processes are taking place there. The political system cannot reach into this sphere directly. These two steps of the argument do claim some plausibility. However, it is the third thesis that is the critical one: there are constellations in which the political processes within society seem perfectly legitimate. 'Private transnationalism' is the term that Schepel employs, but 'societal constitutionalism' seems a preferable notion because it covers national, European and transnational phenomena. However, it too is a notion in need of further explanations. Those (the few) who advocate it accentuate different aspects.[20,31,34] In the version adopted in this essay, societal constitutionalism seeks to respond to three interdependent phenomena: the 'politicization' of markets; the emergence of governance arrangements which need to acknowledge the problem-solving capacities and managerial qualities of the private sphere; and the transformation of nation-state governance in transnational constellations. This is not where the law ends, however. Even where non-governmental actors commit themselves credibly to normative standards, which 'deserve recognition', their legitimacy and autonomy, according to Harm Schepel, rests upon the compatibility of their institutionalization with the legal institutions surrounding them: it is not, therefore, so surprising that standardization organizations seek to establish procedures in which society as a whole can trust, and that sufficiently self-critical law-makers and regulators realize they would not be able to substitute what standardization accomplishes. In short, standardization both integrates and coordinates private governance actors across national and international levels, and reconnects national and international public spheres; standardization is functioning not under their direction, but in their shadow.

(3) Is the weak transnational juridification of social regulation a bad thing that we should try to overcome? It is first of all important to acknowledge the normative arguments against stricter transnational legalization. Their core is that there is simply no political authority that would be entitled to take the same type of decisions for which constitutional states are legitimated. But it is then equally important to consider the responses that law can nevertheless help to organize. The most important among them is a conflict-of-laws inspired approach to the handling of legal differences that result in barriers to free trade. The European experience is encouraging and can be developed further at the WTO level. Conflicts between legal systems, which become apparent in legal differences in the field of social regulation, are usually multi-faceted. They concern political preferences, economic interests, industrial policy objectives, distributional politics, and ethical concerns. A proceduralizing approach to such conflicts has the potential of discovering the nature of the differences and thereby identifying the conditions under which the free trade objective can be defended. The conceivable solutions will regularly be incomplete in that they leave it to the concerned jurisdictions to deal with implications that cannot be handled at the international level. The distributional implications of regulatory decisions are a case in point; their political implications tend to overburden the international system. A strategy of differentiating between the levels of governance, which decentralizes the management of such difficulties, can be advantageous – provided that the international level proceeds with sufficient sensitivity to national concerns.

Conclusion

The type of proceduralized conflict resolution advocated here for international disputes is less juridical than its European counterpart. The search for conflict avoidance through deliberative processes within the EU has become a constitutional commitment. As Jona Israël[18:136–159] recently put it, the EU has turned comity among the European nation states into a duty of cooperation. The European system of multi-level governance is operating within legally defined limits. The law-mediated legitimacy of its new modes of governance – their 'constitutionalization' – is at least conceivable.

At the WTO level, the transformation of *comitas* into mandatory commitments may be, to rephrase a famous reservation against constitutionalization of the WTO,[17] 'a step too far'. Comity is a softer technique. It involves self-restraint in the assertion of jurisdiction and the application of the *lex fori* out of respect for foreign concerns. To invoke such commitments among WTO members is to suggest that court-like independent bodies – such as the WTO's Appellate Bodies – remain legitimized to promote amicable solutions to disputes where they cannot resolve them through adjudication. *Comitas* would suggest a search for a middle ground between law and politics by advising the latter to take the expertise of the former seriously, and by advising the former to be aware of the limited legitimacy of law that does or did not originate in a democratic process. Where the WTO has reached the borderlines of 'judicialization' and does not seem empowered to assess policies and economic interests, it may still function as a forum and as an instigator of fair and workable compromises.

Acknowledgements

The participants in the Bremen-Florence project on 'Social Regulation and World Trade' have all, in one way or the other, contributed to the production of this paper. Christiane Gerstetter and David Gerl helped very intensively with the literature and more. Cormac MacAmhlaigh, a First Year Researcher at the European University Institute's Law Department in Florence, and Chris Engert corrected our English prose. An elaborated version of this contribution will be available in the TranState Working Paper Series at http://www.sfb597.uni-bremen.de/.

References

1. K. W. Abbott, R. O. Keohane, A. Moravcsik, A.-M. Slaughter and D. Snidal (2000) The concept of legalization. *International Organization*, **54**(3): 401–419.

2. Appellate Body Report *EC – Measures Concerning Meat and Meat Products (Hormones)*, WT/DS26/AB/R and WT/DS48/AB/R, 16 January 1998.

3. F. Block (2005) Towards a new understanding of economic modernity. In: C. Joerges, B. Stråth and P. Wagner (Eds) *The Political Construction of Modern Capitalism* (London: GlassHousse), forthcoming.

4. B. Currie (1963) The constitution and the choice of law: governmental interests and the judicial function (first published 1958). In B. Currie (Ed) *Selected Essays on the Conflict of Laws* (Durham, NC: Duke University Press): 188–282.

5. D. De Bièvre (2004) Governance in international trade. Judicialization and positive integration in the WTO (Bonn: Max Planck Institute for Collective Goods), Preprints MPICG WP 2004/7.

6. V. Eichener (2000) *Das Entscheidungssystem der Europäischen Union. Institutionelle Analyse und demokratietheoretische Bewertung* (Opladen: Leske + Budrich).

7. European Commission (1985) *Commission White Paper to the European Council on Completion of the Internal Market*, COM (85) 310 final, 14. June 1985.

8. European Court of Justice *ECJ* (1979): Case 120/78, *ECR [1979]* 649 – *Cassis de Dijon*.

9. J. Freeman (2000) The private role in public governance. *New York University Law Review*, **75**(3): 543–675, 546 and 548.

10. J. Freeman (2003) Symposium: public values in an era of privatization: extending public law norms through privatization. *Harvard Law Review*, **116**(5): 1285–1352, esp. p. 1290.

11. C. Godt (1998) Der Bericht des Appellate Body der WTO zum EG-Einfuhrverbot von Hormonfleisch-Regulierung im Weltmarkt. *Europäisches Wirtschafts- und Steuerrecht*, **9**(6): 202–209.

12. J. Habermas (1985) Law as medium and law as institution. In: G. Teubner (Ed) *Dilemmas of Law in the Welfare State* (Berlin: de Gruyter): 203–220.

13. J. Habermas (1998) Paradigms of law. In: M. Rosenfeld and A. Arato (Eds) *On Law and Democracy: Critical Exchanges* (Berkeley and Los Angeles, CA: University of California Press): 13–25.

14. J. Habermas (2001) Remarks on legitimation through human rights. In: J. Habermas (Ed) *The Postnational Constellation. Political Essays* (Cambridge, MA: MIT Press):113–129, esp. p. 113.

15. J. Habermas (2004) Hat die Konstitutionalisierung des Völkerrechts noch eine Chance? In: J. Habermas (Ed) *Der gespaltene Westen* (Frankfurt a.M.: Suhrkamp):113–193.

16. A. Herwig (2004) Transnational governance regimes for foods derived from biotechnology and their legitimacy. In: C. Joerges, I.-J. Sand and G. Teubner (Eds) *Transnational Governance and Constitutionalism* (Oxford: Hart): 199–222.

17. R. Howse and K. Nicolaïdis (2000) Legitimacy and global governance: why constitutionalizing the WTO is a step too far. In: R. B. Porter, P. Sauve, A. Subramanian and A. B. Zampetti (Eds) *Efficiency, Equity and*

Legitimacy: The Multilateral Trading System at the Millennium (Washington DC: Brookings Institution Press): 227–252.

18. J. Israël (2004) European cross-border insolvency regulation, Florence: European University Institute, PhD Thesis, http://www.xs4all.nl ~ monk/jona/thesis.pdf.

19. C. Joerges (2003) Comitology and the European model? Towards a Recht-Fertigungs-Recht in the Europeanisation process. In: E.O. Eriksen, C. Joerges and J. Neyer (Eds) *European Governance, Deliberation and the Quest for Democratisation* (Oslo: Arena Report 2/2003): 501–540.

20. C. Joerges (2004) Constitutionalism and transnational governance: exploring a magic triangle. In C. Joerges, I.-J. Sand and G. Teubner (Eds) *Transnational Governance and Constitutionalism* (Oxford: Hart): 339–375.

21. C. Joerges, Y. Mény and J. H. H. Weiler (2001) Symposium: Mountain or molehill? A critical appraisal of the Commission White Paper on Governance (New York: New York University, Jean Monnet Working Paper No. 6/01) http://www.jeanmonnetprogram.org/papers/01/010601.html.

22. C. Joerges and J. Neyer (1997) From intergovernmental bargaining to deliberative political processes: the constitutionalisation of comitology. *European Law Journal*, **3**(3): 273–299.

23. M. P. Maduro (1997) *We the Court. The European Court of Justice and the European Economic Constitution* (Oxford: Hart): 150ff.

24. G. Majone (1994) The rise of the regulatory state in Europe. *West European Politics*, **17**(3): 77–101 (see now his *Dilemmas of European Integration. The Ambiguities and Pitfalls of Integration by Stealth* [Oxford: Oxford University Press, 2005]).

25. J. Neyer (2003) Discourse and order in the EU: a deliberative approach to multi-level governance. *Journal of Common Market Studies*, **41**(4): 687–706.

26. F. Nicolas (1995) *Common Standards for Enterprises* (Luxembourg: Office of Official Publications of the European Community): 94.

27. J. Peel (2004) Risk regulation under the WTO/SPS agreement: science as an international normative yardstick (New York: University School of Law, Jean Monnet Working Paper 02/04).

28. O. Perez (2004) *Ecological Sensitivity and Global Legal Pluralism: Rethinking the Trade and Environment Conflict* (Oxford: Hart): 115ff.

29. E.-U. Petersmann (2003) Constitutional economics, human rights and the future of the WTO. *The Swiss Review of International Economic Relations (Aussenwirtschaft)*, **58**(1): 49–91.

30. S. Poli (2004) The EC and the adoption of international food standards within the Codex Alimentarius Commission. *European Law Journal*, **10**(5): 613–630.

31. H. Schepel (2004) *The Constitution of Private Governance. Product Standards in the Regulation of Integrating Markets* (Oxford: Hart).

32. G. Teubner (1983) Substantive and reflexive elements in modern law. *Law and Society Review*, **17**(2): 239–285.

33. G. Teubner (1987) Juridification – concepts, aspects, limits, solutions. In: G. Teubner (Ed) *Juridification of Social Spheres* (Berlin-New York: de Gruyter): 3–48.

34. G. Teubner (2004) Societal constitutionalism: alternatives to state-centered constitutional theory? In: C. Joerges, I.-J. Sand and G. Teubner (Eds) *Transnational Governance and Constitutionalism* (Oxford: Hart): 3–28.

35. J. H. H. Weiler (2001) The rule of lawyers and the ethos of diplomats: reflections on the internal and external legitimacy of the WTO dispute settlement. *Journal of World Trade*, **35**(2): 191–207.

About the Authors

While **Christian Joerges** and **Christine Godt** are the authors, and together with **Josef Falke**, the principal investigators, **Christiane Gerstetter**, **Alexia Herwig**, **Matthias Leonhard Maier** and **Ulrike Ehling** are investigators in our Bremen/Florence research group on 'Social regulation and free trade', one of the 15 current projects at the Research Centre on 'Transformations of the State' (TranState). In this team of lawyers, Ulrike Ehling and Matthias Leonhard Maier are the social scientists. Alexia Herwig is finishing her first book on *A Postmodern Critique of the Regulation of the Trade, Safety, and Consumer Choice Issues Concerning GM [genetically-modified]-Foods Through WTO-Law*, New York: New York University Law School, PhD thesis (2004). Josef Falke has published widely in the field of product standardization, be it European or international, while Christine Godt's principal research focus is on environmental protection, be it international (WTO) or European – both are senior researchers at the Centre for European Law and Politics (ZERP) at the University of Bremen. Christian Joerges has been professor for European economic law at the European University Institute in Florence since 1988, with his research focused on social regulation in the EU and, more recently, at the WTO level, on the Europeanization of private law and also on anti-liberal traditions in European legal thought. For some of his works see items 19 to 22 of the references.

European Review, Vol. 13, Supp. No. 1, 119–137 (2005) © Academia Europaea, Printed in the United Kingdom

THE DEMOCRATIC NATION STATE: EROSION, OR TRANSFORMATION, OF LEGITIMACY

6 Is there a legitimation crisis of the nation-state?

ACHIM HURRELMANN, ZUZANA KRELL-LALUHOVÁ, ROLAND LHOTTA, FRANK NULLMEIER and STEFFEN SCHNEIDER

It is widely accepted that internationalization and the increasing loss of parliamentary control over political power challenge the legitimacy of national democratic systems and their core institutions. We first present results from a study of public communication, which, when examined in the context of theories of legitimation, indicate that these processes do not necessarily lead to the erosion or breakdown of popular support for the nation state. The idea that there is a linear cause-and-effect relationship is overly simple, and a more detailed analysis is called for. Legitimation of a political system through public communication is a back-and-forth process which is determined by the system's specific institutional arrangements and by the fortuitous twists and turns of public debate. Nation states have more extensive, diverse and deeply rooted sources of legitimation than is often assumed.

Legitimacy in the nation-state: what do we know?

The idea of democracy is at the heart of the modern western state, whose institutions reflect what Robert A. Dahl called the 'second democratic transformation', i.e. the transfer of democratic self-government from the city-state to nations and large-scale societies.[6] For a long time, this transfer was remarkably successful. Institutions of representative democracy at the national level secured effective citizen participation in political decision-making and they themselves became a central source of popular support for the nation state's political arrangements.[13] This democratic dimension of the modern state, therefore, is critical to its legitimacy: Both the degree to which political systems enable collective self-government, a measure of legitimacy in the normative sense, and citizen acceptance of state institutions, legitimacy in the empirical sense, greatly depend on the nature and quality of democratic procedures.

These procedures, however, are affected by the transformations of the state discussed in this volume. Two factors are particularly important, the first being the *internationalization of political power*. Many of the nation state's traditional responsibilities have shifted to international or supranational regimes and organizations like the WTO or the EU. This is, in part, a response to challenges that the nation state can no longer effectively tackle on its own. But while such institutions may indeed be capable of more effective problem-solving, the democratic quality of their decision-making procedures is generally quite low. It would be natural to assume, then, that such internationalization jeopardizes the legitimacy of both the nation state and the transnational organizations: as the influence of the former dwindles, and the latter are found wanting in democratic quality, the democratic form of government is at risk of becoming one in which citizens, in Dahl's words, 'participate extensively in political decisions that do not matter much but cannot participate much in decisions that really matter a great deal'.[6]

The second factor in the transformation of the state that strongly influences democratic procedures is the *loss of parliamentary control over political power*, or deparliamentarization. While parliaments have traditionally exerted considerable influence as core institutions of representative democracy, their decision-making functions are increasingly being assumed by national executives, the judiciary, central banks, expert commissions, business corporations, interest groups, etc. Hence, even in areas where the nation state has preserved its responsibilities, democratic control over political decision-making can no longer be taken for granted. To some extent, this trend is itself caused by internationalization, as nation states are generally represented by their executives in supranational organizations. But other factors, such as the growing complexity of legislation, the imperatives of party government or the growing influence of private actors, are also important. They all contribute to a shift of power away from parliaments, and thus away from the core legitimating institutions of the democratic nation state.

As political decision-making moves out of national spheres of sovereignty and parliamentary arenas, many traditional standards of democratic legitimacy are falling by the wayside.[1,3,12,15] However, we question whether these developments have in fact also eroded popular support for the nation state. Are we facing a legitimacy crisis of representative democracy, as many analysts of the viability of the modern western state maintain?[2,10,14] They conclude that the changes in the state's democratic, constitutional, welfare and power structures are severely damaging the sources of its legitimacy. But do we really have empirical proof of such an erosion of support for the nation state and its institutions? Or are we mixing normative premises with dire, yet sketchy empirical findings?

We present here results from a study of media communication in Great Britain, Switzerland, and the United States, highlighting the important role played by public discourses in the construction, reconstruction and transformation of legitimacy. We examine if the hypothesis of an imminent legitimation crisis of the nation state can be corroborated, and to what extent it might have to be differentiated: Do internationalization and deparliamentarization really undermine popular support for the nation state? To what extent is legitimation communication shaped by idiosyncratic national institutional arrangements, political agendas and debates? How diverse and robust are the resources used in the legitimation of national political systems?

Legitimacy discourses and political institutions

Legitimacy is a key resource for every political system. It refers to the acceptance of a specific political order by its own citizens and to the beliefs on which that acceptance is grounded. Easton defined legitimacy as a function of 'diffuse' support and 'specific' support.[7] Diffuse support is created in socialization processes and obtained when the members of a political community are convinced that the institutions and guiding principles of a political order or 'regime', as well as the behaviour of its representatives or 'authorities', correspond to their own moral principles. It is based on values and affective attachments, and relatively insensitive to short-term fluctuations in system performance. Specific support, on the other hand, is based on the relationship between the demands of the citizens and the material outputs of a system. Whereas diffuse support is anchored in beliefs about the political community and the regime, specific support is based predominantly on the citizens' perceptions and evaluations of authorities.

What is important here is that legitimacy, as a function of both diffuse and specific support, is attributed and constructed in an ongoing process of interpretation and reinterpretation, and thus dependent on language. The norms and values central to the perception of a political system as legitimate are established, modified or re-established in public discourses. Such discourses guide and legitimate political action by shaping acceptable, hegemonic, or collectively binding interpretations of social and political events and relationships; they justify or contest normative criteria for the attribution of legitimacy, and debate the extent to which these criteria are met. These discursive processes can result either in the legitimation or in the delegitimation of a political order.

The political institutions at the core of democratic systems of governance play a vital role in shaping our interpretations of the world[11] and are thus in the Janus-headed position of influencing the very legitimation processes of which they are the object. If we want to know more about the resources of support at the disposal of political systems, we need to focus on how institutions influence the discursive construction of legitimacy. Institutional designs are also likely to play a gate-keeper function vis-à-vis internationalization and deparliamentarization and influence the interpretations of these processes.[4] Legitimacy may, however, be so deeply embedded in the institutional structure of a polity that any deficits in its attribution caused by these processes are directed at *specific* policies and/or political actors rather than at the polity's core institutions. Contrary to assumptions in much of the literature, problems induced by these challenges may only scratch the surface of the nation state's legitimacy.

Legitimation statements in public communication

Research on empirical legitimacy tends to privilege two types of methods: public opinion surveys, producing data on individual attitudes and beliefs, and the observation of (non-)conventional political behaviour, such as (non-)voting and protest activities. However, this research does not fully capture the role of discourses in the construction of legitimacy. As both public opinion, including beliefs on legitimacy, and political behaviour are embedded in or framed by public communication, we plead for an alternative method: the analysis of textual data. Here we aim to highlight the potential of this approach. Concentrating on one specific, albeit important segment of public communication, the print media, our study compares legitimacy discourses in political systems characterized by different institutional designs. We examine articles from two top-quality newspapers in each country studied: the *Guardian* and *Times* from the United Kingdom, *Neue Zürcher Zeitung* and *Tagesanzeiger* from Switzerland, and the *New York Times* and *Washington Post* from the United States. Conventionally, discourse is operationalized as a text corpus, but we focus on individual *legitimation statements* produced for or transported by the media. We define a legitimation statement as a statement that denies or affirms the legitimacy of a specific *object*, using a specific *pattern of legitimation*. The structure and content of a legitimation statement is thus characterized by these two parameters.

As *objects of legitimation*, we consider the key institutions and principles of national political systems: the political order, or regime, and the political community as a whole, i.e. the nation and its citizenry; the institutions and principles that characterize the modern western state, i.e. democracy, nation state, constitution/rule of law, welfare state, sovereignty; the form of government, whether it is a monarchy or republic; the three branches of government, i.e. executive, legislative, and judiciary; the electoral system; territorial organization, whether it is federal or unitary; the political class/elite; the party system and the system of interest groups; and type of democracy, whether parliamentary or presidential, representative or direct. Statements about subnational institutions, specific authorities, or individual policies are not included in the analysis.

As *patterns of legitimation*, we consider the substantive criteria a speaker relies on when affirming or casting doubt on the legitimacy of an object. We classify the patterns within two dimensions. In the first, we distinguish between the *input* and the *output* side of political decision-making. A pattern of legitimation is called *input-oriented* if it refers to the process of decision-making, in particular to the actors involved and the procedures followed. A pattern is *output-oriented* if it refers to the results of the process, to their quality and consequences.[a]

In the second dimension, we distinguish between democratic and non-democratic criteria. This distinction is more problematic: different theories of democracy rely on different criteria for a genuine democracy. For our purposes, the distinction between democratic and non-democratic patterns of legitimation should be grounded in an undemanding definition of democracy, such as that proffered by Schmitter and Karl: 'a system of governance in which rulers are held accountable for their actions in the public realm by the citizens, acting indirectly through the competition and cooperation of their elected representatives.'[17] Patterns of legitimation pertaining to decision-making processes or outputs that are essential to the implementation of such a system can then be classified as democratic; patterns that are non-essential – though not necessarily antithetical – to democracy are classified as non-democratic.

On the basis of these definitions, patterns of *democratic input* are those that refer to the decision-making rules that guarantee self-governance of the citizens and respect for these rules, and to the procedural conditions that ensure the 'enlightened understanding'[5] required if citizens are to make adequate use of them. Many discussions of democratic legitimacy focus exclusively on such democratic inputs, but as David Held notes in his 1995 book *Democracy and the Global Order* they can be rendered worthless if a society's power structures 'systematically generate asymmetries of life chances [...] which limit and erode the possibilities of political participation.'[9] Therefore, we have also included patterns of *democratic output* which include references to political results that prevent the development of such 'nautonomy', as Held calls it. These include guarantees of individual liberty and of the material and cognitive conditions for full participation in citizenship, as well as the absence of political results that serve only small sectors of the population or limit the options of future generations.

Patterns of *non-democratic input* and of *non-democratic output* refer to characteristics or results of decision-making processes that may be valued in both democratic and non-democratic systems of government, but are not essential for democratic decision-making and the prevention of nautonomy. If we map patterns of legitimation in both dimensions, we arrive at a fourfold scheme, containing 25 patterns (Table 1).

---

[a] Fritz W. Scharpf[16] distinguishes input- and output-based legitimacy, but his standard for assessing a polity's input legitimacy is 'government by the people', while that for output is 'government for the people'; this confounds the distinction between political inputs and outputs with considerations of the democratic quality of the processes in question.

Table 1. Patterns of legitimation

	Democratic	Non-democratic
Input: Characteristics of political processes	*Popular sovereignty* – all power resides in the citizens *Accountability* – rulers can be controlled and removed *Participation* – citizens can actively contribute to decisions *Legality* – domestic legal rules are respected *International legality* – international legal rules are respected *Transparency* – political processes are public and accessible *Credibility* – political processes conform to stated objectives, no hidden agenda *Deliberation* – political processes are based on the rational exchange of political arguments	*Charismatic leadership* – strong personal leadership *Expertocratic leadership* – leadership by experts *Religious authority* – political processes follow religious principles *Tradition* – political processes follow traditional rules and customs *Moderation* – political style is conciliatory and non-aggressive
Output: Characteristics of political results	*Protection of human rights* – individual and political rights are guaranteed *Democratic empowerment* – material and cognitive conditions of meaningful participation are guaranteed *Contribution to public good* – political results serve the population as a whole *Reversibility* – political results are not irrevocable	*Effectiveness* – solution to common problems *Efficiency* – political results are cost-effective, not wasteful *Distributive justice* – equal distribution of resources and burdens *Contribution to stability* – enhancement of political stability *Contribution to identity* – political results reflect or enhance the political community's sense of identity *Contribution to morality* – political results conform with moral standards *Contribution to sovereignty* – enhancement of a polity's autonomy, capacity, power, or interest *Good international standing* – enhancement of a polity's status in the international sphere

A legitimation statement thus has the structure: [Object X] [is (il)legitimate] [because of Pattern Y]. To generate our text corpus, we select all articles from our six newspapers that contain at least one such legitimation statement.[b] The articles can be news reports, commentaries or features, from any section of the newspapers. In addition to the object, assessment as legitimate or illegitimate, and pattern of legitimation, discussed above, three other variables are coded for each statement: the issue or policy context in which a statement arises – i.e. the way in which it is framed – and the presence or absence of references to internationalization and deparliamentarization.

Monitoring legitimacy: some preliminary findings

The procedure described allows us to monitor legitimacy discourses, examine their structure, and track changes. Tables 2–4 summarize our first results, obtained for January to March 2004.[c] This short time period does not yet allow for an analysis of trends or convey a complete picture of legitimacy discourses in the three countries studied. But it is already apparent that the structures and trajectories of national legitimacy discourses are more complex than is often assumed. And a number of tentative theses about legitimacy discourses, and the factors that influence them, are beginning to emerge.

(1) Delegitimating statements dominate in national legitimacy discourses, but the scope of delegitimation is not uniform across countries

Sixty-three percent of all statements in our text corpus question or deny the legitimacy of their political objects, while only 37% evaluate them positively. These percentages are not necessarily indicative of the all-pervasive legitimacy crisis of western democracies so often referred to in the literature – it is probable that uncritical assessments are less likely to be expressed in discourse than critical ones. Furthermore, there are pronounced differences between the three countries, as evident from Table 2. While critical statements outnumber expressions of support in all three nations, they do so considerably more clearly in the UK (72%)

---

[b] Texts are retrieved from an electronic media database in a two-step procedure, using automated search routines for preselection, and manual interpretation for final selection of texts. Search routines are based on our definition of legitimation statements and are similar for each country, with country-specific adaptations for the various political orders and terminologies.

[c] Our text corpus to date consists of 626 legitimation statements from 399 articles: 102 articles and 173 statements from the two Swiss papers, 134 articles and 207 statements from the British, 163 articles and 246 statements from the American. Relevant articles constitute 0.65% of all articles published during that time (0.69%, 0.78% and 0.58%, respectively, for the three countries). On average, each article contains 1.57 legitimation statements (1.70, 1.54 and 1.51 respectively).

Table 2. Objects of legitimation addressed in British, Swiss and American legitimation statements (rounded to the nearest percent)

	UK			CH			USA		
	% of statements	% of		% of statements	% of		% of statements	% of	
		delegitimation	legitimation		Deligitimation	legitimation		delegitimation	legitimation
Political order	26	68	32	31	66	34	49	49	51
Political community	13	46	54	8	57	43	12	48	52
Democracy	7	79	22	5	38	63	9	68	32
Nation state	1	0	100	2	100	0	0	–	–
Constitution/ rule of law	10	70	30	4	43	57	7	41	59
Welfare state	5	91	9	8	64	36	1	50	50
Sovereignty	0	–	–	2	67	33	0	–	–
Parliamentary democracy	1	100	0	0	–	–	0	–	–
Presidential democracy	0	–	–	0	–	–	0	–	–
Direct democracy	0	–	–	17	30	70	0	–	–
Representative democracy	2	20	80	0	–	–	0	–	–
Other type of democracy	0	–	–	4	67	33	0	–	–
Form of government	4	75	25	0	–	–	0	–	–
Executive	3	100	0	4	100	0	2	83	17
Legislative	6	83	16	1	50	50	4	90	10
Judiciary	8	88	12	0	–	–	6	50	50
Electoral system	2	100	0	1	100	0	2	83	17
Federalism/ territorial organization	6	67	33	5	86	12	1	50	50
Political class	7	93	7	5	86	12	4	100	0
Party system	1	100	0	6	100	0	3	100	0
Organized interests	0	–	–	0	–	–	1	50	50
Total (not rounded)	100	72	28	100	62	38	100	57	43

than in Switzerland (62%) and the US (57%). Evidence of general legitimacy problems, then, is weaker in Switzerland and the US than in the UK.

(2) Legitimacy discourses are shaped by, or reflect, national institutional arrangements and political cultures

Conventional survey research is often limited to measuring quantitative changes in the degree of legitimacy granted to a political order or its elements, whereas an examination of the objects and patterns of legitimacy discourses provides insight into the qualitative nature, sources and foundations of legitimacy. If these aspects of legitimation are indeed shaped by or reflect specific institutional arrangements and political cultures, then the objects and patterns that dominate legitimation statements in the three countries should remain constant over time, at least as long as institutions remain stable. Our data cover too short a period to prove or disprove this hypothesis, but we can see variations in the dominant objects and patterns of legitimation that correspond to the different institutional configurations in the three countries.

The object of legitimation most frequently referred to in all three countries is the political order as a whole (Table 2), but the percentages vary greatly, from 25% of the statements in the UK to almost half in the American sample. The political community is often neglected in discussions of legitimation, but, as it turns out, it also receives relatively frequent consideration in all three countries, as an object of 8–12% of the statements. Beyond these general categories, one would expect that a particular political system's most significant or visible institutions would be objects of legitimation more often than peripheral ones. This expectation is borne out most clearly in Switzerland, where the peculiar Swiss institution of direct democracy (17% of statements) and the welfare state (8%) are frequent objects, while the judiciary – a comparatively peripheral institution in Switzerland – is not addressed at all. In the US, two objects of great importance for the American political system and its self-image, democracy (9%) and the constitution or rule of law (7%), are referred to most often, while the welfare state is the object of only 1% of the statements. In the UK, the form of government (i.e. the monarchy) is a predictably frequent object, but the prominence of the constitution and the judiciary is puzzling until we note that both were recently the subject of intense political debate. This suggests that legitimacy discourses reflect not only entrenched institutional arrangements, but also reform initiatives or debates that move marginal institutions temporarily into the limelight or give them a more central position. Similarly, despite the fact that Switzerland and the US have much stronger federal institutions and traditions than the UK, federalism and territorial organization are objects of legitimation more often in Great Britain – which may well be due to the recent debates about devolution.

The influence of national institutional configurations on legitimation statements is also apparent in the tendency for a political system's core institutions and principles to enjoy much higher legitimacy than those more narrowly associated with specific political actors. For example, despite the overall prevalence of delegitimating communication in the UK, the percentages of supportive statements about the political community (54%), the political order (32%), the constitution (30%), and democracy (21%) are distinctly higher than for the judiciary (13%) and the political class (7%). In the US, more than half of the statements about the political order (51%) and the political community (52%) are positive, and satisfaction with the constitution and rule of law is even stronger, with 59% legitimating statements. Delegitimating and legitimating statements are split fifty-fifty for the US judiciary, but all statements about the political class are negative. In Switzerland, direct democracy (70%) and the political community (43%) are the two objects most likely to be evaluated positively. However, the number of positive statements about the entire political order (34%) and some of its core elements and principles (welfare state, 36%; consensus democracy, 34%) is considerably lower, and only 12% of all statements on federalism are positive. This latter is puzzling and does not seem to fit with the general tendency to approve a system's core institutions and principles. Just as in the other two countries, however, nearly all evaluations of the party system and the political class are negative.

Finally, the distribution of patterns of legitimation used in the three countries (Table 3) provides still further insight into the ways national institutional arrangements and political cultures impact legitimacy discourses. The relatively high importance of accountability and credibility in British legitimacy discourse reflects the lack of formalized checks and balances in the country's political system. Informal conventions of good conduct are the main safeguard against a strong government turning into an 'elective dictatorship', so discussion focuses on the credibility and trustworthiness of government and the accountability of power-wielding institutions and actors. That tradition plays a more important role in the British legitimacy discourses than it does in the other two countries is also very much in line with expectations. In the US, the pattern of legitimation used most often is the protection of human rights, which includes references to freedom, obviously a fundamental American value. A considerable number of statements refer to religious authority and morality, two patterns hardly ever used in the UK and Switzerland, and clearly reflecting the importance of religion in American society and politics. Switzerland's traditions of consensus democracy are apparent in its relatively large number of references to moderation, the public good, stability, and identity. Surprisingly, the pattern of popular sovereignty is used considerably *less* in Switzerland than in the other countries, where it is one of the leading patterns. Almost one fifth of the Swiss statements, on the other hand, refer

Table 3. Patterns of legitimation used in British, Swiss and American legitimation statements (rounded to the nearest percent)

	UK	CH	USA			UK	CH	USA
Democratic input				**Democratic output**				
Popular sovereignty	12	6	12		Protection of human rights	10	9	12
Accountability	10	6	6		Democratic empowerment	1	1	0
Participation	5	2	6		Contribution to public good	1	4	0
Legality	4	2	7		Reversibility	0	0	1
International legality	1	1	1					
Transparency	3	1	2					
Credibility	9	2	1	**Non-democratic output**	Effectiveness	8	18	4
Deliberation	2	4	2		Efficiency	2	1	2
					Distributive justice	5	3	6
					Contribution to stability	5	7	2
Non-democratic input					Contribution to identity	1	5	1
Charismatic leadership	1	1	2		Contribution to morality	1	2	5
Expertocratic leadership	1	1	0		Contribution to sovereignty	1	0	2
Religious authority	0	1	6		Good international standing	0	4	3
Traditional processes	3	1	1					
Moderation	1	4	0	**Rest**	General (no specific pattern of legitimation)	9	7	7
					Other (unclassified)	3	9	8
					Total (not rounded)	100	100	100

to effectiveness. If one considers the potential for political gridlock inherent in the Swiss form of direct democracy, this finding makes more sense: although direct democracy is generally evaluated positively, its downsides nevertheless play a role in the Swiss legitimacy discourse.

> *(3) Legitimacy discourses are often triggered, or influenced, by specific events and controversies that dominate national political agendas and media reporting at a given point in time*

To what extent the described similarities and variations between the UK, Switzerland, and the US are truly stable over time and represent general tendencies remains to be seen. Our preliminary findings may well reflect ephemeral political events and developments that dominated national political debates in the first quarter of 2004. Whether, and to what degree, this is the case will become clearer when we take a systematic look at the issues and policy fields that form the context of our legitimation statements. Such an analysis enables us to identify the types of political debates that were most likely to trigger legitimating or delegitimating public communication. It also allows us to assess the relative influence of entrenched beliefs and institutions on the one hand, and transitory events and conflicts on the other, on legitimacy discourses.

Not surprisingly, some of the topics generating the greatest numbers of legitimation statements in our three countries are the same ones that dominated the political agendas and media reporting during the time period examined. By far the greatest number of statements come from articles having to do with the routine operation, performance, or reform of political institutions (44% of all statements in the UK, 43% in the US, and 39% in Switzerland). However, different institutions are highlighted in each country. In the UK, almost a third of the articles on institutions are about constitutional reform, particularly the Blair government's proposal for the creation of a Supreme Court. In the US and in Switzerland, articles about electoral campaigns, campaign finance, the electoral and/or party system, etc., are the most common. In the US, this is linked to the Democratic primaries and impending presidential election. In Switzerland, the 2003 elections and formation of a new government triggered debates on consensus and direct democracy, federalism, and the polarized nature of the party system.

Newspaper articles may also deal with specific policy fields. We distinguished the following categories: fiscal and economic policy; infrastructural policy; environmental policy; educational, research and cultural policy; social policy; domestic policy (interior ministry policies); and foreign policy. In the US, a large proportion of statements (24%) is linked with foreign policy issues such as the ongoing 9/11 investigations, the 'war on terrorism', and Iraq. Discussions about same-sex marriage and civil unions – triggered by court rulings and local initiatives in Massachusetts, California and elsewhere – resulted in fairly high percentages for domestic policy issues (16% of statements, with more than half from articles about minorities and citizenship). While articles dealing with fiscal and economic policy are almost completely lacking in the American sample (2%), they are quite frequent in Great Britain (13%). In contrast to the US, only 3% of British debates explicitly refer to foreign policy, with debate about Iraq generally framed as an issue of media, communication and government spin doctoring, rather than foreign policy. The predominant domestic policy issues (16%) in the UK were public security and immigration, reflecting controversies about government plans to combat terrorism and reform asylum laws. Similar debates on domestic policy account for a significant proportion of legitimacy communication in Switzerland (10%), but foreign policy is of greater importance (16%), dominated by concern about the Swiss negotiations with the European Union, EU enlargement, and the EU constitution. Fiscal and economic policy (16%) are also important, especially the secrecy of Swiss bank accounts and sluggish economic growth.

Issues that are not prevalent in our text corpus may simply have been absent from the media and from political agendas during the period examined. Or they may have been quite prominent and generated heated debate on the details of a specific policy field, the behaviour of political actors, etc. *without* generating debate on the legitimacy of the political *system*. Hence, the relatively low percentages for social policy (9% in the UK, 5% in the US, and 4% in Switzerland) by no means reflect the share of articles on this policy field in the first quarter of 2004, but rather signify that social policy debates gave rise to a limited number of legitimation statements. This is surprising, given that the erosion of national welfare state systems induced by globalization is often considered one of the most difficult political challenges faced by contemporary western democracies. Apparently, political debate has managed to isolate welfare state reform from the issues of legitimacy potentially at stake. Even more remarkably, statements generated by articles dealing with environmental policy – one of the main topics of public and scientific legitimacy discourses in the 1980s – are almost completely absent during our study period.

The analysis of the issue contexts that give rise to legitimation statements enables us to put our figures on the dominant objects and patterns of legitimation into perspective. In many cases, however, it is still impossible to tell whether institutional factors or transitory events and conflicts have a greater influence. For example, in the British case, some of the objects of legitimation referred to most often – the constitution and the rule of law (10%), the judiciary (8%), democracy (7%), and the political class (7%) – are of central importance for the British political system, but were also at the centre of the debates on judicial reform and government 'spin doctoring' that dominated politics in early 2004. In the US, foreign and domestic policy issues, such as the war on terrorism, the Guantanamo prison camp, internment of 'enemy combatants' without due process, military tribunals, and same-sex marriage are visibly tied to a heightened scrutiny of key institutions, such as the constitution and the rule of law, the executive, the judiciary, and even the legislative branch. Similarly, while religion undoubtedly plays a crucial role in American politics, the number of references to religious authority in the period under review here may also be more specifically linked to a Supreme Court case argued in early 2004 which focused on the words 'under God' in the pledge of allegiance. On the other hand, we found that even the most prevalent issue contexts do not always translate into a high frequency for the particular objects or patterns of legitimation that might appear most closely associated to the policy debates in question. Most remarkably, although debates on electoral issues generate a large number of legitimation statements in the US, the electoral system itself hardly ever appears as an *object* of legitimation (2%) in these statements.

(4) The legitimation resources of national systems of government are more diverse than many contributions to democratic theory suggest

If the range of sources for legitimacy beliefs is underestimated, then the extent to which western democracies are besieged by crises of legitimacy is easily overestimated. The many patterns of legitimation citizens may use when assessing the legitimacy of their political orders was shown in Table 3. If we group the individual patterns according to their two dimensions, i.e. input versus output, and democratic versus non-democratic (Table 4), we see that democratic input and non-democratic output are the patterns most often used in all three countries. In the UK, democratic input patterns are used in 47% of all statements and non-democratic outputs patterns in 24%. In the US, the figures are 37% and 25% respectively. Interestingly, the situation in Switzerland is exactly reversed, as non-democratic output is the most common pattern here. In all three countries, non-democratic input and democratic output patterns are used much less frequently (from 6% to 14%). Despite this diversity, discussions in democratic theory tend to focus only on democratic input.

A comparison of the extent to which legitimating and delegitimating statements make use of the four categories of legitimation criteria is even more revealing. Statements concerning political inputs are delegitimating to a much larger extent than those concerning outputs. This difference is particularly dramatic in the UK, where 81% of the input-based statements, but only 57% of the output-based ones, are negative. Patterns in the US and Switzerland are similar, with 63% of input-based and 46% of output-based statements delegitimating in the US, and 70% and 58% respectively in Switzerland. If only the input-based patterns most commonly used in democratic theory were considered, these figures would indicate a problem with the legitimacy of the political systems examined. But taken together, they rather suggest that output-based arguments play a reaffirming role in legitimation discourses that may temper or prevent a full-blown legitimation crisis.

For the UK and the US, this interpretation is further supported by the fact that statements using democratic patterns of legitimation are much more likely to be delegitimating than those using non-democratic patterns (75% versus 62% in the UK; 61% versus 48% in the US). In these two countries, then, statements based on democratic input patterns are delegitimating to a greater extent than those from any other category. In Switzerland, however, democratic patterns are used to question or deny an object's legitimacy in only slightly more than half the

Table 4. Delegitimating and legitimating statements within aggregate patterns of legitimation (rounded to the nearest percent)

	UK			CH			USA		
	% of statements	% of delegitimation	% of legitimation	% of statements	% of Deligitimation	% of legitimation	% of statements	% of delegitimation	% of legitimation
Democratic input	47	81	19	25	65	35	37	70	30
Non-democratic input	6	75	25	6	90	10	9	36	64
Democratic output	12	52	48	13	36	64	14	35	65
Non-democratic output	24	59	41	41	64	36	25	51	49
Sum democratic	59	75	25	38	55	45	50	61	39
Sum non-democratic	30	62	38	46	68	32	34	48	52
Sum input	52	81	19	31	70	30	46	63	37
Sum output	36	57	43	53	58	42	39	46	54
General	9	74	26	7	58	42	7	39	61
Unclassified	3	100	0	9	69	31	8	90	10

statements (55%), whereas those using non-democratic patterns are negative in two thirds of the cases (68%). This indicates that satisfaction with the democratic quality of the political order is higher in Switzerland than in the UK or the US.[d] Citizens' support for the political system may still be quite strong even in the latter, but according to the standards of normative democratic theory the sources of that support are not the most desirable.

(5) There is little evidence for the hypothesis that internationalization and the loss of parliamentary control over political power are at the root of the nation-state's problems of legitimation

If internationalization and deparliamentarization really have an influence on legitimacy discourses, this should be visible in either (or both) the context or content of a legitimation statement. The internationalization of political decision-making, for example, might mean that foreign policy issues become more likely to trigger legitimation debates than other topics, or that certain objects (e.g. sovereignty, the nation state) and patterns of legitimation (e.g. international legality, good international standing) become predominant in legitimacy discourses. Similar indicators can be identified for deparliamentarization, but in neither case do they establish a *direct* connection between internationalization or deparliamentarization and the content of a statement. Any conclusions based on these indicators are necessarily speculative, so we also monitor *explicit* references to processes of internationalization and deparliamentarization in the immediate context of our legitimation statements. For this purpose, internationalization is defined as the transfer of responsibilities to political structures beyond the nation state, and deparliamentarization as the transfer of responsibilities from the national parliament to a non-parliamentary domestic institution.

These explicit references in our text corpus are negligible (less than 2%) except for Switzerland, where 16% of the statements refer to internationalization. More than two thirds of those statements are actually relegitimating, which makes some sense when considered in the context of public debate about Switzerland's relations to the EU. Switzerland is usually compared favourably with the EU, and legitimated on the basis of democratic criteria, in such statements. In this case, objections to further European integration are linked to expressions of support for the national political order, a finding which corroborates the hypothesis that internationalization contributes to the erosion of legitimacy in a national political

---

[d] Delegitimation or legitimation based on democratic patterns of legitimation could, theoretically, be grounded in substantively non-democratic arguments, e.g. if a person were to refer to popular sovereignty in an argument such as 'our political system is illegitimate because it gives the people too much power'. Our coding procedure allows us to monitor such an unexpected non-democratic usage of democratic patterns of legitimation, and it is, in fact, extremely rare.

order. A number of statements do, however, indicate that the inverse, the growing isolation of Switzerland, also contributes to its delegitimation.

The loss of parliamentary control over political power is mentioned even less frequently than internationalization, present in only 1% of statements in the US and Switzerland, and 5% in the UK. These latter generally occur in debates about expanding judicial and executive powers, and are mainly critical of these two branches of government.

Given the limited reference to either internationalization or deparliamentariza-tion, our data provide little evidence that these processes play a major role in delegitimation in the countries studied. We cannot completely rule out, however, that they are influential background processes, even when not explicitly referred to in legitimacy discourses.

Has the legitimacy of the nation-state been transformed?

There is no doubt that the transformations of the modern western state through globalization and transnational integration affect processes of legitimation. As the structures and institutions of political decision-making change, the nation state faces serious challenges to its legitimacy. However, such challenges do not necessarily weaken the popular support of the state, or lead to a crisis of legitimacy. A number of factors may intervene.

Our analysis shows that legitimation communication is highly volatile, reflecting current political agendas and debates. While in many cases, we cannot differentiate between the short-term effects of fickle fluctuations in policy agendas and the long-term effects of institutional configurations or of internationalization and deparliamentarization, it is clearly an oversimplification to suggest that changes in the legitimacy of national systems are exclusively caused by the latter. Additionally, we have seen that institutional arrangements and political cultures shape the precise form of legitimation communication in every political system. Different institutional designs may therefore be more or less susceptible to delegitimation, and it would be worthwhile to determine which systems of democratic governance are best suited to deal with the challenges to legitimacy posed by internationalization and deparliamentarization. And finally, this study makes it clear that a wide range of resources needs to be taken into account when assessing a political system's popular support. Many discussions of democratic theory focus exclusively on aspects of democratic input, which are strongly affected by internationalization and deparliamentarization. Democratic input, however, is not the only, and perhaps not even the most reliable, source of legitimacy that a democratic nation state can draw on.

Our theoretical considerations and first empirical findings indicate that it may be premature to predict a serious crisis of legitimacy in the modern state, as such.

Rather, the crisis may be limited to specific political systems. Internationalization and the decline of parliaments do not automatically jeopardize or erode the state's legitimation resources. It seems more reasonable to expect a *transformation* of legitimacy and legitimation in the modern state – a process wherein the content and structure of the arguments used to justify systems of democratic governance change without completely destroying a nation state's legitimacy. This suggests that the scenario of an upcoming 'end of the nation state'[8] is at least premature in the democratic dimension. It remains to be explored, however, whether empirical findings can be translated into normative ones: The democratic quality of the nation-state might be gradually diminishing even though public acceptance of its institutions can be shown to be stable or unrelated to internationalization and deparliamentarization.

Acknowledgement

We are grateful to Susan Gaines for all her help in 'transsubstantiating' this article into English.

References

1. H. Abromeit (1998) *Democracy in Europe. Legitimising Politics in a Non-State Polity* (New York, NY and Oxford, UK: Berghahn): 19ff.
2. M. Albrow (1998) *Abschied vom Nationalstaat. Staat und Gesellschaft im Globalen Zeitalter* (Frankfurt a.M.: Suhrkamp): 280ff.
3. A. Benz (1998) Postparlamentarische Demokratie? Demokratische Legitimation im kooperativen Staat. In: M. Greven (Ed) *Demokratie – eine Kultur des Westens?* (Opladen: Leske + Budrich): 201–222.
4. A. Busch (2003) *Staat und Globalisierung. Das Politikfeld Bankenregulierung im internationalen Vergleich* (Wiesbaden: Westdeutscher Verlag).
5. R. A. Dahl (1989) *Democracy and its Critics* (New Haven, CN etc: Yale University Press): 111f.
6. R. A. Dahl (1994) A democratic dilemma: system effectiveness versus citizen participation. *Political Science Quarterly*, **109**(1): 23–34.
7. D. Easton (1965) *A Systems Analysis of Political Life* (New York: Wiley).
8. J. M. Guéhenno (1995) *The End of the Nation State* (Minneapolis, MN: University of Minnesota Press).
9. D. Held (1995) *Democracy and the Global Order. From the Modern State to Cosmopolitan Governance* (Stanford, CA etc: Stanford University Press): 171.
10. S. Hix and T. Raunio (2000) Backbenchers learn to fight back: European integration and parliamentary government. *West European Politics*, **23**(4): 142–168.

11. J. G. March and J. P. Olsen (1989) *Rediscovering Institutions. The Organizational Basis of Politics* (Oxford, UK: Oxford University Press).
12. A. Maurer (2001) National parliaments in the European architecture: from latecomers' adaptation towards permanent institutional change? In: A. Maurer and W. Wessels (Eds) *National Parliaments on their Ways to Europe: Losers or Latecomers?* (Baden-Baden: Nomos): 27–76.
13. P. Norton (1990) Parliaments: a framework for analysis. *West European Politics*, **13**(3): 1–9.
14. P. Norton (1996) Conclusion: addressing the democratic deficit. In: P. Norton (Ed) *National Parliaments and the European Union* (London: Frank Cass): 177–193.
15. F. W. Scharpf (1998) Demokratie in der transnationalen Politik. In: U. Beck (Ed) *Politik der Globalisierung* (Frankfurt a.M.: Suhrkamp): 228–253.
16. F. W. Scharpf (1999) *Governing in Europe. Effective and Democratic?* (Oxford, UK etc: Oxford University Press).
17. P. C. Schmitter and T. L. Karl (1996) What democracy is … and is not. In: L. Diamond and M. F. Plattner (Eds) *The Global Resurgence of Democracy* (Baltimore, MD: Johns Hopkins University Press): 49–62, esp. p. 50.

About the Authors

Roland Lhotta is Professor for Political Science at the Helmut-Schmidt University of the (German) Federal Armed Forces in Hamburg. His research focuses on the constitutional state in international comparison, and some of his German publications are: Föderalismus und Demokratie in der 'postnationalen Konstellation': Verfassungstheoretische und dogmatische Herausforderungen für die deutsche Staatsrechtslehre, *Jahrbuch des Föderalismus* (Baden-Baden: Nomos, 2001): 35–55; *Föderalismus in der Bundesrepublik Deutschland* (Wiesbaden: Verlag für Sozialwissenschaften, 2004, 2nd revised edn); *The Federalist Papers* (Baden-Baden: Nomos, 2005, forthcoming). **Frank Nullmeier** is Professor for Political Science at the Centre for Social Policy Research, University of Bremen. He focuses on politics in a sociology of knowledge perspective, and until now mostly on German domestic policy. His publications are, amongst others, *Politische Theorie des Sozialstaates* (Frankfurt a.M. etc: Campus, 2000); (with F. W. Rüb) *Die Transformation der Sozialpolitik. Vom Sozialstaat zum Sicherungsstaat* (Frankfurt a.M. etc: Campus, 1993); (with R. Edmondson) Knowledge, rhetoric and political action in context. In: R. Edmondson (Ed), *The Political Context of Collective Action: Power, Argumentation and Democracy* (London: Routledge, 1997): 210–238. Together Lhotta and Nullmeier direct the TranState research group on 'Transformation of democratic legitimation via internationalization and deparliamentarization' in which Bremen University political scientists **Steffen Schneider**, **Zuzana Krell-Laluhová** and **Achim Hurrelmann** and **Achim Wiesner** work as investigators.

European Review, Vol. 13, Supp. No. 1, 139–160 (2005) © Academia Europaea, Printed in the United Kingdom

7 National and transnational public spheres: the case of the EU

BERNHARD PETERS, STEFANIE SIFFT, ANDREAS WIMMEL, MICHAEL BRÜGGEMANN and KATHARINA KLEINEN-VON KÖNIGSLÖW

While many important social processes cut across national borders and have transnational institutions to regulate them, democratic participation still occurs almost exclusively within individual nation states. Public information and debate are essential ingredients of democracy, and their confinement to the individual national public sphere threatens the democratic aspirations and legitimacy of transnational institutions. Therefore, it is often argued that the European Union can only achieve greater legitimacy if there is a Europeanization of national public spheres. Has public discourse in fact Europeanized in the last decades? Here we present results from a study of major national newspapers from five European countries. Europeanization is defined in three dimensions: Europeanization of contents, Europeanization of public identities, and Europeanization of communication flows. Our results show that national public spheres are, in fact, quite resilient and that change is slow or halting. We discuss several possible explanations for this resilience, and go on to question the assumption that the legitimacy of European institutions depends on Europeanization of public discourse.

The European Union (EU) is the most prominent, albeit in many respects unique, case of the development of a transnational or multilevel political system. Within the institutional framework of the EU, considerable political powers and competencies have been pooled at the transnational level. This has long been done by stealth, as it were, based on a considerable degree of elite consensus and the acquiescence of national voters and publics. This situation has been changing, however. Concerns about a 'democratic deficit' of the EU and a corresponding lack of legitimacy have come to the fore, both in public debates and in the scholarly literature. The question of how EU decision-making could be made more accountable to EU citizens and how democratic control and participation on the EU level could be improved has led to an intense and wide-ranging debate about the social and cultural preconditions for such democratization. Prominent authors have maintained that basic preconditions are lacking. Dieter Grimm, Fritz W.

Scharpf, Peter Graf Kielmansegg and others have pointed to the underdevelopment of a *European public sphere* or a shared space of public communication, as well as to the lack of a common European identity and of intermediary institutions for interest articulation and aggregation.[11,15,23,24] In their view, attempts to make EU decision making more democratic by strengthening the power of the European Parliament or similar measures are bound to fail if the mentioned preconditions are not given. This suggests the possibility that current transformations of the European system of nation states may lead to a primarily administrative political superstructure with fragmented decision powers, a deficient democratic dimension, and chronic problems of legitimacy. In response to these concerns, a field of research has developed that focuses on the development of the mentioned preconditions for a democratic and legitimate political order on the European, transnational level. Is there any evidence that a European public sphere might be developing?

Civic participation and public discourse – two strands of research

Within the recent literature that discusses the legitimacy of EU institutions, the realities and possibilities of public participation and, in particular, the development of a European public sphere, two basic strands can be distinguished. We call them the civic participation and the public discourse approach.

The *civic participation approach* looks at ways in which individuals or groups from civil society try to influence EU decision-making, both by public protest or petitioning, by lobbying or by formal and informal participation in policy making.[3,27] The most important stage for this latter kind of participation is the complex and variegated system of committees or panels in Brussels, set up mostly by the European commission and designed to aid in the preparation of policy proposals or directives (see the essay by Joerges and Godt). Empirical findings on civic participation in EU policy-making are mixed. Cooperation of social movements and movement organizations on the European level remains limited,[21] while the inclusion of experts and civil society representatives in the committee system, as well as the workings of this system, have been evaluated more positively. In particular, the role of policy *deliberation* in these contexts has been interpreted as a means to improve decision-making and make it potentially more legitimate.[12,19]

While this line of research is certainly important for the question of how the 'democratic deficit' of the EU can be reduced and its legitimacy strengthened, it will not be our main topic here. Instead, we will follow what we call a *public discourse approach*. In this approach, the public sphere is interpreted as a field of communication that is accessible to mass publics. In this perspective, civic activities become part of the public sphere to the degree that they are represented in public communication, primarily in the mass media. NGOs or other civil actors then become public speakers together with politicians, experts, intellectuals, and journalists. *Public discourse*, however, represents only a specific segment of public communication. Research on public discourse focuses not on information, or 'news', but on public commentary, interpretation, and debate.[3,5,6,13,20] The term discourse, then, is similar to Habermas's notion of *Diskurs*, or to recent uses of the term 'deliberation' in theories of 'deliberative democracy'.[2,8,16] Discourse, in this sense, occurs if opinion statements are supported by some kind argumentative backing, or by some presentation of evidence.

If we look for *public* forms of discourse, we find them partly in discussions during informal encounters and in public meetings. In the electronic media, there are forms of news commentary, news magazines, and documentaries with elements of analysis, commentary, and sometimes advocacy, as well as various discussions and talk shows. Both in the electronic and print media, we also find a considerable amount of *reported* opinions with some deliberative content. In the print media, we find much deliberative content in non-fiction books as well as in the periodical press in the form of newspaper commentary, opinion pieces, analytical or advocatory reporting, essays, or other genres of more sustained argument, especially in the *Feuilleton* or in quality journals and magazines. This media discourse is certainly the most important and influential part of public discourse.

Why should one focus on the *discursive* part of public communication? There might be normative and empirical reasons. Normative conceptions of public discourse or deliberation play an import role in recent theories of democracy and legitimacy. Empirically, it might be interesting to examine the degree to which the reality of public discourse deviates from the normative model, or what conditions would support or hinder the realization of the normative model. Apart from that, it seems plausible to assume that public discourse is the primary medium for the development of public knowledge, values, interpretations, and self-under-standings, and for change and innovation as well as reproduction or transmission over time in the inventory of ideas and arguments that are available in a given public sphere. To put it more generally, public discourse can be regarded as a primary mechanism for cultural reproduction and change. Public discourse in this sense has historically developed in *national* public spaces. Can we observe the development of a common *European* discursive space, a common sphere of opinion formation and public debate?

Dimensions of transnationalization or Europeanization of public discourse

Researchers who study the development of a European public sphere have long agreed that the existence of such a sphere is not a yes or no question. In fact we are dealing with processes of Europeanization that are both gradual and multidimensional.[30] There are several forms or aspects in which public discourse can become Europeanized. There is no complete agreement, however, about the relevant dimension, their delineation and their relationship and respective importance. In an attempt at conceptual synthesis, we focus on three broadly defined dimensions, which subsume some more specific aspects that play a role in the literature:

- *Europeanization of contents*. This dimension includes all ways in which the *topics* addressed in public discourse, and the *manner* in which they are discussed, can become more European (or more transnational in other ways). Indicators for a Europeanization of contents would be growing numbers of references to the EU as such and to EU institutions and policies, but also to the affairs of other EU member states, as well as an increasing similarity of public agendas and frames of reference within the public spheres of EU countries.
- *Europeanization of public identities*. Here we talk about the basic *orientation* of public conversation and debate. Do the contributions take a national or a European perspective? Are they addressed to a national or to a European public? Who is the community among which public discourse, debate or contestation is taking place? Whose affairs are the participants talking about?
- *Europeanization of communication flows*. An emerging European public sphere is integrated horizontally to the degree that communicative exchanges cross national borders, to the degree that there is a real exchange of opinions and ideas originating in different places, in short: that public discourse flows across a European (or other transnational) space of public communication. This can occur in several direct or indirect ways, as we will see later.

We will next discuss these dimensions in more detail, report some findings concerning their development from the literature and from our own research, and discuss the importance of these findings and the relevance of the three dimensions for the constitution of a European pubic sphere. As yet, there is no truly longitudinal study on developments in several European countries over a more extended time period. Our empirical study seeks to fill this gap. So far, we have analysed the political sections of quality newspapers from five EU member states: Germany (*Frankfurter Allgemeine Zeitung*), France (*Le Monde*), Great Britain (*The Times*), Denmark (*Politiken*), and Austria (*Die Presse*). We have analysed press articles for two constructed weeks in the years 1982, 1989, 1996 and 2003. Because we are primarily interested in public *debates*, we have sampled articles with a recognizable opinion component and have excluded mere 'news'.

Following that, we will briefly take up two additional aspects: we will ask about possible *causes* for the development or non-development of a European public sphere and briefly look at possible *consequences* – especially the likely effects for the legitimacy of the European Union.

Europeanization of contents

The first way in which the contents of national public discourse can become more transnational or European is by including more and more international or European *topics*. Reports, analysis, and comments on 'foreign affairs' are a very common and elementary way in which national public spheres can become international in outlook. These foreign affairs can include relations between governments (i.e. matters of foreign policy), but also all other kinds of relations or exchanges with other countries, as well as 'internal affairs' (political, economic, social, cultural) of those countries. One might also think of reports about international organizations or transnational political bodies like the EU, or of references not to particular countries, but to world regions, e.g. 'the West'. If we look at Europeanization, references to the EU or EU institutions but possibly also to 'Europe' and to other EU member states and their 'external' and 'internal' affairs would be of special interest, especially in comparison with references to other international organizations (e.g. NATO) or transnational bodies, to other (non-EU) countries or other regions (again, 'the West').

Another way in which the contents of national pubic discourse could become more European would be a convergence of *public agendas* in different countries. Public debates could converge with respect to the selection of topics that are under debate within the same period. Different publics in different public spheres would thus deliberate in parallel, as it were. They could also come to debate over common affairs. Publics in different EU member states could debate EU policies or institutional developments of the European Union in this parallel fashion.

A third, more profound convergence of discursive contents would consist in a growing similarity of *discourse constellations* in different countries. By this we mean the ways in which issues are framed by the various parties that are involved in public debates, as well as the constellation of parties or the patterns of cleavages over certain issues. Debates on abortion, for example, were based on different discourse constellations in different countries – different cleavages and alignments of warring parties, and different frames as used by these parties.[7] As such, specific debates in different countries can be compared with respect to the greater or lesser similarity of these configurations. Again, we could look for convergence over time within a specific set of countries and consider this another dimension of transnationalization or, if we find the phenomenon among European countries and their public spheres, as a case of Europeanization. Not only would the

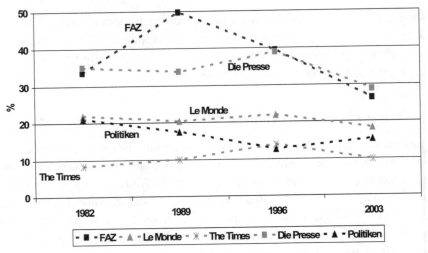

Note: N (all discursive articles – including press reviews, i.e. 'press roundups' – in the sample) = 3,059

Figure 1. Share of articles on European countries by newspaper (in percent).

same topics be debated in different national spheres at the same time, but also by roughly the same set of differing camps and on the basis of similar problem definitions or frames.

Let us now look at some findings. There are some studies that have looked at the similarity or dissimilarity of newspaper agendas in European countries as well as similarities or dissimilarities of frames of reference.[14,25,26,28] These studies, however, lack longer time frames. So the results are somewhat inconclusive with respect to *changes* in these aspects. It has not been systematically analysed so far whether agendas, framing and cleavage patterns are really converging over time or not. Our own study has a longer time frame, but concentrates on European topics in newspaper articles and their relative importance in different EU countries over time.

In our quantitative content analysis, we have coded all articles focusing on *foreign countries*. The main geographical focus of the article was determined on the basis of the countries referred to in the headline and lead paragraph. Figure 1 shows to what extent other *European countries* have appeared in the formation of opinions in each country. First of all, the data show that there is generally no positive trend towards Europeanization. All five national newspapers demonstrate either no clear pattern or even a slight decline over time in their attention to other European countries. Figure 2 illustrates the extent to which the articles discuss *non-European countries*. As we can see, four out of five national newspapers report more on non-European countries than European ones. European countries appear more often only in *Die Presse*, which is the result of its elaborate

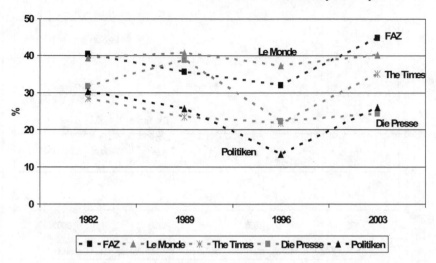

Note: N (all discursive articles, including press reviews, in the sample) = 3,059

Figure 2. Share of articles on non-European countries by newspaper (in percent).

commentary on German affairs. Overall, the United States appears most frequently, followed by Russia or the Soviet Union. As in the case of the European countries, no continuous trend of internationalization can be observed.

Another sort of international content consists of references to international institutions. Here we have coded any *European or international institution* referred to in the entire article (not just the headline or lead paragraph). We have distinguished between EU institutions – such as the European Commission, the Council of Ministers, and the European Parliament – and other international institutions, for example, NATO, the OECD, and UN institutions in order to establish a standard of comparison. Figure 3 demonstrates the extent to which *European institutions* have entered public discourse. In most cases the European Union (EU) is mentioned without further specification of its political institutions. Among the different European institutions, the European Commission plays the largest role, only in Denmark is the European Parliament referred to almost as frequently. Comparing across time, we can observe a clear trend of Europeanization, as the percentage of articles referring to European institutions increases up to at least 20% in four out of five newspapers. Overall, the appearances of the European Union, in general, and of the European Commission increased more than three times from 1982 to 2003, while the European Parliament has remained at a relatively low level since 1989. Compared with the trend towards an increasing discussion of EU institutions, our data do not reveal a similar trend towards a growing visibility of other *international institutions*. Neither the UN nor NATO

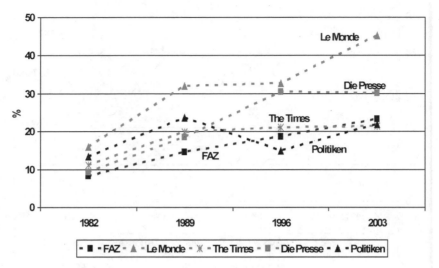

Note: N (all discursive articles in the sample) = 2,964

Figure 3. Share of articles on European institutions by newspaper (in percent).

is, on average, mentioned as often as the EU, nor do references to international institutions consistently increase over time.

Finally, we can look at newspaper content that refers not to countries or institutions as such, but to *policies* concerning foreign affairs or to the policymaking of international institutions themselves, in particular the EU. Figure 4 compares the share of discursive articles that discuss European politics with those that concern other international politics. The light-shaded line shows the relative share of references to EU institutions, while the heavy-shaded line represents the contributions related to non-EU issues of foreign policy and international relations. A trend of increasing 'EU'-ization can be observed, although at a relatively low level. While the share of articles concerning European politics was around 2% in 1982, it has climbed during the 1980s and 1990s and has now almost reached the 10% level. The figure also makes clear that the level of debate over European politics has in no way 'exceeded the level of coverage characteristic of normal foreign politics', as suggested by Eder and Kantner.[29] In fact, coverage of European politics remains at a lower level than coverage of international affairs. Furthermore, it never challenges the dominance of debates about domestic politics.

To sum up these findings: we do find increasing attention to EU institutions and their activities as well as to national policy making concerning the EU. However, attention to EU policy making has not surpassed attention to 'classical' foreign policy issues. In addition, there is no increase in mutual attention between national

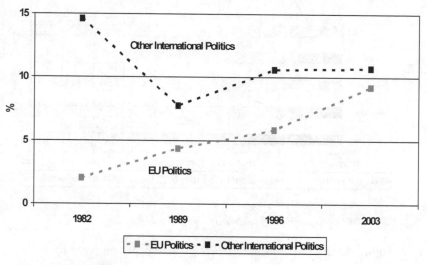

Note: N (all discursive articles in the sample) = 2,964

Figure 4. EU and international politics as the articles' main themes (in percent).

publics in the EU – and attention to countries outside the EU, in particular the US, is stronger than attention to EU neighbours. So we find some degree of *vertical, segmented Europeanization*, where national publics pay attention to EU policies and institutional affairs, but not necessarily to each other. Apart from that, our data do not indicate that national publics are integrated into some kind of overarching European public sphere.

Europeanization of public identities

In national public debates we not only find references to one's own national political entity and political institutions, but also implicit or explicit self-identifications as national publics – as national communities of discourse whose members discuss certain topics among each other. In these processes of identification, certain forms of common cultural characteristics, collective identities, or shared historical experiences are referred to as a shared background. This is frequently accompanied by demarcation from other groups. A milestone for the transnationalization of public debates would be the extension of the imagined collective 'We' beyond national borders, for example, if speakers referred to themselves as part of 'Europe' or 'the Western community', and if corresponding disassociations, such as those against the 'East' or 'South,' or possibly against 'America' and others, became more important.

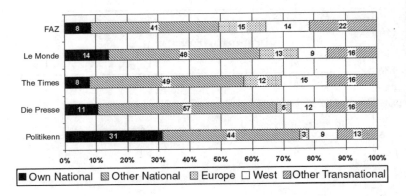

Note: N (all collective identity labels in the sample) = 2,092

Figure 5. Collective identity labels by newspaper (in percent).

Do we actually find the development of such a common European identity in public discourse within the European Union? Are EU affairs treated as genuinely common affairs of all EU members and are solutions to problems and conflicts debated within such a European frame of reference? Or are the issues on the political agenda still debated solely from the respective national viewpoints?[a] There is much conceptual debate as well as some empirical research on the development of a European collective identity. But this research is primarily based on survey research and does not tell us much about the collective identifications that play a role in public discourse. An exception is research directed by Thomas Risse that looks at identity projections in public debates – and in some cases finds a distinctive European perspective.[20] But because of the very short time frames in this study, inferences to processes of change are not possible.

Let us therefore look at some indicators for the development of a supranational, European public identity from our own research. Certainly, the expression of identity by speakers is usually rather implicit, and, therefore, can be analysed more meaningfully with qualitative methods. Yet we have developed two indicators that have proven reliable for quantitative content analysis: 'We' references (operationalized as 'we', 'us', etc.) and references to national or transnational collective identities such as 'the Italians' or 'the West' (collective identity labels). Despite the narrow operationalization of these variables, we were able to identify 1,510 'We'-references referring to national or transnational collective identities and 2,092 collective identity labels.

---

[a] A 'European perspective' in public discourse should not be confused with a positive attitude towards the EU as an institutional framework or a political project. Nor does it necessarily mean an orientation to a European 'common good' or common interest. The existence of a European orientation only means that the EU is taken as the relevant frame of reference, that political controversies are seen as controversies within the membership of the EU, where legitimate demands of other EU members have to be taken into account.

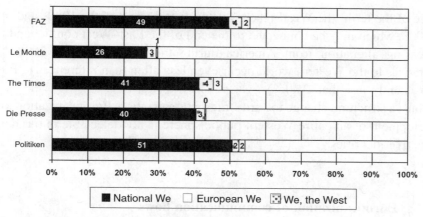

Figure 6. 'We'-references by newspaper (in percent).

The data have been analysed with three questions in mind. First, how self-referential in character is national public discourse? Is there a trend to mention one's own collective identity ('we Germans' or 'the Germans') more or less often than before? Are there differences between countries? Figure 5 shows that almost every third mention of a collective identity label in *Politiken* refers to its own nation (31%). The other newspapers follow far behind, led by *Le Monde*, with barely over 14%. In contrast, only 8% of all cases of collective references in *FAZ* are to its own nation. In the long term, we see no clear trends, neither across nor within countries. Comparing the number of collective labels with the number of 'We'-references also produces interesting distinctions (see Figure 6). When the conservative *FAZ* refers to 'we', half of the time it is referring to 'we, Germans,' as does *Politiken*. This shows that although Germans are supposed to have Europeanized their nation-state identity, at least *FAZ* still strongly identifies with its own national identity, as do *The Times* and *Die Presse* (41%; 40%), while somewhat less so *Le Monde* (26%).

Secondly, we consider the question of Europeanization: how has the collective identity 'Europe' developed in public debates? 'The Europeans' as a collective identity label barely appears in the national discussions. While roughly one out of every tenth reference to a collective identity refers to Europe, only *FAZ* displays a somewhat higher affinity to the collective identity of Europe (15%). Concerning 'We'-references, our data similarly do not reveal a general trend towards explicit identification with Europe. Although the percentage is increasing from 1% in 1982 to 6% in 2003, due to the low absolute numbers and broad variations over time, this does not create a significant trend.

The third question considers whether other collective identities such as the US ('the Americans') or 'the West,' appear more often than 'the Europeans'. The usage of the term 'the West' reaches its peak at the end of the 1980s and wanes in 2003, which may be connected to the end of the East–West conflict and to an increasing alienation from America during the war in Iraq in 2003. 'We' references to the Western world occur even less often than references to Europe (consistently less than 3%).

Thus, a structural change towards transnationalization, Europeanization, or the development of an entire Western public sphere is not detectable in our data on collective identities.

Europeanization of communication flows

Flows of communication across national borders are the most obvious way in which national publics and public spheres can become internationalized. An elementary form of transnational circulation of contributions or arguments is the reception of such products in another country and the reference to it in one's own contributions, be it by quotations or other references, by agreement or opposition. Another elementary form of communication beyond national borders is the import and export of cultural products or contributions *in toto*. These communication processes are evident if books, press products (periodicals or single articles), films, and TV comments are imported or exported (original or translated version). Contributions by foreign authors in print or electronic media can also be a sort of cultural export and transnational communication. Such flows of communication are more hidden, however, if the diffusion of ideas or other cultural elements takes place in personal contacts or by individual observation of other countries' public spheres, e.g. by reading periodicals or books. Such encounters or observations might influence authors or other cultural producers, but they may not explicitly refer to them either. Of further interest is coverage of supporting or critical comments in deliberative contributions from other national contexts, ranging from simple quotations to foreign press reviews to explicit discussion.

In order to analyse transnational communication flows we distinguish between transnational discursive contributions and discursive references. Discursive contributions are articles written by authors from abroad or interviews. Discursive references are direct or indirect quotations of more than one sentence. This length offers speakers the chance not only to express opinions but also to give at least some kind of justification.

Discursive contributions form a substantive share of our sample with every fourth discursive article being an interview or a guest contribution. Particularly in *Le Monde* and *Politiken*, intellectual and political elites as well as ordinary citizens (*Politiken*) contribute to political debates. However, *transnational* discursive contributions are rare: about 90% of all guest contributions are of

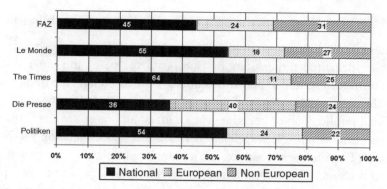

Note: N (all discursive references in the sample) = 2,640

Figure 7. Origin of discursive references by newspaper (in percent).

national origin. *Le Monde* stands out in that it has a stronger tendency of inviting foreign authors from outside of Europe.

In contrast to foreign contributions, *discursive references* made by foreign speakers are often present in public debates. First, foreign speakers have been cited continuously for at least 20 years among the considered newspaper sources. In *Die Presse, FAZ* and *Politiken*, foreign speakers appear more often than national ones (64%; 56%; 55%, see Figure 7). *The Times* comes in last with only about one third of all discursive references coming from speakers from outside the United Kingdom (37%). There is movement over time, but no clear tendency in one direction or another. The highest number of international references was recorded for 1989 (except in *Politiken*). This can be easily explained by the end of the socialist regimes in Eastern Europe. References by speakers from the former East Germany have been coded as foreign, which would explain the sudden increase in foreign references in *Die Presse* and *FAZ*. The United States is the most common source of foreign discursive references. The only exception here is *Die Presse*, which prefers to cite Germans.

Can we now conclude that there has been a structural change in the public sphere through the transnational circulation of contributions? The answer is a clear no. There are no clear trends towards more contributions by European or other foreign speakers or more discursive references from foreign sources. The high number of American voices also leads us to conclude that the national public spheres in Europe show a consistent and strong degree of Americanization.

Interpretation: do we see an emerging European public sphere?

To put these findings in perspective, it is useful to consider the importance of each of the three principal dimensions of Europeanization for the emergence of a common European sphere of public discourse. To recapitulate: the first dimension refers to the degree that national discourses pay attention to European affairs and that national public debates become synchronized and more similar with respect to thematic frames and cleavage patterns. The second dimension refers to the emergence of a European outlook in national public debates. And the third dimension is about actual communicative interchanges between national publics. While we find a partial increase in the first dimension, primarily a growing attention to EU affairs, both the development of a European outlook or public identity and the development of cross-border flows of communication within Europe are weak or non-existent.[b]

Can we nevertheless conclude that a positive development in the first dimension is enough to speak of an emerging European public sphere and suffices as a precondition for the further democratization of the European Union? Some authors seem to assume as much.[4] The plausibility of this assumption depends upon the way one understands the basic features and functions of a public sphere. If one only looks to the *informational* function of public communication, increasing attention to EU affairs might be regarded as sufficient. In this view, public communication has to provide citizens with information about common, public affairs, to enable them to make informed political decisions and hold political authorities accountable. In addition, public officials should be informed about citizen's opinions. This is certainly an important aspect of public communication in democratic political systems.

However, there are important limits to such an understanding of public discourse. Public discourse is not just about the dissemination of information, but also about collective opinion building through open discussion, about a collective search for solutions to common problems, about the generation of new public ideas, interpretations and collective self-understandings. For this to happen on a European level, a growing attention to EU affairs and a convergence of national public discourses, a growing similarity of agendas and discussion frames alone is not enough. A search for common solutions on the European level requires the adoption of some kind of European perspective, instead of merely national ones. And the formation of public opinion and the production and dissemination of new ideas and self-understandings on the European level should be based on communicative interchanges across national boundaries. *Parallel* public debates

---

[b] In addition, we found rising attention to EU affairs without much increase in attention toward the affairs of other EU countries. This might be a sign that every national public looks at EU affairs from its own point of view without much interest and regard for other countries, their interests, opinions and more general conditions.

in different countries (separate but equal, as it were) do not really constitute a *common* public space. If two groups of people deliberate in separate rooms on the same questions, they do not constitute a common public sphere. Accordingly, we can speak of a shared, European universe of discourse only if there are communication flows, flows of ideas and arguments across national borders, criss-crossing the whole European sphere. In our view, then, the density of cross-border communication flows of various sorts, as described above, and the distributive pattern of these flows are the most important single measure for the emergence of a transnational or, more specifically, a European public sphere. The empirical findings are negative so far; the grid of transnational or European cross-border flows of communication currently seems to be rather weak.[c]

Concluding thoughts: causes and consequences

So far, we have only been concerned with the detection and description of possible patterns or trends of Europeanization.[d] As we have seen, genuine Europeanization of public discourse seems to be very limited so far, and national public spheres remain by far the most important fora for public debate. This observation leads to the question of what causes or constraints lead to the staying power of national public spheres and what consequences this predominance of national public spheres might have for transnational or multilevel political systems like the EU.

As to what causes the apparent 'underdevelopment' of a transnational, European public sphere, or conversely, the staying power of the national, several explanatory hypotheses have been proposed. Apart from the rather obvious problem of language barriers, it has been pointed out that EU policy-making is lacking institutional features that could further public debate on a European level; in particular, a clear-cut confrontation between a governing and an oppositional political camp.[9] It has also been argued that a primary cause for low public interest in EU policies lies in the character of EU policy-making itself: Most of it occurs in policy areas *that do not attract much public attention at the national level either.* Andrew Moravcsik has argued for this proposition in a recent article: 'Of the five most salient issues in most West European democracies – health care provision, education, law and order, pension and social security policy, and taxation – none

---

[c] Does this mean that we put more stringent conditions on the realization of a European public sphere than are in fact realized in *national* public spheres? We do not think so. National public discourses are certainly segmented and stratified in many ways. However, there exists a common national agenda of debate and contestation. National politics, national governments, parties, intermediary organizations, and associations provide topics and input. National mass media function as channels or carriers of public discourse. In the background, there is something like a public culture, a repertoire or reservoir of symbols, meanings, knowledge, and values that are relevant to the public. Public debates implicitly assume the existence of a debating 'we' or 'us', a community of discourse that includes both friends (members of one's own camp in a debate) and adversaries.

[d] This is true for virtually the whole research literature on the Europeanization of public spheres.

is primarily an EU competence'.[18] Such an argument calls the diagnosis of a *lag* in the Europeanization of public spheres into question, of course. It refers, however, only to the low salience of *EU politics* and cannot explain why transnationalization of public spheres seems to progress very slowly, if at all, in other, non-EU issue areas or dimensions. Given the assumed trends of globalization or denationalization in many economic, social and cultural areas, this might still be seen as an anomaly.

Here, we would like to sketch another, more general kind of explanation. It will be much harder to confirm or disconfirm, but that should not render such conjectures entirely useless. National public spheres are characterized by specific communication infrastructures as well as by cultural features that manifest themselves in interpretation patterns, relevancy structures, collective memories and other cultural resources. However, these differences do not exist independently from other features of the respective national societies. In many cases, they are linked to social practices and institutional structures that impact the character of the public sphere and the mode of cultural reproduction. Put differently, public spheres have a *social and cultural foundation* that extends well beyond the framework of media markets and media organizations. Many other structures affect intellectual production and its reception, collective interests, and problem definition and hence play a role here. They include educational and research facilities, journalism and other professions, networks (and cliques) of producers of cultural and intellectual property, structures for interest articulation and aggregation, such as political parties, interest groups, and social organizations and milieus. All of these interlocking infrastructural conditions are not easily reproduced on a European level. Of course, this is no argument against cultural exchange or against efforts to increase cultural exchange, dialogue and cooperation. It just means that it is unlikely that we will get a comparatively tightly integrated public sphere on the European level any time soon.

If we now look at the *effects* that the staying power of the national and the weak development of a transnational, European public sphere have on the *legitimacy* of a transnational, multilevel political system like the EU, we first have to note that most statements about the legitimacy problems of the EU are not really empirical statements about some *cause* of illegitimacy. Instead, they are mostly normative *evaluations* of EU realities: the EU has a 'legitimacy problem' or 'legitimacy deficit' because it does not have the *normatively* required features of democracy and a public sphere.[1,22] Such statements can be contested on normative or empirical grounds. It could be argued, for instance, that the underlying picture about the powers of the EU is inaccurate and that EU policy-making is of a kind that is just not very suitable for public debate and democratic decision-making, but can safely be left to various kinds of independent agencies with some kind of democratic mandate and some degree of accountability to democratic bodies.[17,18] Such arguments can by disputed by questioning the veracity of the empirical picture it gives of the EU, and by criticizing the applied normative standards. However, we will not pursue this line of argument here.

Let us look instead at possible *empirical* relationships between the development of a European public sphere, on the one hand, and the empirical legitimacy, either acceptance or support for the EU, on the other. Does the EU suffer from a lack of legitimacy that is caused by the underdevelopment of a common European public sphere? There is no credible answer to this question yet. Of course, we have data on limited or diminishing support for EU institutions and policies in some countries. However, it is far from clear that this has to do with a demand for more democratic participation or a perceived lack of public discourse *on the EU level*. Maybe people just are not in favour of more political centralization on a European level and are loath to give up their national democracies – and public spheres, for that matter – or to see them weakened further? Do we have theoretical reasons to suppose that the development of a stronger European public sphere will increase support for the European Union? We could say that public deliberation is necessary to produce a high degree of reasoned acceptance about basic features or actual policy decisions within a political system. To put it differently, a higher level of public deliberation will, on average, produce more reasoned and stable agreement on contested political matters than it will at a lower level.

Now this is a somewhat problematic empirical conjecture. Although the very idea of public deliberation includes the consideration that participants try to convince each other and thereby strive toward consensus by moving through dissidence, it is doubtful that such a result is in fact often achieved.[10,31] There are many constraints restricting the possibility of arriving at rational consensus in public controversies. Typically, public controversies, especially in the mass media, have a triadic structure: The adversaries address a public to gain endorsement. Seldom do the adversaries address each other directly. There is also a lack of social constraints that would press for an agreement. This is different from many other situations in which practical decisions have to be reached out of necessity, as well as from close social relationships or milieus where unresolved dissidence may create a disturbance. Quite to the contrary, public actors live on controversy and dissidence. Not only the struggle for public attention, but also the struggle for intellectual and moral leadership in their own camp often puts a premium on intransigence and the demonstration of particular sensitivities. The speakers present themselves as honourable and committed protagonists of the group values they represent. They also seek to demonstrate profound diagnostic capabilities and powers of observation. This often leads to a somewhat dramatized or accusatory style. Sometimes this may not prove very supportive for gaining agreement or endorsement beyond the boundaries of one's own camp.

Empirical evidence, thus, seems to indicate that public discourse very seldom leads to the harmonious solution of real conflicts. Argumentative processes of persuasion may not even lead to reciprocal and explicitly confessed definitive changes in the opinions of the participating protagonists. One, therefore, cannot expect any automatic increase in acceptance (or empirical legitimacy) of controversial political decisions.[e] A lively discursive public sphere would, first, appear to multiply questions and uncertainties and increase dissidence. Insofar as it produced innovative ideas and proposals, it would probably bring about an increase in the variety of opinions rather than their reduction. This variation may be reduced in the course of the development of public controversies by virtue of polarization, simplification, generalization, and camp building – initially leading to a consolidation of dissent.

On the other hand, however, debates that do not lead to generally accepted solutions or general accord may still clarify the difficulties and different aspects of the topic under debate, at the very least discrediting some of the bad arguments and clarifying some other aspects. Under favourable circumstances, such debates may not end up exerting such a polarizing effect, but perhaps may lead to a certain mutual recognition of the differences between, or the seriousness of, respective positions. This, in turn, may facilitate the search for institutional compromise or the acceptance of such compromise.

Above all, though, one should imagine the effect of public discourse – with regard to the influence of ideas or convictions held by the public – more as a *shift* of the opinion spectrum, rather than as a *contraction* of this spectrum. Certain positions or arguments will eventually become implausible, lose influence, or disappear altogether from the public stock of argumentation. Others will gain influence within the spectrum. At the same time, new ideas, new problems or problematizations, and new controversies will appear. Nevertheless, this process may contain elements of convergence or of reaching consensus in a very general sense. Certain ideas, convictions, normative principles, and stocks of knowledge become more or less settled as generally – if not universally – acceptable, proven, and convincing without consensus necessarily being explicitly declared.

Some cultural processes of change that have taken place or are in the process of taking place in the West over the past decades provide us with plausible examples. Just think of the changed attitudes toward gender or familial relations, of environmental issues or minority rights, or, more specifically, the development of the public view of Nazi history in Germany.[f] These more gradual and diffuse

---

[e] This may be different in the case of local, transparent public spheres or in the case of advisory panels that are under great pressure to arrive at solutions and that, by means of repeated co-presence, exert great reciprocal pressure for persuasion and accommodation.

[f] Case studies of the abortion debate and of the public discussion of surrounding narcotics policy did not, however, reveal any change in the balance of argumentation during the periods investigated. But it remains rather unclear just how typical these two examples are.[31]

changes in the cultural repertoire, changes in the stock of public argumentation, developments in the interpretation of central principles or values, and changes in specific collective self-interpretations should be perceived as the primary potential effects of public discourse, rather than short-term agreement on specific controversial political issues.

To return to the relation between public discourse and legitimacy: following the account of public discourse just given, it seems likely that public discourse influences above all the general normative expectations and criteria by which people judge political orders. Consensus or convergence in this respect is a long-time process, and the resulting convergence in normative standards may provide one condition of political legitimacy. A decent and lively public discourse may also generate, in the long term, some general mutual respect and tolerance despite continuing disagreements over many of the questions being debated. Nevertheless, this effect seems to be more contingent and dependent on the specific qualities of public discourse and the nature of the disagreements.

Thus, any expectations about a short- or medium-term increase in the empirical legitimacy of the EU that would be a result of increased Europeanization of public discourse does not look very plausible. In the long run, the development of a unified European public space might very well bring about cultural changes that are broadly supportive of political integration. However, this is very hard to know, and even in the medium term such a cultural, discursive integration of Europe does not seem to be very likely.

This leaves us with somewhat paradoxical results concerning the relations between public discourse and legitimacy in the EU. One the one hand, there is no clear indication that the EU is suffering from a deficit of empirical legitimacy *because* of a deficient European public sphere. There are even plausible arguments to the effect that the demands of EU policy-making on legitimacy and publicity are not all that strong. On the other hand, it seems rather less than certain that a stronger European public sphere will lead to more legitimacy for the EU, at least in the short run. In any case, relations between legitimacy, democratic participation and public discourse need to be analysed more thoroughly on both the theoretical and the empirical level.

Acknowledgement

Comments and advice by Achim Hurrelmann are gratefully acknowledged.

References

1. T. Banchoff and M. Smith (Eds) (1999) *Legitimacy and the European Union* (London: Routledge).

2. J. Bohman and W. Rehg (Eds) (1998) *Deliberative Democracy* (Cambridge, MA: MIT Press).

3. K. Eder, K.-U. Hellmann and H.-J. Trenz (1998) Regieren in Europa jenseits öffentlicher Legitimation? Eine Untersuchung zur Rolle von politischer Öffentlichkeit in Europa. In: B. Kohler-Koch (Ed) *Regieren in entgrenzten Räumen* (Opladen: Westdeutscher Verlag): 321–344 (Supplement no. 29, *Politische Vierteljahresschrift*).

4. K. Eder and C. Kantner (2000) Transnationale Resonanzstrukturen in Europa. Eine Kritik der Rede vom Öffentlichkeitsdefizit. In: M. Bach (Ed) *Die Europäisierung nationaler Gesellschaften* (Wiesbaden: Westdeutscher Verlag): 306–331 (Supplement no. 40, *Kölner Zeitschrift für Soziologie und Sozialpsychologie*).

5. K. Eder and C. Kantner (2002) Interdiskursivität in der europäischen Öffentlichkeit. *Berliner Debatte Initial*, **13**(5/6): 79–88.

6. K. Eder and H.-J. Trenz (2003) Transnational resonance structures: searching for the link between national governance and European policy-making. The case of justice and home affairs. In: B. Kohler-Koch (Ed) *Linking EU and National Governance* (Oxford, UK: Oxford University Press): 111–134.

7. M. M. Ferree, W. A. Gamson, J. Gerhards, D. Rucht, W. L. Bennet and R. M. Entmann (2002) *Shaping Abortion Discourse: Democracy and the Public Sphere in Germany and the United States* (Cambridge, UK: Cambridge University Press).

8. J. S. Fishkin and P. Laslett (Eds) (2003) *Debating Deliberative Democracy* (Oxford, UK: Blackwell).

9. J. Gerhards (1993) Westeuropäische Integration und die Schwierigkeiten der Entstehung einer europäischen Öffentlichkeit. *Zeitschrift für Soziologie*, **22**(2): 96–110.

10. J. Gerhards, F. Neidhardt and D. Rucht (1998) *Zwischen Palaver und Diskurs. Strukturen öffentlicher Meinungsbildung am Beispiel der deutschen Diskussion zur Abtreibung* (Wiesbaden: Westdeutscher Verlag).

11. D. Grimm (1995) Does Europe need a constitution? *European Law Journal*, **1**(3): 282–302.

12. C. Joerges (2002) 'Deliberative supranationalism' – two defenses. *European Law Journal*, **8**(1): 133–151.

13. C. Joerges and J. Neyer (1997) Transforming strategic interaction into deliberative problem-solving: European comitology in the foodstuffs sector. *Journal of European Public Policy*, **4**(4): 609–625.

14. D. Kevin (2003) *Europe in the Media* (Mahwah, NJ: Lawrence Erlbaum).

15. P. G. Kielmansegg (1994) Läßt sich die Europäische Gemeinschaft demokratisch verfassen? *Europäische Rundschau*, **22**(2): 23–33.

16. S. Macedo (Ed) (1999) *Deliberative Politics: Essays on Democracy and Disagreement* (New York: Oxford University Press).

17. G. Majone (1998) Europe's 'democracy deficit': the question of standards. *European Law Journal*, **4**(1): 5–28.

18. A. M. Moravcsik (2002) In defence of the 'democratic deficit': reassessing legitimacy in the European Union. *Journal of Common Market Studies*, **40**(4): 603–624.

19. C. Kantner (2003) Transnationale Öffentlichkeit und Demokratiefähigkeit der Europäischen Union. Unpublished PhD Dissertation, Humboldt Universität, Berlin.

20. T. Risse (2003) An emerging European public sphere? Theoretical clarifications and empirical indicators, http://www.fu-berlin.de/atasp/ EUSA Paper.

21. D. Rucht (2000) Zur Europäisierung politischer Mobilisierung. *Berliner Journal für Soziologie*, **2**: 185–202.

22. F. W. Scharpf (1999) Demokratieprobleme in der europäischen Mehrebenenpolitik. In: A. Busch (Ed) *Demokratie in Ost und West* (Frankfurt a.M.: Suhrkamp): 672–694.

23. F. W. Scharpf (1999) *Governing in Europe: Effective and Democratic?* (Oxford, UK: Oxford University Press).

24. F. W. Scharpf (2003) Problem-solving effectiveness and democratic accountability in the EU (Cologne: Max-Planck-Institute for the Study of Societies, MPIfG Working Paper 03/01).

25. H. A. Semetko and P. M. Valkenburg (2000) Framing European politics: a content analysis of press and television news. *Journal of Communication*, **50**(2): 93–109.

26. H. Sievert (1998) *Europäischer Journalismus. Theorie und Empirie aktueller Medienkommunikation in der Europäischen Union* (Opladen: Westdeutscher Verlag).

27. P. Statham and R. Koopmans (1999) Challenging the liberal nation-state? *American Journal of Sociology*, **105**(3): 652–696.

28. H.-J. Trenz (2004) Media coverage on European governance: exploring the European public sphere in national quality newspapers. *European Journal of Communication*, **19**(3): 291–319.

29. H.-J. Trenz, K. Eder and C. Kantner (2000) Transnationale Resonanzstrukturen in Europa. Eine Kritik der Rede vom Öffentlichkeitsdefizit. In: M. Bach (Ed) *Die Europäisierung nationaler Gesellschaften* (Wiesbaden: Westdeutscher Verlag): 306–331, esp. p. 307 (Supplement no. 40, *Kölner Zeitschrift für Soziologie und Sozialpsychologie*).

30. M. van de Steeg (2002) Rethinking the conditions for a public sphere in the European Union. *European Journal of Social Theory*, **5**(4): 499–519.

31. H. Weßler (1999) *Öffentlichkeit als Prozeß: Deutungsstrukturen und Deutungswandel in der deutschen Drogenberichterstattung* (Opladen: Westdeutscher Verlag).

About the Authors

Stefanie Sifft (political science, case study: Denmark, UK), **Andreas Wimmel** (political science, case study: Germany), **Katharina Kleinen-von Königslöw**

(communication research, case study: Austria) and **Michael Brüggemann** (communication research, case study: France) are investigators in the TranState research project on 'The transnationalization of public spheres and its impact on political systems'. **Bernhard Peters**, the principal investigator, is Professor of Political Science and Codirector of the Institute for Intercultural and International Studies (InIIS) of the University of Bremen. Recent publications by group members include: B. Peters, A new look at 'national identity', *Archives Européennes de Sociologie*, **43**(1): 3–34 (2002); B. Peters, Collective identity, cultural difference and the developmental trajectories of immigrant groups. In: R. Sackmann, B. Peters and T. Faist (Eds) *Identity and Integration. Migrants in Western Europe* (Aldershot, Hampshire, UK: Ashgate, 2003): 13–35.

European Review, Vol. 13, Supp. No. 1, 161–185 (2005) © Academia Europaea, Printed in the United Kingdom

THE INTERVENTION STATE: THE SHIFTING WELFARE COMPONENT

8 Welfare state transformation in small open economies[a]

HERBERT OBINGER, STEPHAN LEIBFRIED,
CLAUDIA BOGEDAN, EDITH GINDULIS, JULIA
MOSER and PETER STARKE

We examine whether a fundamental change in the core dimension of modern 20th century statehood, the welfare state, has become evident in response to changed exogenous and endogenous challenges. By combining quantitative and qualitative approaches we take stock of social policy development in four advanced welfare states – Austria, Denmark, New Zealand and Switzerland – over the last 30 years. Neither spending patterns nor structural changes support a 'race to the bottom thesis', according to which the changed environment of welfare state policies has led to a downward spiral in benefit provision. On the contrary, we show that social spending levels have risen, mainly due to a catch-up of former welfare state laggards. In structural terms, a blurring of welfare regimes can be observed. This twofold process can be described as dual convergence.

Introduction

The welfare state is intrinsic to statehood in contemporary advanced democracies. However, rising unemployment, increasing public debt, declining economic growth, an ever more competitive economic environment and changing demographics have increased the pressure on advanced welfare states over the last decades. How have welfare states responded to these changing conditions? What patterns of welfare state adaptation can we observe and what are their causes? Does politics still matter for social policy-making or is there a market-driven development towards a residual welfare state model?

These are the key questions to be addressed in this essay. By combining quantitative and qualitative approaches we examine the process of welfare state restructuring in four small open economies (Austria, Denmark, New Zealand and

---

[a] For an unabbreviated version of this paper (including a comprehensive list of references) see Herbert Obinger *et al.*[17]

Switzerland) between 1975 and 2004 and compare the outputs of social policy reform over this period to clarify whether a changed international economy and various endogenous pressures have contributed to a transformation of the welfare state. If increased exit options for mobile factors threaten mature welfare states, then, particularly small nations face high pressures to redesign their welfare state arrangements. By welfare state transformation we mean major policy changes in generosity and structures of benefit provision, funding principles and patterns of regulation. In addition, we discuss whether such policy changes reflect a more profound transformation of the state's role in welfare provision characterized by shifts in the division of labour between state, market and family and/or shifts of competencies to lower levels of government or supranational institutions.

Since the impact of globalization and endogenous challenges are likely to be mediated by national political and institutional configurations, we argue that the patterns, directions and the extent of welfare state transformation are decisively shaped by political institutions, political parties, policy legacies and specific problem pressures of welfare regimes. To examine the impact of politics on the process of welfare state restructuring, countries were selected that evince a substantial variety in their basic political and institutional features, including different welfare regime patterns.[7]

Since many retrenchment efforts only take effect in the long run and social policy changes typically occur in an incremental fashion as welfare states behave like 'elephants on the move'[13] we focus on long-term developments in pension, unemployment, health and family policy over the last 30 years. In the next section we examine the development of total social expenditure, programme-related spending patterns and funding principles over the period of investigation. In the following section we analyse national trajectories of welfare state adaptation between 1975 and 2004 in four brief case studies. In the final section we compare the national adjustment paths and seek to clarify whether the process of welfare state restructuring in the four countries examined ended up in a transformation of the (welfare) state. In addition, we briefly discuss the role of political variables in explaining policy change.

The macro-quantitative evidence: social spending development

A view on social expenditure trajectories between 1980 and 1998 suggests that the welfare state is not on the retreat. Figure 1 illustrates that social expenditure levels have increased rather than declined in all countries over this period. In addition, welfare state effort, measured as the proportion of social spending to total public spending, has remained constant or even increased. Only in New Zealand did the relative weight of the welfare state decline.

(a)　　　　　　　　　　　　　　　　　　　(b)

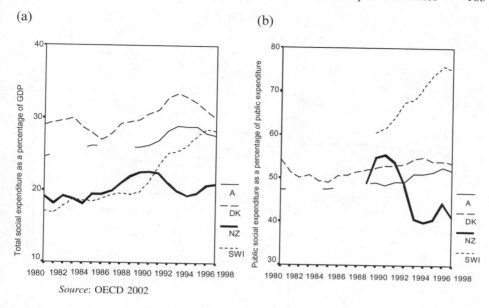

Source: OECD 2002

Figure 1. Social expenditure as a percentage of GDP (a) and of total public expenditure (b).

A similar picture emerges if real total expenditure per capita is calculated and total spending is broken down in its programme-related components. Real spending per dependent also reveals a continuous increase in expenditure levels. Figure 2 shows time series for real expenditure on old age cash benefits per person aged 65 and over, family cash benefits and family services per person aged 15 and younger as well as spending on active and passive labour market policy per unemployed. In addition, the bold line exhibits the development of real total social expenditure per capita. Adjusting expenditure to programme-specific caseloads by and large confirms the general trend that spending either remained constant or even increased. This also holds for health expenditure per capita not reported in Figure 2. Again, the only exception is New Zealand where spending on old age pensions has steadily declined over time.[b] Spending efforts on unemployment compensation and activation measures per unemployed show a greater variation in all countries but these fluctuations are mainly driven by the business cycle.

Although disaggregated spending trajectories show a more nuanced picture compared with the development of total social expenditure, we can conclude that the social spending profiles in the four nations under scrutiny are not indicative of a race to the bottom. All the indicators employed rather suggest a remarkable stability of spending efforts.

---

[b] However, this calculation of pension expenditure per person over 65 overstates the real value for New Zealand for most of the period because, between 1975 and 1992, retirement age was 60, and was then lifted to 65 over a period of nine years.

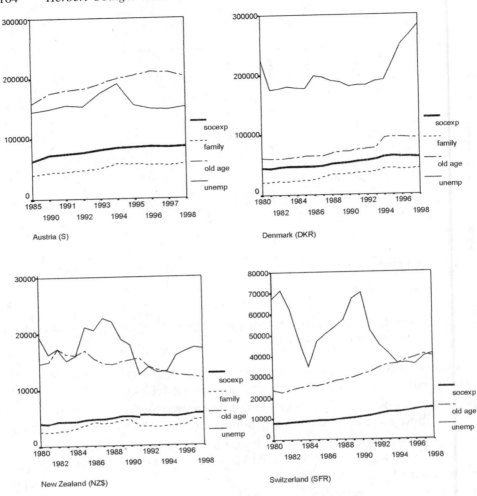

Source: OECD 2002.
Note: Data on family expenditure in Switzerland are not available.

Figure 2. Programme-specific expenditure per dependent in national currencies at constant 1995 prices.

As Figure 3 illustrates, social expenditure dynamics have been mainly driven by catch-up. Growth rates were highest in laggard countries and lowest in those nations that already maintained mature welfare states in 1980. The initial social spending level explains more than 50% of the cross-national variation in social expenditure growth between 1980 and 1998. In addition, this chart illustrates that only Ireland and the Netherlands have reduced social spending over this period.

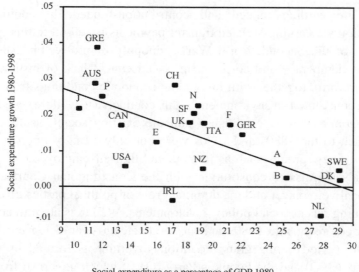

Source: OECD 2002

Figure 3. Social expenditure growth 1980–1998.

Given this evidence, welfare states have converged towards a national steady state rather than to the bottom.

In all four countries, public social spending makes up the bulk of total social expenditure, whereas mandatory private benefits contribute to no more than 2% of GDP. Similar to spending, the broad patterns of welfare state funding remained largely unchanged. The welfare state in New Zealand and Denmark is still almost entirely tax-financed, while the share of social security contributions as a percentage of GDP has slightly increased in Austria and Switzerland since 1980.

Nonetheless, the remarkable stability of spending and funding patterns does not rule out that major policy changes in regulation and benefit provision have occurred over the last 30 years. To address this issue in more detail, case studies are needed. The next section provides a brief summary about the adjustment paths in four small open economies.

Case studies

Austria

Judged by its structural make up, the Austrian welfare state is commonly classified as conservative:[7] entitlements are regularly tied to employment status, while benefits are earnings-related and contribution-funded. In addition, status preservation via earnings-related transfer payments is central to this type. In the aftermath of the Second World War, a duopoly of pro-welfare state parties, consensus democracy and corporatism, a consequent lack of institutional veto points to reform, together with favourable economic conditions from the 1950s onwards, constituted an environment highly conducive to welfare state expansion. New programmes were established and the existing social insurance benefits dating back to the 1880s and 1920s were not only steadily improved but also extended to new groups such as farmers and the self-employed.

Austria's permissive constitution with the Constitutional Court as the only institutional veto player and the dominant role of political parties go a long way in explaining recent social policy developments. Welfare state retrenchment did not occur before the mid-1980s and was moderate but ever increasing in intensity during the period of the grand coalition governments formed by the Social Democrats (SPÖ) and the People's Party (ÖVP) which governed from 1986 to 2000. The most substantial benefit cuts were imposed by the centre-right government that took office in 2000. The reform of old-age pensions and unemployment insurance are the most prominent examples that illustrate the ever-increasing intensity of retrenchment over time.

The Austrian *pension system* is fragmented along occupational lines and provides benefits for aged or disabled employees and their survivors. Benefits are funded by earmarked contributions and federal grants. The General Social Insurance Act (GSIA) of 1955 is the legal base of old age, health and accident insurance for blue and white-collar workers. With the GSIA as a model, old age pensions were gradually extended to farmers, entrepreneurs, artists and professional groups such as lawyers and doctors. Civil servants are covered by a special and initially more generous scheme.

The politics of labour shedding via early retirement regulations and invalidity pensions in a greying society exposed pension insurance to profound fiscal stress. In 1998, almost 50% of the social budget was devoted to old age pensions and survivors' benefits, making the Austrian pension system one of the most expensive in the OECD. Moreover, the imperative of budget consolidation in the shadow of the Maastricht Treaty was an impetus to curtail the federal grants delivered to pension insurance.

Increasing both contributions and the ceiling for contributory payments as well as changing the pension formula were repeated exercises to cope with demographic changes and fiscal austerity. The pension reform of 1987 (and that of 1993) extended the calculation base from 10 to 15 years. In addition, contribution-free credits in periods of tertiary education were abolished and eligibility to survivors' pensions for childless survivors was tightened. The pension reform launched in 1993 was more balanced: benefit adjustment was changed from the dynamics of gross to that of net wages, while child raising periods were credited for benefit calculation up to a maximum of four years per child. The 1997 pension reform aimed at curtailing early retirement and increasing the effective retirement age, while eligibility to invalidity pensions was tightened. In addition, the calculation of pensions for civil servants was partly harmonized with that based on the GSIA.

Retrenchment was further intensified by the centre-right coalition that came to power in 2000. In an effort to bring the actual age of retirement (which was 57.6 years in 1999) closer to the threshold of 65 years stipulated by law, early retirement pensions based upon invalidity were abolished and eligibility for early retirement was tightened by imposing benefit deductions. Survivors' benefits were curtailed, whereas pension contributions for civil servants and pensioners were raised. A further reform followed in 2003. This draft was unprecedented in terms of the intensity of the benefit cuts suggested. The government proposed to calculate pensions on the basis of an employee's full employment record instead of the best 15 years as under the previous system. This proposal was equivalent to a benefit cut of up to 30%. In addition, the government increased its efforts to contain early retirement by cancelling early retirement pensions for employees with long contribution records and for the long-term unemployed. Given widespread opposition, the reform was slightly watered down but the government used its parliamentary majority to pass the bill in June 2003. However, the government also imposed structural reforms that will take full effect in the long-run. A reform of severance payment in 2002 paved the way for a greater role of fully funded private and occupational pensions. In addition, civil servant pensions are to be fully harmonized with the regulations of the GSIA. However, the decision-making process on this issue is at present still in flux.

The main route to cope with rising *unemployment* was to curtail benefits and to increase contributions. Until the mid-1990s, the latter strategy clearly dominated as contribution rates have been raised from 2.10% in 1980 to 6.00% in 1994. Unemployment insurance reforms combined selective improvements with modest benefit cuts until 1993.[25] The mid-1990s witnessed a shift of emphasis in labour market policy. While contribution rates were stabilized at 6%, the government increasingly relied on benefit cutbacks. Reform of unemployment compensation was characterized by modest cuts in the net replacement rate and stronger sanctions in the case of unwillingness to work. There was also a moderate shift towards active labour market policy. Special unemployment allowance for the elderly unemployed with a long insurance record – a benefit to bridge the time gap until retirement – was abolished in the course of the austerity packages in the mid-1990s. The centre-right coalition reduced family supplements for the unemployed by around a third (with the partner's income no longer taken into account) and imposed a uniform net replacement rate of 55%. In addition, the federal grant to unemployment insurance was cancelled.

Cost explosion was a major theme underpinning the reform of *health insurance*. In contrast to unemployment and pension insurance, this social insurance branch was not subject to fundamental reform. Similar to pension insurance, health insurance is occupationally fragmented and contribution-funded. However, with a coverage of 99% of the resident population it is de facto a universal system. Hospitals are financed through general revenue and health insurance. The main route to cope with increased health expenditure was to extend co-payments beyond farmers, civil servants and the self-employed. In 1988, the government imposed co-payments to cover the so-called 'hotel costs' in case of hospital treatment. As of 1997, patients have to pay a contribution amounting to €3.60 on each health insurance voucher, whereas co-payments for cures were imposed in 1996. The centre-right coalition continued and intensified this policy. User charges for hospital treatment and prescription charges were raised and a new user charge for out-patient treatments in hospitals was established. In addition, free health co-insurance for childless couples was abolished.

A further attempt to curb expenditure was to reorganize hospital funding. Hospital funding is characterized by a considerable fragmentation between the federal government and the nine *Länder*, and was seen as contributing to inefficient investment, duplication of effort and over-capacities. In 1997, the federal government and the *Länder* agreed on a state treaty to reduce the cost explosion in the health sector through improved co-ordination in hospital planning and financing.

There were, however, areas in which benefits were increased or extended. A major breakthrough was the introduction of federal care allowance for the permanent disabled in 1993. This new programme is entirely tax funded and anchored a structurally unique pillar in the Austrian social security system. Finally, in 1998, compulsory health (and pension) insurance was extended to the so-called new self-employed (*Scheinselbständige*).

Income support to families is generous compared with other OECD countries. Most cash benefits are funded by the Compensation Fund of Family Expenses, which is fed by employers' contributions and payments from the public purse. These funds are used, for example, for family allowances and free school books. Cash benefits, such as family allowances, are universal. Retrenchment in this field occurred with two austerity packages launched in the mid-1990s, which abolished birth allowances and imposed co-payments for school books.

Recent years have witnessed several efforts to overcome the shortcomings with regard to day-care facilities for children. In the late 1990s, the grand coalition provided special grants to subordinate governments to enhance the number of childcare facilities, which are the responsibility of the *Länder* and municipalities.

Despite a declining number of children, the number of day-care facilities has increased since the 1980s. However, there is still a substantial mismatch in coverage between rural areas and urban agglomerations.[24]

Parental allowance was subject to numerous reforms. Initially, this was an insurance-based lump-sum benefit for mothers, paid for 12 months subsequent to maternity allowance that replaced the full salary for eight weeks after birth. The grand coalition extended parental allowance from one to two years in 1991 but reduced it from 24 to 18 months in the mid-1990s. The centre-right government finally replaced this benefit by the universal child care benefit which is granted for a period of up to three years as a non-employment-related lump-sum transfer provided that both parents take care of the children.

In sum, the majority of changes, at least over the last two decades, have been about cutting benefits, reducing entitlements and increasing contributions, although there were also selective benefit enhancements (e.g. care allowances) and an increase in coverage. Overall, the contribution-benefit nexus and the pressure for labour market participation (activation) have been intensified. Unger and Heitzmann[26] therefore argue that the Austrian welfare state returned to its conservative roots. Although there is no doubt that the insurance principle was strengthened recently, this judgement ignores crucial developments, which rather suggest that the Austrian welfare state is less conservative today. Two salient features typical for conservative welfare states are on the retreat, although these developments will take full effect only for the younger cohorts. First, the profession-specific differences between blue-collar and white-collar workers have been levelled-out over time and occupationally fragmented pension systems are to be harmonized in the long-run. Secondly, and more importantly, the principle of status-preservation has been hollowed out. This not only holds true for unemployment compensation, which guarantees comparatively low replacement rates, but also for old-age pensions in the wake of the 2003 pension reform. Moreover, care allowances for the disabled have increased service-orientation, and childcare facilities were enhanced over recent years. Finally, the new child benefit marks a break with the employment-centred design of the welfare state, because its approach is universal and no longer linked to an earlier employment record.

The Austrian experience also suggests that parties do matter in more subtle ways in times of austerity. The social democrats are by no means pure defenders of the welfare state. Together with their Christian democratic coalition partner they launched two austerity packages in the mid-1990s, which imposed substantial cuts in social and public sector spending. However, compared with the centre-right coalition that took office in 2000, retrenchment was moderate since the grand coalition governments in Austria were characterized by a greater ideological distance between the incumbent parties than was the case for the succeeding centre-right coalition. Operating under a permissive constitutional setting and by deliberately bypassing the traditional system of social partnership, the latter therefore was able to implement more far-reaching policy changes.

Denmark

In the last decade, this small country in the north of Europe has gained much attention as a role model for successful welfare state restructuring. As a social democratic welfare state,[7] Denmark has offered universal and generous benefits promoting equality and diminishing stigmatization. Welfare state provision is almost entirely tax-financed and public services play an important role. Since the municipalities are the principal agent in financing and providing these social services, the local level has traditionally been a cornerstone of the Danish welfare state. Nonetheless, the question of more or less decentralization is a recurrent topic in welfare state reforms.

The Danish parliament is unicameral. Broad coalition cabinets and minority governments are characteristic. With the election of 1973, five new parties moved into parliament leading to a period of political instability: between 1973 and 1993, eleven governments held office and nine elections took place. From 1975 to 1982, the Social Democrats governed in changing (minority) coalitions. In 1982, the first conservative prime minister since the Second World War came to power. Until 1993, the Conservatives controlled the cabinet in changing coalitions. At the beginning of their term in office a number of social benefits were frozen. Owing to high inflation and rising wages this meant de facto a severe cut back (see Figure 1). Nevertheless, the principle of universalism, generosity and the state's role in welfare provision remained unchanged. In actual fact, '[...] the Danish welfare state was further expanded in a social democratic direction'[10] under conservative rule. In 1993, the Social Democrats returned to power. They reacted immediately to the welfare crisis caused by fiscal pressure and high unemployment with several reform packages and successfully reduced public debt as well as unemployment. But in the 2001 election a liberal-conservative coalition succeeded and, for the first time since 1924, the Social Democrats were not the biggest parliamentary group. In their election campaign, both the liberals and the conservatives had refrained from their former neo-liberal rhetoric and promised improvements in maternity and paternity leave as well as in hospital funding.

The Danish welfare state has traditionally been characterized as women and *family*-friendly, providing day-care services for children in order to integrate women into the labour market. Women's participation in the labour market as well as the proportion of children in public day-care is high compared with other European countries. The provision and funding of day-care for children lies with the municipalities as well as the administration of the child benefit, which is granted to all families with children under the age of 18. Supplementary cash benefits exist for families in special need. Apart from a short period from 1977 to 1986,[c] the child benefit has always been universal and flat rate since its introduction in 1952. In contrast to the general policy of cut backs, family allowance was increased during the 1990s.[14] Parental leave has been gradually prolonged since the 1970s. In 1984, the 14 weeks of maternity leave were extended by another 10 weeks that now either mother or father can take. Leave provision was further increased in 1992. In 1999, two extra weeks became available exclusively for men. Another extension in 2002 is to give both parents together the possibility of up to 52 weeks of paid absence. Simultaneously, the liberal-conservative government introduced the possibility to be granted an allowance if parents choose to opt out of public day-care. These measures were introduced as both a family and a labour market policy instrument in order to reduce labour supply and to cope with the shortage in day-care facilities. Despite a comparatively high labour market participation of women, the reform of 2002 has been criticized for not promoting gender equity.

Labour market policies in Denmark, especially measures for the *unemployed*, recently received much attention, because of their innovative character.[6] The Danish 'miracle'[20] gained prominence as a counter-strategy to neo-liberal cut-back rhetoric even though some researchers criticize the reforms' outcomes.[27] On the one hand, Denmark offers a flexible labour market with only little regulation, and on the other hand high social security. This 'flexicurity'[6] is accompanied by a still voluntary unemployment insurance, which is organized by 35 state-recognized unemployment insurance funds and administered by the unions.

Up until the 1980s, labour market policies were aimed at reducing labour supply, for example through government-financed early retirement schemes. These programmes still continue to exist but there has been an important shift during the 1990s to reintegrate the unemployed in the labour market. Activation has been the guiding principle of the reforms and a number of new instruments, which followed the principle of entitlement and obligation, were introduced. The individual recipient has the obligation to participate in training schemes and other measures. And he has the right to choose his 'individual action plan'. Two issues already on the agenda in the reform era during the 1960s were further pushed forward: decentralization and bringing administration and recipients closer together. Measures such as closer local cooperation between employers, the unemployed and the local employment service should reduce unemployment caused by a labour market mismatch. In order to increase flexibility, the possibility to move between periods of employment, unemployment and periods spent on

---

[c] In order to reduce spending on family allowance, the Social Democrats introduced a means test whereas the opposition planned a universal cut back of benefits by 10%. In 1986, the centre-right majority in parliament re-introduced universal child allowance.

caring for children or on further training was improved. The duration of unemployment benefit receipt was shortened in the reform era from up to ten years in 1994 to four years in 1999. As outlined in their 2003 action plan, 'More people in Work', the liberal-conservative government introduced measures to harmonize and simplify the rules governing municipal action to improve the re-integration of the unemployed into the labour market. With the same argument they made social assistance the responsibility of the Ministry of Employment, emphasizing the obligation to work. Shortening of benefit duration, rising obligations and work requirements for benefit receipt is the overall trend in labour market policy in the period between 1975 and 2004. However, benefits are still generous in a comparative perspective. State regulation increased rather than diminished, although welfare provision was further decentralized.

The Danish *pension system* was also subject to a number of changes concerning benefit rates and the organizational structure. At first glance, theses changes seem only minor, producing differences in degree, not in kind.[14] However, in a long-term perspective these changes can be regarded as path breaking.[9] The '*Folkepension*', a universal flat-rate pension scheme at age 67,[d] was introduced in 1956. This basic pension scheme still exists today, but step-by-step the labour market related tier of the Danish old age pensions system was further expanded. Already in 1964, 'supplementary mandatory pension insurance' was introduced (ATP). The umbrella organization of the Danish trade unions (LO) called for further occupational pensions and, in 1993, almost all professions represented by the LO were covered by supplementary pension schemes that were financed by employers and by employees. Two further schemes were established. The '*Lønmodtagernes Dyrtidsfond*' (LD), consisting of funds from a tax on cost-of-living adjustments in labor contracts between 1977 and 1979, was established in 1980 and would be paid out to workers in lump sums at pension age. It will be depleted around 2035 and has never played an important role. The 'Temporary Pension Savings Scheme' (SP) in 1998, on the other hand, has been subject to recent reforms and party conflict. Whereas the former has never played an important role, the latter has been subject to recent reforms and party conflict. In 1999, the social democratic government changed the scheme from an earnings-related to a flat-rate pension saving, but in 2002 the newly elected bourgeois government reversed this, stopping the redistributive effect. Today, the Danish pension system consists of three pillars: a public tax-financed 'Folkepension', several contribution-based occupational schemes and privately organized individual insurance schemes. Consequently, the universal, tax-financed pillar has lost importance and Danish old age pensions have become more dependent on previous labour market participation.

---

[d] The retirement age was lowered to 65 in 1999 in order to decrease the number of people in early retirement. The aim was to reduce costs because old-age pension benefits are lower than early retirement benefits.

In contrast, the *healthcare* system has not seen a major restructuring in the period under investigation. Two important changes were already imposed in the early 1970s: counties and municipalities were made responsible for the healthcare system and a universal Health Care Reimbursement Scheme replaced the health insurance system. Every Danish inhabitant is entitled to services. General practitioners act as gatekeepers to specialists or hospital treatment. The system is tax-financed with only minor co-payments for medicine and for some forms of special treatment. In March 2001, the social democratic government introduced new rules for pharmaceutical co-payments. As a measure of cost containment the size of reimbursement now depends on the individual's personal consumption per year. People using a lot of drugs and people in need of long-term medication receive more compensation than the rest. Although no overhaul of the healthcare system has taken place, a number of regional initiatives altered the way in which healthcare is delivered. There is a tendency to increase efficiency, reduce waiting periods for hospital beds, and improve quality and patient rights.

In sum, only minor cutbacks in welfare benefits were carried out and Denmark continues to be one of the most developed and most comprehensive welfare states in the OECD, with social expenditure at approximately 30% of GDP. Yet, the welfare state has lost some of its salient regime characteristics. Elements from the liberal welfare state ('workfare') were adopted as well as from the conservative regime type (linkage to previous employment in old age pensions, expansion of cash benefits and leave schemes in family policy). In other respects Denmark sticks to the social democratic path. Unemployment insurance has kept its universal and generous character because coverage and replacement rates have remained high, although eligibility rules were tightened. The child benefit and the basic old age pension ('Folkepension') have remained universal and flat-rate. There is neither a clear shift of competencies to lower levels of governments nor to supranational institutions. The state preserved its dominant role in the provision and funding of welfare programmes. Although the number of institutional veto players is low, fundamental policy change did not occur because of a broad welfare state consensus among the governing parties. In addition, minority governments made the political compromises necessary and hindered more radical reforms, changing the overall character of the Danish welfare state.

New Zealand

New Zealand's welfare state has undergone significant change in all of its constituent programmes since 1975. In structural terms, the welfare state has usually been grouped among the 'liberal' welfare regimes[7] due to a range of means-tested benefits and below-average social expenditure growth rates during the post-war period. Yet, some programmes deviate from this liberal pattern: in 1975, healthcare provision, family benefits and part of the public pension were universal and accident compensation was partly earnings-related and insurance-based. Looking exclusively at direct provision of transfers and services by the state, however, might not be sufficient. For much of the post-war era, a high degree of 'social security' in a wider sense was achieved in New Zealand – and even more so in Australia – through a combination of atypical policy instruments and favourable economic conditions *without* relying much on direct social expenditure. On the one hand, both countries had lower demand for social security, by virtue of a high degree of economic development, male full employment, a rather 'young' demographic profile and high home ownership rates. On the supply side, on the other hand, trade protectionism and a highly regulated system of wage setting led to high wages – set at a level sufficient to support a wife and family – and to an egalitarian income structure. Consequently, Francis Castles[4] called the Australasian welfare regime the 'wage earners' welfare state'.

In the 1970s, this system of production and protection came under heavy strain, mainly due to shifts in the world economy[19] and various social changes such as rising female labour participation and family change.[4] The Labour government of the 1980s (1984–1990) famously responded to the economic problems by what might be the most rapid and radical economic liberalization an OECD-country has seen in recent years, thereby accelerating the demise of the 'wage earners' welfare state'. Labour's conservative successors continued this policy and dismantled the system of wage regulation. Reform-minded governments were helped by the extremely permissive institutional environment of New Zealand's Westminster-style political system, where, prior to the constitutional changes of the 1990s, the Prime Minister and the cabinet were usually supported by a single-party majority in parliament and unhindered by institutional veto points such as a second chamber, federalism or a constitutional court. This gave reformers the opportunity to push through legislative changes at a remarkable speed and virtually unhindered by political opponents. In 1993, however, the country changed its electoral system from a single-member plurality system ('first past the post') to proportional representation, which makes single-party majority governments less likely, and recent experience in New Zealand is a case in point. Since 1993, no government has been able to rely on a single-party majority in parliament. For most of this period, coalitions and/or minority governments have been the rule. Arguably, institutional change has made radical short-term policy reversals much more difficult as governments now depend on other parties' support.

Today, after the economic reforms, New Zealand no longer has a comprehensive system of 'social protection by other means'.[4] Yet, there is still a 'core' welfare state, i.e. direct cash transfer programmes and social services. In the following, the focus will be above all on changes in this field.

The mid-1970s saw a massive expansion of public involvement in the field of *pensions* when the conservatives introduced National Superannuation, a generous universal flat-rate pension at age 60. Today, New Zealand's pension system is still universal in principle, albeit at a markedly lower benefit level and with a qualifying age of 65 years. However, it would be wrong to conclude that pension reform in New Zealand was a path-dependent, incremental adjustment process towards a somewhat less generous scheme within a stable institutional framework. Superannuation has, in fact, been subject to almost constant short-term reforms by left and right-wing governments alike. Labour, for instance, introduced a highly unpopular 'claw back' tax for better-off pensioners – the Superannuation Surcharge – in 1986 in an attempt to curb the burgeoning cost of Superannuation. This policy was abandoned in 1998 by a conservative-led coalition. Since 1975, the pension scheme has seen numerous changes of the benefit adjustment mechanism and a rapid increase in the eligibility age from 60 to 65 years between 1992 and 2001.[22] Financing the old-age pension has been on the agenda throughout the 1990s. The centre-left coalition eventually established a Superannuation Fund in 2001 aimed at pre-funding part of the future pension expenditure for the baby-boom birth cohorts. Today, universal Superannuation is still the central instrument of public pension policy. There is still no 'second tier' earnings-related scheme and private provision remains completely voluntary and is not subject to special tax incentives.

New Zealand's public *health* sector, established in 1938 along universal lines,[f] has remained intact in terms of the overall principles of entitlement but the instruments of service provision have been considerably restructured in the 1990s. In 1993, the conservative government introduced a 'purchaser–provider split', hoping to increase the system's efficiency. Four Regional Health Authorities (RHAs) were to act as the main purchasing organizations, each with a single budget to buy primary and secondary health services and disability support on behalf of the population – three areas which until then were separately financed. In terms of provision, the change was just as radical: The government regrouped public hospitals and community services into 23 profit-oriented Crown Health Enterprises and made them compete with private hospitals, general practitioners (GPs) and voluntary organizations in an internal market for contracts with the RHAs.[2] It turned out that the new system, if anything, did not increase the efficiency of public healthcare provision. As a consequence, the right-wing coalition watered down the quasi-market structure as early as in 1997.[2] More importantly, in 2001, the Labour-led government established 21 District Health Boards responsible for both funding *and* provision of services in their districts, thus abandoning the purchaser–provider split of 1993. To a certain extent, the private sector is still involved in delivery of public services but the reach of the

---

[f] From 1938, the government has never been able to fully integrate general practitioners' services into the scheme but they are partly subsidized. In reality, primary care has always been a state-regulated but nonetheless predominantly private affair.[5]

controversial 'market model' is now significantly limited.[11] On the level of individual entitlement rules, change has been much scarcer. Hospital care is still universal. At the same time, state subsidies for primary care – which have always covered only part of the usual GP charges – were targeted to low-income groups and the chronically ill. Co-payments for medicine consist of a general prescription charge and, for some drugs, additional charges, depending on the extent to which certain drugs are subsidized. Since 1997, children under six get GP visits and pharmaceuticals free of charge.

The major needs-based benefits, such as *unemployment* benefit, sickness benefit or Domestic Purposes Benefit (DPB), which is mainly claimed by lone mothers, have undergone significant changes since 1975.[g] The single most important event was the incoming conservative government's 1991 budget, with extensive cuts between 5% and 27% across a range of benefits.[23:5] The government tightened eligibility criteria, particularly for young and unemployed people. In addition, there has been a marked tendency towards 'activation' and 'workfare' policies. The subsidized employment schemes of the 1970s and early 1980s were scrapped in 1985 on grounds of possible market distorting effects.[12] Governments of the 1990s put more emphasis on individual obligations in order to end so-called 'welfare dependency'. Work testing was introduced by conservative governments for most working-age beneficiaries – not just those on unemployment benefits but also many lone mothers and spouses of unemployment beneficiaries. Recipients were expected to take up paid work or participate in community work or training schemes, and sanctions for non-compliance were tightened. In 2000, the Labour-led coalition reduced some of the work obligations for the sick and for lone mothers but kept the overall strategy. Furthermore, the government is now increasingly trying to move beneficiaries into work through intensive case-management, combining tight monitoring and access to a wider range of employment and training opportunities.

Apart from the 'family wage', one of the pillars of the 'wage earners' welfare state', the post-war income assistance for *families* in New Zealand, was based on the universal Family Benefit. However, governments failed regularly to adjust benefit rates to rising price levels, thus allowing its real value to decline markedly.[21:255] The last adjustment was made in 1979, twelve years before its abolition. Instead of universal payments, New Zealand governments from the mid-1970s onwards increasingly relied on means-tested assistance. First, this was done in the form of tax rebates for low-income families, until the introduction of

---

[g] In housing policy, the early 1990s also mark a major turning point. The government withdrew from direct provision of state rentals with reduced rents for low-income households and, instead, tried to intervene solely through income support, with the new Accommodation Supplement. This reform was partially reversed in 2000.[15]

Family Support, a major means tested programme under Labour in 1986. Beginning in 1986 with the Guaranteed Minimum Family Income, a negative income tax scheme for the working poor, family policy in New Zealand has become increasingly dual in character, in the sense that working families can claim additional in-work-benefits – usually in the form of tax credits – whereas families with both parents out of work have to rely exclusively on Family Support, the basic financial assistance scheme.[16] Income transfers are accompanied by social services, notably child-care services, which have seen a significant expansion since the 1970s[21] and for which low-income families can claim government subsidies.[23] Unpaid parental leave was introduced in New Zealand in the 1980s and only in 2002 did the government finally set up a comprehensive paid parental leave scheme, which was enhanced further in 2004. In May 2004, the Labour government announced a huge spending boost for family cash transfers and services, without abolishing means tests. Arguably, this is the most significant welfare state expansion of the last 25 years.

The overall picture of welfare state change in New Zealand is one of substantial transformation, with the first government of the conservative Prime Minister Bolger (1990–1993) marking the major policy turning point of the 1975–2004 period. The impact of this period of deep benefit cuts and entitlement changes as well as the reorganization of the healthcare sector is also reflected in the slump in social expenditure at the beginning of the 1990s (see Figure 1). Although aggregate social expenditure relative to GDP increased again afterwards and is slightly higher today than in 1975, for most of the key programmes, including the old-age pension, benefit levels have declined relative to average wages and eligibility has been tightened. During the 1980s and 1990s, both Labour and conservative governments introduced cuts in social programmes and, for much of the period, if anything, partisan differences on the issue of welfare retrenchment seem to have been a matter of degree rather than of kind. The shift towards needs-based assistance in family policy or workfare and activation policies illustrate this point.

In terms of its structural characteristics, the welfare state seems quite resilient in the long run. Pensions and healthcare are still essentially universal, and – with the longstanding but minor exception of accident compensation – social insurance-based policies are non-existent. Means-testing is now even more prominent than in 1975. Family policy is the only field that has seen an outright shift in principle from universal benefits towards means-tested assistance. On the whole, and despite the end of the 'wage earners' welfare state', income maintenance is still a mix of citizen-ship-based and needs-based programmes but with a noticeable tilt towards the latter.

Switzerland

Switzerland, prior to the 1970s, has generally been assigned to the liberal world of welfare. Only old-age and disability insurance were mandatory for the whole population, and accident insurance only for certain groups. Private providers played an important role, especially in healthcare. Additionally, Switzerland only spent a comparatively low share of GDP on social provision. It was also a laggard with regard to the date when the core programmes of the welfare state were finally introduced.

The impressive increase in social expenditure in Switzerland since the 1970s (see Figure 1) raises the question of whether the Swiss welfare state has experienced fundamental change over the last three decades.

The Swiss political system is characterized by a strong horizontal and vertical fragmentation of power. The Swiss federal government, a collegial body where all major parties are represented with a share unchanged[h] since 1959, is not responsible to parliament. Federalism disperses power vertically and provides various opportunities for the cantons to influence federal policy-making. In addition, several instruments of direct democracy enable citizens to overrule any major decision at the federal level: a referendum is compulsory for all amendments to the constitution; through the optional referendum, the people can challenge parliamentary bills or decrees; and with the people's initiative, citizens may seek a decision on an amendment to the constitution.

The Swiss *pension* scheme rests on a 'three pillar model' which became officially recognized in 1982. The first pillar is a state-run, mandatory old age and survivors' insurance (AHV), covering the entire resident population and providing minimal financial security for retirement. It is mainly financed on a pay-as-you-go basis through parity contributions of employers and employees and state-subsidies. Since 1965, means-tested supplementary benefits exist to support needy recipients. The second pillar consists of fully-funded occupational pensions. It is compulsory for employees above a certain income level and is to guarantee the previous standard of living when combined with AHV. The third pillar is made up of voluntary savings supported by tax relief and has remained largely unchanged during the period under review.

Most changes have occurred in the first pillar. It was mainly the pressures imposed by the economic crisis of the 1970s and the growing financial troubles of the AHV compensation fund that caused two reforms. These reforms share several features: they combined cuts with expansion of benefits, and they were challenged by optional referenda or people's initiatives. However, these reforms were only incremental with the basic programme principles remaining un-

---

[h] The elections of 2003 provoked the first change of the so-called 'magic formula' when, as a result of changed patterns of electoral support, the Christian Democrats lost one seat to the right-wing Swiss People's Party.

changed.[1] The most important modification took place in the 1990s and combined major improvements for women (splitting of pensions for couples and granting credits for care and upbringing) and for low-income groups with restrictive measures. Specifically, the retirement age for women was gradually increased, which was strongly contested by the left. Two tax reforms to raise revenues for AHV could not put an end to the financial problems of the first pillar. Therefore, another revision – which was rather restrictive with its main focus on cost-containment – was accepted by parliament in 2003. The reform went together with an increase in value-added tax on behalf of AHV (and invalidity insurance) to be decided on in a mandatory referendum because it required a constitutional amendment. While the left attacked pension reform via referendum, bourgeois parties argued against a tax increase. Both proposals were rejected by the voters in May 2004.

The second pillar was also subject to a reform in recent years. Faced with unfavourable financial and stock market developments, cuts such as the increase in retirement age for women and a reduction of the minimum conversion rate[i] were coupled with a reduction of income limits required for mandatory insurance, resulting in better coverage for part-time and temporary workers. However, pure retrenchment took place for the first time when the federal government reduced the guaranteed interest rate in 2003.

Until the 1990s, *health* insurance was voluntary. The federal government subsidized (mostly) private sickness funds, which act as carriers of health insurance, and regulated only minimum benefits. Health insurance is financed through non-income related premiums and public subsidies. While the problem of increasing healthcare costs had already put the question of reform on the political agenda in the mid-1960s, apart from the introduction of a strong component of co-payments in 1964, the Swiss system of healthcare remained generally unchanged until the 1990s. Since then, several crucial changes have occurred. Health insurance became mandatory for the entire resident population in 1994. Although nearly the whole population had been covered before, this was a system-shift, which entails an enlarged role for the federal state in social policy. The reform was marked by a tendency to combine expansive with restrictive measures. While competition between providers was strongly enhanced, the reform again increased co-payments. The scope of benefits in-kind covered by health insurance was somewhat enlarged and explicit discrimination of women was eliminated with the abolition of gender-related premiums. Similar to New Zealand, state subsidies were targeted to low-income groups and, additionally, cantons were empowered to implement policy.

---

[i] The minimum conversion rate is used to convert individual savings in the second pillar into annual pensions.

Because the cost-containment achieved by the reform of 1994 was not considered sufficient, further modification of health insurance was put on the political agenda. In 2003, the lower chamber of parliament dismissed a minor revision mainly focusing on hospital financing, while the federal government imposed strongly contested retrenchment: mandatory co-payments were again enhanced and maximum deductions for optional co-payments were reduced. However, the federal government has drafted several additional encompassing reform 'packages' in 2004.

Federal *family* policy is the stepchild of social policy in Switzerland. Its development is marked by both sovereign and parliament preventing an enlargement of federal involvement. This applies especially to social protection in the case of motherhood and harmonizing regulations in the field of family allowances.[j] Here, apart from federal benefits for small farmers and agricultural employees, various cantonal allowances exist which differ in type, level and conditions for entitlement.

Since maternity insurance was lacking at the federal level, the canton of Geneva created a cantonal insurance in 2000, with other cantons intending to follow. This illustrates how Swiss federalism makes it possible for individual cantons to step in when the decision-making process is blocked at the federal level. As a tax reform which, amongst other things, was aimed at lowering the tax burden of families failed in a referendum in 2004, the people will have to decide on two family policy initiatives soon. A relatively modest maternity insurance proposal was attacked by a referendum from the right-wing Swiss People's Party. In addition, a harmonizing law on family allowances has been proposed by way of a people's initiative.

In retrospect, the only real expansion of federal family policy since the 1970s occurred in 2002, when, as a result of a social democratic parliamentary initiative, temporarily limited financial support for childcare outside the family was enacted.

In 1975/76, only about 20% of the wage earners were covered by voluntary *unemployment* insurance. Voluntary insurance with federal subsidies to private, public and parity funds was sufficient until the 1970s, because economic growth and spectacular low levels of unemployment acted as functional equivalents for social insurance. Unemployment figures could be kept low by regulating labour supply, even in the 1970s. In times of decreasing demand for labour, restrictive work and residency permit regulations were used to make foreigners leave the labour market. Additionally, the lack of an infrastructure for non-family childcare discouraged women from entering the labour market. However, the oil crisis showed that voluntary insurance was not able to cope with rising unemployment.

---

[j] Until today, three attempts to create a federal maternity insurance have failed in optional referenda, the last one in 1999.

Making unemployment insurance mandatory in 1976 was a system-shift that resulted in a stronger involvement of the federal state in Swiss social policy.

The economic crisis of the 1990s hit Switzerland stronger than every cyclical slump since the 1930s. Unemployment figures rose dramatically and unemployment insurance ran into debts. The traditional way of regulating labour supply had become less effective because of the introduction of mandatory unemployment insurance, the increasing number of foreigners with permanent residency permits and modified employment patterns of women.[18] As a result of these pressures, reform seemed inevitable. Since the 1990s, mandatory unemployment insurance was subject to several reforms, all of them inducing incremental changes which generally balanced cuts and expansion, while a rather restrictive reform (1997) was prevented by a referendum launched by the political left. Important modifications include the enhancement of activation in labour market policies and the buffering of gender discrimination. Replacements rates were reduced, but now depend on social criteria such as disability. Equally, targeting was strengthened as the duration of benefits was limited but simultaneously related to the age of recipients. In the face of declining unemployment figures in 2002, temporary emergency measures imposed in the crisis of the mid-1990s (e.g. higher premiums) were ended. Finally, the qualifying period was doubled and the maximum number of daily allowances was further reduced.

On the whole, all core programmes were subject to major changes since the mid-1970s. This is especially astonishing with regard to Switzerland's dense political structure, providing reform opponents with many opportunities to block changes. However, the great number of veto players can, to a large part, explain the dominant pattern of Swiss social policy reform since the 1970s: in particular, consensus democracy and direct democracy paved the way for balanced reforms that distribute gains and losses evenly among the electorate.

The impact of parties on social policy is problematic to disentangle in Switzerland's consensus democracy since the federal government traditionally consisted of the four major parties. However, a clear partisan effect shows up in referenda, with the left generally attacking retrenchment and the bourgeois parties being successful in mobilizing against expansive measures.

In the long run, however, the role of the federal state in social policy was expanded by making unemployment and health insurance compulsory. This increase in coverage, programme maturation and low economic growth caused a huge increase of social expenditure during the period under scrutiny. Despite some benefit cuts, replacement rates are comparatively generous. Only family policy is characterized by few results when compared with legislative attempts, which is why the country remains a European laggard in the domain of family policy.[3]

Summing up, Switzerland has come closer to the conservative model of welfare capitalism. Nevertheless, strong liberal traits remain, for example the important role of co-payments and private carriers in health insurance or the substantial element of social control in unemployment insurance.

Comparative perspectives

In this essay we have compared social spending efforts and national reform paths in four open economies over the last 30 years. Despite a markedly changed international political economy and significant policy changes, the role of the state in social provision is holding its own. The welfare state is still a bastion of the nation state. Judged by spending efforts, the extent of governmental involvement in social affairs is greater than ever before. Moreover, there was neither a devolution of social responsibilities nor a profound supranational standard setting in social policy that would have affected the major programmes of income support run by the nation state.

However, underneath the aggregate level of social expenditure, social policy developments in the countries examined are indicative of a creeping transformation of welfare states that becomes apparent in the long-term analysis. This transformation has less to do with a changed role of the state but more with the ways and instruments of social provision, as today all countries rely on a welfare mix that is less clear-cut than several decades ago. Admittedly, welfare state development is highly path dependent, but incremental policy changes have added up to path departures in some areas of social policy.

Our findings also suggest more subtle partisan effects compared with the 'golden age of the welfare state'. Depending on the specific balance of power in reforming countries, both left and right-wing governments started retrenchment and have adopted new views on social policy. In terms of institutional effects, the empirical evidence is more consistent. In the short run, formal political institutions have an influence on the range and speed of single reform measures, as exemplified by the course of social policy in New Zealand. In the long-term, countries with a dense institutional structure (e.g. Switzerland) may be equally capable of achieving extensive policy changes.

The broad developmental trajectories of social policy identified in this essay can be described as a *dual convergence* of welfare states. On the one hand, social spending levels have not only increased in almost all countries but also converged, mainly because of the catch-up of former welfare state laggards. First and foremost, this process is driven by belated programme maturation in these countries. On the other hand, welfare states have also structurally converged in the sense that the regulatory patterns in which states provide benefits are less distinctive compared with the golden age. Hence, welfare states have become more similar as they have lost some of their salient structural characteristics that underpinned Esping-Andersen's regime typology[7] resulting in a 'blurring of regimes'.[8] The nations examined have also pursued common policy routes: activation and workfare in labour market policy, enhanced co-payments in health insurance as well as a shift of emphasis to family policy are cases in point. Both activation and co-payments can be regarded as a reallocation of responsibilities from the state to the individual. Nevertheless, it would be wrong to conclude that the state's overall role in welfare provision has declined. In all four countries the state has become more active in family policy, both via increased income support to families and extended social services. These common policy routes contribute to the blurring of regimes that is taking place underneath the surface of welfare state resilience. However, the exact causes underpinning this creeping transformation of welfare states and its implications for the welfare state will be explored in more detail in future research.

References

1. K. Armingeon (2001) Institutionalising the Swiss welfare state. *West European Politics*, **24**(2): 145–168, esp. p. 158.
2. T. Ashton (1999) The health reforms: to market and back? In: J. Boston, P. Dalziel and S. S. John (Eds) *Redesigning the Welfare State in New Zealand* (Oxford, UK: Oxford University Press): 134–153.
3. G. Bonoli (1999) La réforme de l'Etat social Suisse: Contraintes institutionnelles et opportunités de changement. *Swiss Political Science Review*, **5**(3): 57–77, esp. p. 73.
4. F. G. Castles (1996) Needs-based strategies of social protection in Australia and New Zealand. In: G. Esping-Andersen (Ed) *Welfare States in Transition: National Adaptations in Global Economies* (London: Sage): 88–115.
5. P. Crampton (2001) Policies for general practice. In: P. Davis and T. Ashton (Eds) *Health and Public Policy in New Zealand, Auckland* (Oxford, UK: Oxford University Press): 201–218.
6. P. Egger and W. Sengenberger (Eds) (2003) *Decent Work in Denmark: Employment, Social Efficiency and Economic Security* (Geneva: International Labour Office).
7. G. Esping-Andersen (1990) *The Three Worlds of Welfare Capitalism* (Cambridge, UK: Polity Press).
8. R. E. Goodin and M. Rein (2001) Regimes on pillars: alternative welfare state logics and dynamics. *Public Administration*, **79**(4): 769–801, esp. p. 771.
9. J. Goul Andersen and C. Albrekt Larsen (2002) Pension politics and policy in Denmark and Sweden: path dependencies, policy style, and policy outcome (Aalborg University, Denmark: Centre for Comparative Welfare Studies, CCWS Working Paper 27).

10. C. Green-Pedersen (1999) The Danish welfare state under bourgeois reign. The dilemma of popular entrenchment and economic constraints. *Scandinavian Political Studies*, **22**(3): 243–260, p. 243.

11. Health Reforms 2001 Research Team (2003) Interim Report on Health Reforms 2001 Research Project (Wellington: Health Services Research Centre, Victoria University of Wellington).

12. J. Higgins (1999) From welfare to workfare. In: J. Boston, P. Dalziel and S. S. John (Eds) *Redesigning the Welfare State in New Zealand* (Oxford, UK: Oxford University Press): 260–277, esp. pp. 262–263.

13. K. Hinrichs (2001) 'Elephants on the move'. Patterns of public pension reform in OECD countries. In: S. Leibfried (Ed) *Welfare State Futures* (Cambridge, UK: Cambridge University Press): 77–102.

14. J. Kvist (1999) Welfare reforms in the Nordic Countries in the 1990s: using fuzzy-set theory to assess conformity to ideal types. *Journal of European Social Policy*, **9**(3): 231–252.

15. L. Murphy (2003) Reasserting the 'social' in social rented housing: politics, housing policy and housing reforms in New Zealand. *International Journal of Urban and Regional Research*, **27**(1): 90–101.

16. P. Nolan (2002) New Zealand's family assistance tax credits: evolution and operation (Wellington: New Zealand Treasury, Working Paper 02/16).

17. H. Obinger, S. Leibfried, C. Bogedan, E. Gindulis, J. Moser and P. Starke (2004) Beyond resilience: welfare state changes in Austria, Denmark, New Zealand and Switzerland (Bremen: University of Bremen, Research Centre Transformations of the State, TranState-Working Paper 06/2004).

18. M. G. Schmidt (1995) Vollbeschäftigung und Arbeitslosigkeit in der Schweiz. Vom Sonderweg zum Normalfall. *Politische Vierteljahresschrift*, **36**(1): 35–48.

19. H. Schwartz (2000) Internationalization and two liberal welfare states: Australia and New Zealand. In: F. W. Scharpf and V. A. Schmidt (Eds) *Welfare and Work in the Open Economy,* vol. II: *Diverse Responses to Common Challenges* (Oxford, UK: Oxford University Press): 69–130.

20. H. Schwartz (2001) The Danish 'Miracle'. Luck, pluck or stuck? *Comparative Political Studies*, **34**(2): 131–155.

21. I. Shirley, P. Koopman-Boyden, I. Pool and S. St. John (1997) Family change and family policies: New Zealand. In: S. B. Kamerman and A. J. Kahn (Eds) *Family Change and Family Policies in Great Britain, Canada, New Zealand, and the United States* (Oxford, UK: The Clarendon Press at Oxford University Press): 207–304.

22. S. St. John (1999) Superannuation in the 1990s: where angels fear to tread? In: J. Boston, P. Dalziel and S. St. John (Eds) *Redesigning the Welfare State in New Zealand* (Oxford, UK: Oxford University Press): 278–298.

23. S. St. John and K. Rankin (2002) Entrenching the welfare mess (Auckland: University of Auckland, Department of Economics, Policy Discussion Paper No. 24).

24. Statistik Austria (2002) *Krippen, Kindergärten & Horte 2001/02* (Wien: Bundesregierung).
25. E. Tálos and K. Wörister (1998) Soziale Sicherung in Österreich. In: E. Tálos (Ed) *Soziale Sicherung im Wandel* (Wien: Böhlau): 209–288.
26. B. Unger and K. Heitzmann (2003) The adjustment path of the Austrian welfare state: back to Bismarck? *Journal of European Social Policy*, **13**(4): 371–387, esp. p. 384.
27. W. van Oorschot and P. Abrahamson (2003) The Dutch and Danish Miracles revisited: a critical discussion of activation policies in two small welfare states. *Social Policy and Administration*, **37**(3): 288–304.

About the Authors

Herbert Obinger is Associate Professor and **Stephan Leibfried** Professor for Political Science, both at the Research Centre on Transformations of the State (TranState) and the Centre for Social Policy Research (CeS). As principal investigators they belong – together with **Claudia Bogedan** (case study: Denmark), **Edith Gindulis** (quantitative comparisons), **Julia Moser** (Switzerland) and **Peter Starke** (New Zealand), who are the investigators – to the TranState research group 'Small states in open economies'. Major books by some of the authors are: H. Obinger, S. Leibfried and F. Castles (Eds) *Federalism and the Welfare State. New World and European Experiences* (Cambridge, UK: Cambridge University Press, 2005); E. Rieger and S. Leibfried *Limits to Globalization. Welfare States and the World Economy* (Cambridge, UK: Polity, 2003) and S. Leibfried (Ed) *Welfare State Futures* (Cambridge, UK: Cambridge University Press, 2001; first as *European Review* **8**(3) (2000): 277–446).

European Review, Vol. 13, Supp. No. 1, 187–212 (2005) © Academia Europaea, Printed in the United Kingdom

9 The changing role of the state in healthcare systems

HEINZ ROTHGANG, MIRELLA CACACE, SIMONE
GRIMMEISEN and CLAUS WENDT

This article focuses on two major questions concerning the changing
role of the state in the healthcare systems of OECD countries. First,
we ask whether major changes in the *level* of state involvement (in
healthcare systems) have occurred in the past 30 years. Given the fact
that three types of healthcare system, each of which is characterized
by a distinct role of the state, evolved during the 'Golden Age', we
discuss how this distinctiveness – or more technically, *variance* – has
changed in the period under scrutiny. While many authors analysing
health policy changes exclusively concentrate on finance and
expenditure data, we simultaneously consider financing, service
provision and regulation. As far as financing is concerned, we observe
a small shift from the public to the private sphere, with a tendency
towards convergence in this dimension. The few data available on
service provision, in contrast, show neither signs of retreat of the state
nor of convergence. In the regulatory dimension – which we analyse
by focusing on major health system reforms in Germany, the United
Kingdom and the United States – we see the introduction or
strengthening of those coordination mechanisms (hierarchy, markets
and self-regulation) which were traditionally weak in the respective
type of healthcare system. Putting these findings together we find a
tendency of convergence from distinct types towards mixed types of
healthcare systems.

The economic recession following the oil price shocks of the 1970s triggered a
broad range of cost containment measures in the social polices of all TRUDIs,
an acronym for democratic, constitutional, interventionist states explained in
some detail in the first essay in this volume. National governments, however, have
also shown major difficulties in curtailing public financing as well as provision
in the field of welfare policy. This particularly holds true for the healthcare sector,
in which the difficulties of cutting back state involvement, among other things,

are particulary related to the fact that the legitimacy of health systems is largely based on their capability to provide a satisfactory standard of healthcare for all citizens, irrespective of their ability to pay for it.

Keeping in mind that the state has played a distinct role in the healthcare systems of all developed welfare economies in times of welfare expansion, this article addresses the changing role of the state in the healthcare systems of OECD countries under the condition of 'permanent austerity'.[30] In doing so, the article focuses on two principle questions. First, it asks whether there are major changes in the *level* of state involvement in healthcare systems. Second, it discusses whether the role of the state in the three types of healthcare systems, i.e. national health services, social insurance systems and private (insurance) systems, has increasingly *converged*.

Taking this twofold focus, the article aims at a more systematic evaluation of the changing role of the state in the healthcare systems of advanced capitalist countries. Hence, in the next section we introduce a three-dimensional framework for analysing the role of the state in the healthcare sector, which is then applied to the healthcare systems of the 'Golden Age' of welfare state expansion. In the subsequent two sections the development in the last three decades is analysed with respect to our quantitative and qualitative dimensions. In the final section we draw conclusions on the changing role of the state in financing, providing and regulating healthcare services.

The role of the state in healthcare systems

Conceptualizing and measuring the changing role of the state in healthcare systems

With respect to the role of the state in healthcare, many comparative studies have exclusively concentrated on *financing* and *expenditure*.[6, 7, 25, 26, 27] Following their line of argumentation, the involvement of the state in a healthcare system can be measured as the ratio of public to total health expenditure. A focus purely on financing, however, neglects whether state agencies also provide healthcare, or whether these services are provided by private entities such as hospitals or self-employed doctors. A second role that the state can play in healthcare systems, therefore, is that of *provider of services*. Thus, the share of public services is a good indicator for measuring this dimension of potential state activity. Even if the state neither finances nor provides services directly, there is a third role it can play: it can be more or less engaged in the *regulation* of the relationships between providers, financing agencies, and users – or it can leave this task to corporate self-regulation mechanisms or to the markets. When considering the bilateral relationships between the three major stakeholders of a healthcare system, i.e.

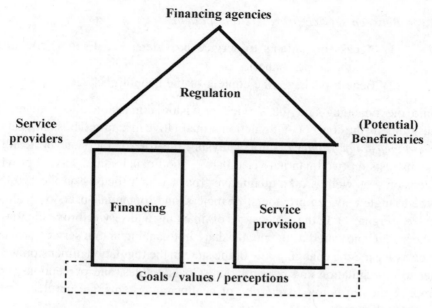

Source: OECD Health Data 2002.

Figure 1. Financing, service provision, and regulation in healthcare systems.

financing agencies, service providers, and (potential) beneficiaries, at least six major areas of regulation evolve and are subject to potential change (see also Figure 1):

Between (potential) beneficiaries and financing agencies

(1) Coverage: the inclusion of (parts of) the population in public and/or private healthcare systems.
(2) System of financing: the financing of healthcare by public (taxes, social insurance contributions) and/or private (private insurance contributions, out-of-pocket payments) sources.

Between financing agencies and service providers

(1) Remuneration of service providers: the specific system of provider remuneration.
(2) Access of (potential) providers to healthcare markets: access to financing agencies.

Between service providers and patients

(1) Access of patients to service providers, i.e. doctors (and further healthcare personnel).
(2) Benefit package: the content of the benefit package.

While the financing and the service provision dimension allow quantitative measurement, the concept of regulation is qualitative in nature. Thus, the proposed *three-dimensional framework* for analysing the role of the state in healthcare systems rests on two quantitative 'pillars' – the financing and service provision dimension – as well as on a qualitative 'roof', which focuses on the regulation of the triangle between providers, financiers, and (potential) users of healthcare services (Figure 1). In the dimensions of financing and service provision, the role of the state is measured as the public share in financing and in service provision. When assessing the changing role of the state in the regulation dimension we also refer to de-regulation and re-regulation. Goals, values, and perceptions, which comprise the *normative foundation* of healthcare systems, are not dealt with in this essay, however.

Types of healthcare systems and the role of the state in the context of welfare state expansion

During the 'Golden Age' of welfare expansion, states pushed for the inclusion of more and more parts of the population into the healthcare systems. Thus, with the notable exception of the US, by the mid-1970s almost the whole population had access to healthcare services in OECD countries. Nevertheless, there were considerable differences between healthcare systems: there were such systems that can be characterized as National Health Services (NHS) (such as in the UK); healthcare systems that can be characterized as social insurance systems (such as Germany); and healthcare systems that can be characterized by a high share of private healthcare and health insurance markets (such as the US). Table 1 summarizes the differences among the types of healthcare systems in a stylized and pointed way: *NHS-type healthcare systems* rely on the state more than the other two systems. In this system, the state is responsible for service provision, financing and regulation. Here, financing is based on taxes and regulation is generally executed hierarchically through a comprehensive planning model. By contrast, *social insurance-type healthcare system* services are provided by public providers, non-governmental, not-for-profit organizations, and private for-profit enterprises. Financing is public, not through the general budget, but through social insurance funds which are public para-fiscal agencies, and merely based on social insurance contributions. While social (security) law provides some regulatory framework, in a social insurance system detailed regulation – including access to

Table 1. Types of healthcare systems with respect to the role of the state.

Type of healthcare	Underlying values and principles	Financing	Service Provision	Regulation
National health service	*Equity:* Equal access to services for everyone	*Public:* taxes according to income (direct taxes) and consumption (indirect taxes)	Public providers	*Dominant Regulatory Mechanism:* hierarchy; comprehensive planning and tight control by the state
Social insurance system	*Solidarity:* Equal access to services for all members of insurance funds	*Public:* contributions according to income	Private and public providers	*Dominant Regulatory Mechanism:* collective bargaining; legal framework and some control by the state
Private (insurance) system	*Principle of equivalence:* service according to ability to pay	*Private:* premium according to individual risk	Private providers	*Dominant Regulatory Mechanism:* markets; limited control of insurance and service provision by the state

healthcare markets, remuneration systems and the detailed definition of the benefit catalogue – is, however, left to negotiations between sickness funds and service providers. *Private healthcare systems*, finally, are characterized by private financing (with an emphasis on private insurance), service provision by private for-profit enterprises, and a limited degree of public regulation. The coordination between providers, financiers, and (potential) users is largely left to the market and – to some extent – to the courts.

In order to conduct an empirical analysis, the United Kingdom is considered to be the representative of a national health service system, Germany is assigned to the social insurance system and the United States represents the private insurance system. We assume that during the period of welfare state expansion, healthcare systems were close to the constructed, stylized types.

A changing role of the state in the healthcare systems beyond the Golden Age?

Starting with the oil price shocks, the last three decades have seen major changes in the context of the healthcare systems of all TRUDIs. First of all, in the course of the recession of the late 1970s and early 1980s, the economic context of healthcare systems changed from growth to stagnation, and from affluence to austerity. Although the economy recovered thereafter, in the healthcare sector the perceived need for cost containment remained, leading to the subsequent introduction of cost containment measures.[2,3,8,17,22] Besides the changing economic situation, healthcare systems are currently also situated in a context of increasing globalization. Generally speaking, this pushes national governments to compete for 'global capital, companies and labour especially by lowering taxes, by deregulating the labour markets and by cutting social provisions'.[18] More specifically, the context of health systems has also changed through the accelerating innovation process in the sphere of medical technology on the one hand, and the profound demographic changes in all highly industrialized countries on the other.[36, 39] Due to the outlined transformations in the context of modern healthcare systems, the pressures on post-war healthcare systems have multiplied. Hence, the major question we focus on in this article is how the role of the state in the healthcare systems has changed since the Golden Age. Using the typology of healthcare systems outlined above we examine both whether the role of the state is growing or declining; and whether the distinct types converge with respect to the role of the state.

Therefore, we first analyse whether the state retreats from healthcare financing and/or service provision, as one might assume. Second, we explore whether retrenchment policies (if existing) have led not only to a reduction in public spending, but also in total healthcare spending and service provision; or whether such a cut is substituted by an increase in private spending and service provision. The third issue we address is whether austerity policies have so far led to more state regulation, e.g. in order to control costs or to guarantee equity in a more privatized system, or whether they are also accompanied by a retreat of the state from regulation.

Given the fact that the three types of healthcare system are characterized by a distinct role of the state, we finally ask whether these three models are equally affected by the changing context of the post-1970s, and whether the differences between distinct 'families of systems' remain. Here, our focus is on whether the types move towards each other (convergence), or away from each other (divergence), or whether they move in the same direction without revealing any changes in the distance between each other (level effects). In the quantitative dimensions these developments are measured by parameters of dispersion (convergence/divergence) and means.

In order to move towards a more universal conclusion, the last question is of particular interest: similar reactions by distinct types of healthcare systems to the changing context variables would indicate the existence of a best-practice solution for problems caused by a changing environment.[1, 10] Non-convergent developments or parallel upward/downward trends of the three types of healthcare systems, on the other hand, would indicate the prevalence of distinct solutions[2,3] due to processes of path dependence and system inertia.

The changing role of the state in financing and providing healthcare

The changing role of the state in healthcare financing

Ever since the OECD published the first edition of its healthcare data in 1985, most international comparisons have centred on the financial dimension. Thus, there is a comparatively rich database for the analysis of the changing role of the state in the financing of healthcare. Based on data of 21 TRUDIs,[a] Figure 2 shows a massive growth in total healthcare financing in the early 1970s. This growth process was almost completely fed by an increase in *public* healthcare spending. From the mid-1970s, cost-containment became the prevailing policy in all healthcare systems. Nevertheless, total healthcare financing still continued to grow, although at a much slower pace. This time however, the process was driven by increased *private* healthcare financing: while public healthcare spending increased by 21% (from 5.0 to 6.0% of GDP) between 1975 and 2000, the private complement rose twice as fast, i.e. by 42% (from 1.6% to 2.3% of GDP).

While the slow-down in growth rates of public healthcare financing was compensated by private spending until 1995, total healthcare spending has been stagnating since the mid-1990s. Even if we cannot observe a decrease in public healthcare financing (in relation to the GDP) on the aggregate level from 1975 to 2000, owing to a much higher growth rate of private healthcare expenditure, the *share* of public healthcare financing out of total healthcare financing declined

---

[a] Included are those cases that had already developed a high standard of democratic, constitutional and welfare institutions in the 1960s and early 1970s. Based on this definition, 23 of the 30 current OECD members qualify for inclusion. The Czech Republic, Hungary, Korea, Mexico, Poland, as well as the Slovak Republic are excluded, since they only became OECD members in the 1990s. Turkey is also excluded as it cannot be regarded as a welfare state. France and Belgium, however, are excluded from the group of 23 countries due to a lack of data. Since data are often not available for the 1960s, we concentrate on the period from 1970 until 2000.

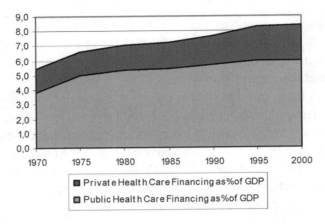

Source: OECD Health Data 2002.

Figure 2. Healthcare financing as a percentage of GDP in 21 OECD countries.

from 75.8% in 1980 to 71.8% in 2000. Thus, there is a *relative retreat* of the state from healthcare financing, but to a very limited extent.

While Figure 2 refers to all countries under consideration, Figure 3 disaggregates the data with respect to the types of healthcare systems.[b] Once again checking what happens after 1975, we observe a declining share of public healthcare financing in NHS systems, a growing share of public financing in the private US system, and no clear tendency for social insurance systems. So the role of the state was strengthened where it was weakest and it was weakened where it was strongest before. In short, on the level of 'families of healthcare systems' there are at least tendencies of convergence towards more mixed systems.

When ranking the countries according to their share of public healthcare spending (as a percentage of total healthcare spending), we find a similar picture: countries with a below-average share of public financing increase their share to a relatively high extent, while countries with an above-average share of public financing reduce their public spending.[41] This is in agreement with Peter Flora's[11] 'growth to limits' thesis, but it is, of course, not sufficient proof. The process is driven by a highly significant closely negative correlation between the average annual growth rate of public health expenditure (as a percentage of GDP) and the

---

[b] In accordance with the respective share of health care financing by taxes, social insurance contributions, and private funds, Austria, Germany, Japan, Luxembourg, Netherlands, and Switzerland are classified as social insurance systems while Australia, Canada, Denmark, Finland, Greece, Iceland, Ireland, Italy, New Zealand, Norway, Portugal, Spain, Sweden, and the United Kingdom are classified as NHS-systems. The private health care system type is represented only by the US.

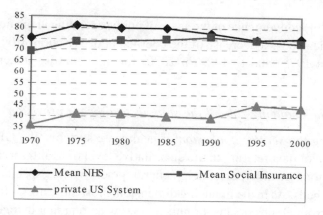

Source: OECD Health Data 2002.

Figure 3. Public healthcare financing as a percentage of total healthcare financing.

respective figure at the beginning of the observation period (Figure 4).[c] As a result, those countries with the lowest public expenditure on health in 1970 have the highest average (geometrical mean) annual growth rate. Thus, a 'catch-up' of the laggards has taken place. With respect to social expenditure, a similar catch-up can be identified (see Obinger et al. in this volume for details). The result is a

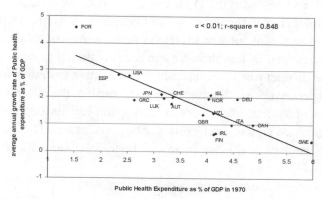

Source: OECD Health Data.

Figure 4. Correlation between average annual growth rate in public healthcare financing as a percentage of GDP from 1970–2000 and public healthcare spending in 1970

---

[c] The figure is based on data for 18 countries. Due to missing data for 1970 Australia, Denmark and the Netherlands are excluded.

(tendency of) convergence of the share of public spending in the field of healthcare that is indicated by a decrease of the coefficient of variation[d] from 21.6 (in 1970) to 18.5 (in 1975) and to 14.5 (in 2000) for the countries under consideration.

The changing role of the state in healthcare provision

Concerning the *service dimension* of healthcare systems, the OECD provides a wide range of data relating to the quantitative level of health services, such as for example total health personnel, general practitioners, specialists, nurses, or in-patient beds. As in the financing dimension, most indicators – for instance, total health personnel, physicians, or nurses – show an ongoing increase in healthcare services, and a slowdown of the increase only in the 1990s.[28] Owing to the decreasing average length of stay, however, the number of in-patient beds per 1,000 inhabitants is declining.[37] However, there is hardly any information on the role of the state in healthcare provision. Only for hospital beds is a differentiation between public and private services available. While the number of hospital beds is declining, the public share remains relatively stable. For the 16 countries that the OECD provides data for at some point in time, the public share grew, on average, from 67.1% of all hospital beds in 1970 to 70.4% in 1975. For the rest of the observation period up to 2000, the share remains slightly above this level (72.7% in 2000). When restricting the analysis to those 12 countries for which data are provided for all the years between 1970 and 1995, one obtains even less variation: at any time from 1975 to 1995, the share of public beds remained between 67.7% and 68.9% (OECD Health Data 2002, own calculation).

Distinguishing between the three types of healthcare system, we find a public share in hospital beds of about 80% in NHS systems, a share of about 55% in social insurance systems, and of less than 20% in the private US system, which again emphasizes the distinct role of the state in the respective systems. While there is a slight convergence process in the financing dimension, the differences between the three types of system in the service dimension remain relatively constant. Generally, there is no sign of a retreat of public services – and hence, of the state – from the provision of healthcare in any of the three systems focused on in this article.

Further data are necessary to provide a clear picture of the 'role of the state' in the provision of healthcare services. It is, however, remarkable that the reduction of hospital beds has been much higher in NHS systems than in social insurance systems – without a major change of the public–private mix.[41] This

---

[d] The coefficient of variation is calculated by dividing the standard deviation of the distribution by its mean. It is given here as a percentage, i.e. multiplied by 100. Other measurements of dispersion lead to a similar result. So, between 1970 and 2000 the range has decreased from 55 to 37 (reduction of 33%) and the interquartile range is reduced from 25 to 8 (reduction of 68%) (own calculations according to OECD Health Data 2002).[22]

indicates that the state has not only reduced public hospital beds, but may also have regulated the reduction of private hospital beds to a similar extent.

The changing role of the state in regulating healthcare systems

When focusing on the third dimension of healthcare systems, i.e. the regulation of the system, in the context of this essay it is not possible to compare the six relations introduced earlier extending to funds for financing, service providers, and (potentially) beneficiaries (coverage, financing, access to the healthcare market, remuneration methods, access of patients to service providers, and benefit package) for all countries. We therefore select three 'representative' countries to sketch changes of regulatory measures in different types of healthcare systems: the United Kingdom (NHS system), Germany (social insurance system), and the United States (private insurance system). In doing so we not only examine whether the role of the state in regulation has increased or decreased, and whether the healthcare systems have converged in this respect; but we also investigate which role the state had in bringing these changes about.

Coverage

Since the introduction of the NHS in 1948, the whole population of the UK is covered. In Germany, nowadays about 89% of the population are covered by the social insurance system. Additionally, about 2% of the population are covered by special systems, and about 9% by private insurance. The latter scheme includes civil servants whose healthcare expenses are partly covered directly by their employers. Consequently, almost the whole population is covered by insurance. In the US, about 70% of the population has private insurance. Private insurance is either employment-based (61%) or privately purchased (9%). The lowest income groups as well as senior citizens and the disabled are covered by the main public insurance programmes, Medicaid and Medicare (25%). In 2002, 15%[e] of the US population were without health insurance.[23] For the period of analysis from 1970 to 2000, no changes took place in the British NHS since there was no need to include further parts of the population, and since a policy of exclusion (for example, of higher income groups) did not exist. Germany's health insurance system experienced a process of inclusion since its first implementation in 1883. Within the period under consideration, coverage was extended by the inclusion of farmers, handicapped persons, students, and artists, thus further strengthening the role of social insurance.[40] In the US system, an important extension of public coverage had already taken place in the 1960s, when Medicare was introduced

---

[e] Due to double counting, these figures do not add up to 100%.

for senior citizens and opened to the disabled (in 1973). Furthermore, Medicaid was introduced for low-income groups. The most significant process of inclusion in the Medicaid programme since 1970 took place in the late 1980s when the eligibility of pregnant women and infants was mandated by Congress. Additionally, the federal government extended public coverage in 1997 with the introduction of the State Children's Health Insurance Program (SCHIP).

In the United Kingdom, there was a considerable increase of subscribers for *private health insurances* in the period from 1979 to 1981 due to a promotion of private health insurance by the new Conservative government.[16] Apart from tax relief for the elderly, however, the government introduced hardly any measures to stimulate the expansion of private coverage to the major part of the population.[40] Today, about 15% of the British population has a supplementary private insurance. In contrast to the UK, both a supplementary private coverage as well as an exclusive private coverage are possible in Germany. While the inclusion of further groups of the population in the public health insurance system during the 1970s reduced the group of potential subscribers to private health insurance, this group was enlarged again by the introduction of an exit option from social insurance for employees and high-income blue collar workers in 1989 (Healthcare Reform Act). Today, about 9% of the population possess exclusive, and a further 9% supplementary private insurance coverage.[31] In the United States, the share of people with private insurance has slowly decreased since its peak in 1980. The vast majority of private coverage is employment-based, with a strong linkage of insurance to the workplace. The 1985 Consolidated Omnibus Budget Act (COBRA) gave workers under certain circumstances, such as voluntary or involuntary job loss or transition between jobs, the right to choose to continue group health benefits provided by their group health plan. In 1996, the Health Insurance Portability and Accountability Act (HIPAA)[5] guaranteed a greater portability and continuation of group health insurance coverage and also limited the insurers' ability to exclude pre-existing conditions.[f]

By and large, we observe an increase in public *coverage* by state regulation in Germany and the United States since the 1970s, indicating a strengthening of the role of the state in these countries. At the same time, private coverage has increased in the UK and decreased in the US. While the increase in public coverage in the United States and Germany was the result of state regulation, the increase in private coverage in the United Kingdom was an effect of some financial incentives and promotion by the state.

---

[f] Pre-existing conditions are physical or mental conditions already existing before an individual receives health insurance coverage. Some insurers refuse coverage or increase rates (risk adjustment) due to pre-existing conditions.

Financing

Cost containment has been a core feature of British health policy since the very beginning of the NHS.[19] Although the increase in total health expenditure has been lower than in many other developed healthcare systems, in 1976 the government introduced a so-called cash limits system. 'This meant that if the cost of providing any particular level of public provision rose faster than assumed by the Treasury [...] there would be no automatic supplementation as in the past', but a compensatory cut in the input of real resources.[19:83] Another major change took place when market principles were introduced with the NHS and Community Care Act in 1990. While the central funding and control system remained, the government advocated an improvement of efficiency through the implementation of a purchaser–provider split: health authorities (purchasers of healthcare), GP fundholders[g] (purchasers and providers) and hospital trusts (providers) started to negotiate contracts that were to set the volume and prices of services within the internal healthcare market. The introduction of internal markets has been of the utmost importance for the relation between financing agencies and service providers. Private insurance has been promoted by the government since the early 1980s, but no major changes in regulatory measures can be detected with respect to financing by private insurance.

In the German health insurance system, contribution rates are traditionally fixed by each insurance fund. While this model of self-regulation did not change in the first phase of cost-containment policy that took place in the second half of the 1970s, we find increasing government intervention from the late 1980s onwards, when 'constant contribution rates' became a catchword in health policy.[33] Even if the scope for self-regulation remained wide, it increasingly took place in the 'shadow of (state) hierarchy' (Fritz Scharpf). During the 1980s and 1990s, the government increasingly intervened in the collective agreements between associations of doctors and insurance funds. The ability of funds to fix contribution rates at their discretion was restricted by the Healthcare Structure Act (1992), the Healthcare Reorganisation Act (1997), and the Healthcare Modernization Act (2003). A second major example of state regulation in the field of healthcare financing is the introduction of free choice of sickness funds for the insured population, and thus the introduction of competition between the main funds of financing. The launch of competition between sickness funds, and of a corresponding risk-adjustment mechanism, established through the 1992 Health-care Structure Act, for the first time introduced competition as a coordinating mechanism in its own right. While the reduction of the number of sickness funds can partly be seen as an effect of higher competition, neither contribution rates

---

[g] GP fundholders are general practitioners (GPs) who are responsible for purchasing NHS services for their patients. This includes GPs taking part in the Standard, Community and (pilot) Total Fundholding schemes.

nor total healthcare financing were stabilized in the period following the implementation of competition between funds in 1996. Starting in the 1990s, the German government not only increased direct intervention within the social insurance system but also within the field of private insurance. By and large, the state thus started to use private insurance companies as a means to achieve public social policy goals, thereby inducing some tendencies towards convergence between these systems.[38]

In the United States, the federal government sets contribution rates, co-payments and deductibles for Medicare enrolees. The contribution-like payroll tax for hospital insurance as part of Medicare has remained unchanged since the early 1980s. The Medicaid programme, by contrast, is tax-financed. In the private schemes, the state governments have the authority to regulate the insurance business, for example by setting the reserve requirements. Additionally, private healthcare financing is heavily regulated by governments' tax policy.[15] While state governments may also regulate premium increases and other aspects of the insurance industry, private insurance premiums are generally set by insurance companies and, in the case of powerful employers, subject to negotiations. Self-insurance, a healthcare financing technique in which employers pay claims out of an internally funded pool, was heavily promoted by federal government and therefore, in 1974, exempted from state regulation. The Employee Retirement Income Security Act (ERISA) of 1974 exempted employers who self-insure their health benefit plans from taxation and control. Although the development of health maintenance organizations (HMOs) was market-driven, HMO Acts of 1970 and 1973 were designed by the federal government to encourage the spread of managed care. From the late 1980s and early 1990s on, federal government has been actively encouraging Medicare beneficiaries to receive their healthcare through managed care organizations, i.e. insurers executing a higher degree of hierarchical control over providers. The states also started to shift Medicaid recipients into managed care plans.[35] While we thus witness some public de-regulation, more control of providers was introduced into the private healthcare market through the development of managed care.

With respect to the regulation of *healthcare financing* we thus see an increased role of the state in regulating healthcare financing in Germany, where direct state intervention can be observed in private and in social health insurance. In Britain, the central role of the state was even strengthened through the introduction of cash limits. Only in the US do we observe some de-regulation in the private insurance sector through the introduction of ERISA. However, on the other hand, a more hierarchical control was introduced through managed care, which was initiated by private entrepreneurs but later on promoted by favourable state regulation.

Remuneration

In the United Kingdom, general practitioners are traditionally paid by a combination of general allowances and a certain amount of money for each person enrolled on their 'list' (capitation). In 1990, new contracts were implemented through state regulation, and the proportion of GPs' income that was derived from capitation payments was increased from 46% to 60%. The introduction of the GP fundholder status further increased the influence that GPs had on their income, as it gave fundholding practices the opportunity and the incentive not only to buy services from the cheapest service provider, but also to provide certain services such as diagnosis tests in their own practice. Most hospitals that, for many years, had received a fixed budget per year, in the early 1990s opted out of direct control of NHS health authorities. Instead, they chose the status of hospital trusts as this granted them higher autonomy to develop their own management structures, allowed them to decide on the number and structure of hospital personnel, or to negotiate individual labour contracts.[13, 32]

In Germany, levels of remuneration in the outpatient sector are traditionally negotiated between the regional associations of panel doctors as monopolist, on the one hand and a wide range of sickness funds on the other. In a number of subsequent reform steps, the state gradually reduced differences between sickness funds and forced them to negotiate together, thus transforming the monopoly into a bilateral monopoly, which mobilized some countervailing power.[4] In the 1990s, the federal government intervened directly in the corporatist self-regulating structure by introducing a (partial) flat-rate payment system for family doctors, fixed budgets for drug prescriptions etc. (Healthcare Structure Act 1992). In the hospital sector on the other hand, the state tried to initiate some corporatism by assigning power to formally private hospital associations.[9] In effect, the state intervened in the self-regulating negotiation system, intending to strengthen it by changing the rules of the game.

In the United States, physicians who under traditional indemnity insurance schemes were usually paid on a fee-for-service basis were confronted with completely changed incentive schemes in managed care systems. Depending on the respective managed care model, primary care physicians and specialists may either be employed by the managed care organization (staff model) or are contracted by the managed care organization (group models). Physicians can be paid on the basis of salary, a (discounted) fee-for-service, or a capitation fee.[24] Until the 1970s and early 1980s, hospitals in public as well as in private health insurance schemes were paid on a retrospective cost-reimbursement basis. Public insurers were the first to implement major payment reforms during the 1980s to overcome these negative incentives for cost containment. In 1983, the prospective payment system on DRG (Diagnosis-Related-Groups) basis was introduced, initially exclusively for Medicare treatment, but later it was extended to all plans.

Summing up the developments in terms of the regulation of *remuneration*, we see that methods were modified in the US managed care system from a previously dominant fee-for-service method to payments by salary, discounted fee-for-service, or capitation. In Germany, the fee-for-service method of remuneration was maintained for self-employed medical doctors, but a flat-rate component was introduced for family doctors in the 1990s. GPs in the United Kingdom are still financed on a per capita basis. As GP fundholders, however, self-employed doctors gained a higher influence on their income. We therefore observe a development from highly diverse methods of remuneration in the three types of healthcare systems to a more common 'mixed model of remuneration'. With respect to hospital financing, a first prospective payment system on a DRG basis was introduced in the United States in 1983, and Germany is currently following the US example. In the UK, too, fixed budgets for hospitals were abolished, and today hospital trusts negotiate with health authorities and GP fundholders on the number and price of hospital treatment based on healthcare resource groups (HRGs), a classification scheme similar to DRGs. As far as the role of the state is concerned, the introduction of internal markets and competition in the NHS has led to the establishment of independent NHS Trusts. Consequently, there is less state control on service provision. In Germany, the state invested a lot of effort into making corporatist self-regulation mechanisms more effective, while in the US the state took no active part in promoting changes in the remuneration systems.

Access of service providers to the healthcare market

Within the British NHS only general practitioners but not specialists have the freedom to establish a practice for ambulatory medical care, thus becoming independent contractors – specialists, however, are free to provide services for private patients in private practice although they are employees of a health authority or a hospital trust. Access for general practitioners, too, is strictly regulated by government-determined limits on their number and location, and by financial incentives to increase the number of practices in under-doctored areas.[12] While the number of general practitioners is still closely controlled by central government, the method of access changed dramatically in the last decade of the 20th century. Since the status of a GP fundholder depends on a certain number of patients on the practice list, most GPs today work in group practices, a few even as salaried employees. In the hospital sector, a similar development took place. While the number and location of hospitals are still highly controlled by state authorities, the number of beds and health personnel can increasingly be decided by semi-independent hospital trusts that have to earn their revenue from contracts won with district health authorities or GP fundholders.[13, 16]

In Germany, the constitutional court overruled the restriction of access for medical doctors to the healthcare market in 1960. Within the self-regulated corporate system, only indirect control of the number and location of general practitioners and specialists as well as the restriction of access to medical schools was possible for many years. In 1992, however, a retirement age for doctors in office practice was introduced for the first time, and the association of panel doctors gained the power to refuse the entry of new doctors to office practice if the region was judged to be oversupplied with self-employed doctors. For hospitals, however, the Länder were always in control of capacity planning. Although, since 1989, hospitals have formally contracted with sickness funds, de facto public 'hospital plans' are actually still in place. Up to now, all attempts to strip the Länder of this power have failed.

In the United States, the increase in the number of medical doctors was promoted by large federal outlays for the training of medical school students in the 1960s and 1970s. The number of private practices also increased steadily. In 1997, however, the total number of outpatient practices for which Medicare makes direct payments was limited by the Balanced Budget Act.[20] Further restrictions were set by government (in the case of Medicare or Medicaid) or by self-regulation in managed care plans.[24] In the inpatient sector an important regulatory measure was introduced by the National Health Planning Act in 1974, which created a system of state and local health planning agencies, largely supported by federal funds. The law required all states to adopt certificate-of-need (CON) laws by 1980, subjecting expansion as well as new entry into the hospital market to certification. Although federal funding of the programme was eliminated in 1986, about 30 states have partially continued the CON process.[21]

Concerning the regulation of *access of service providers to the healthcare market*, Germany and the United States increased state control, while the United Kingdom eased state restrictions by introducing fundholding models. On the one hand, in the US, hierarchical control mechanisms to channel the access of medical doctors were introduced through managed care systems. On the other hand, in Britain, the hierarchical planning and control system of the British NHS has been extended by the introduction of partly independent fundholding settings and NHS trusts. The British government still controls the number and location of general practitioners, but the means of access has changed dramatically. Just like GP fundholder practices, most general practitioners, today cooperate with other health service providers in group practices and negotiate on contracts with health authorities and hospital trusts. Thus, negotiation partly replaced hierarchy.

Finally, in the German system, only in the 1990s were some limits for the entry of new doctors for office practice introduced by state regulation.

Access of patients to healthcare services

In the national health system of the United Kingdom, access to healthcare services is constrained by a reliance on primary care physicians as health system gatekeepers. As a rule, patients are only permitted to select or change their primary care physician once per year, and for access to specialists, patients need a referral from their GP. For British patients it is therefore hardly possible to track multiple physician contacts. Apart from the proliferation of medical practices and the decline of average list size, patients' access to service providers has been facilitated by allowing patients under certain circumstances to change their GP more than once a year. This new rule was introduced in 1990 to increase competition between doctors and make them more responsive to their patients' needs. Since the average size of practices has been increased through the introduction of GP fundholding practices, the access of patients to different service providers in group practices (GP fundholding practices, total fundholding practices etc.) has been improved.

In the German health insurance system, access to health services and the right of patients to choose their own doctor (general practitioner and specialist) has always been an important feature. While the de facto possibilities for 'doctor hopping' increased in the late 1980s and early 1990s, in the second half of the 1990s the government introduced legislation that allowed various types of managed care elements as gate-keeping models, as well as for provider networks and other forms of integrated care. Providers and sickness funds, however, only hesitantly seized these opportunities. With the US experience in mind, in the latest piece of legislation the government even extended possibilities for managed care through the introduction of disease management programmes as well as through the improvement of models of integrated care. When effective, these models will strengthen funds that want to become players rather than payers. On the other hand this will lead to selective contracting between funds and groups of doctors, thus introducing elements of competition and market coordination.

In the United States, the access of patients to healthcare providers is restricted in several ways. Generally, in managed care, the choice of healthcare provider is limited to a pre-selected network of providers. For further investigation, three different forms of managed care organizations have to be considered according to their difference in regulating access to patients. In health maintenance organizations (HMOs), enrolees have no choice of provider and receive access to specialists only through the primary care provider. In preferred provider organizations (PPOs) there is no such gatekeeper. Members may also choose to opt out of the network of providers but at the cost of higher out-of-pocket payments. In case of point-of-service (POS) plans there is a primary care provider as gatekeeper, and again members have the freedom to opt out when choosing a higher co-payment.[24]

As far as the regulation of the *access of patients to service providers* is concerned, our preliminary analysis shows developments towards a similar model in all three countries. In the British NHS, general practitioners have been the first-contact service providers since the introduction of the NHS. In Germany, however, patients still have free access to general practitioners but sickness funds are encouraged to implement gate-keeping models and other forms of managed care. In the US, access of patients to services and the choice of providers has also been restricted under managed care plans – by state regulation (in the case of Medicare/Medicaid) or by self-regulation measures in managed care programmes. The role of the state varied in bringing about those changes: in Germany, funds were given more control through legislation; in the UK, the state induced internal markets; while in the US, once again, markets were the driving force in bringing about more hierarchy.

Benefit package

In the United Kingdom, there has never been a benefit catalogue on the macro level. Health authorities and service providers are free to decide about appropriate services within given budgets. Since cost-containment can be executed through budgets, there is no need for cuts in a formal benefit catalogue to limit expenditure. Consequently, restrictions of benefits through waiting lists as well as through the denial of certain services on a local and/or regional level are the result. The effect, however, was described as 'postcode prescription', alluding to the fact that access to certain services depended on the area in which the patient lived. In order to improve (regional) equity, the National Institute for Clinical Excellence (NICE) was introduced in 1998. The NICE is an independent institute, consisting of representatives from all stakeholders of the healthcare system, that provides guidance on all types of services, but with a strong emphasis on pharmaceuticals. The NICE appraisal process for services follows a well-publicized, standardized procedure, including a health technology assessment (HTA) report, normally commissioned from a university or a research institute. NICE guidance is fairly binding, although regional health authorities still have some discretion and providers may follow a different course if they argue their case. Although cost control is still guaranteed through budgets, NICE places a higher relevance on cost-effectiveness than, for example, the respective German bodies do.[34] The establishment of NICE limited the power of managers and the medical profession.

In Germany, cuts in the benefit package have been a constantly used measure of cost-containment. During the 1970s and 1980s, numerous deductibles and co-payments were introduced through legislation.[29] Although there was some rhetoric claiming that they were introduced in order to limit moral hazard behaviour, they were in fact just aiming at cost-containment. Only in the 1990s did efficiency considerations become more prominent, and the design of the benefit package started to follow the methods of evidence-based medicine and HTA. In the Healthcare Reorganization Act of 1997, the Federal Committee of Physicians and Sickness Funds was given the power to evaluate existing and new technologies and services with respect to effectiveness and cost-effectiveness, and to decide whether they should be part of the publicly financed benefit package.[14] In the latest healthcare reform, taking effect in January 2004, these powers were consolidated and formalized with the new Joint Federal Committee, representing doctors, hospitals and sickness funds. In its decisions about benefit catalogues the Committee is advised by a newly founded independent German Institute for Quality and Efficiency in Healthcare. Thus, once again the state intervened in order to strengthen corporatist self-regulation following publicly decreed goals.

In the US, decisions about benefit packages are as fragmented as the whole system. There are some federal and state regulations concerning benefit packages for private insurances. For the part of the population relying on private health insurance through their employer, decisions about benefit packages are mostly up to employers and insurance companies. Even for public programmes, namely Medicare and Medicaid, procedures and criteria for benefit decisions vary between programmes and states. Evidence-based medicine and health technology assessments were established through the public Agency for Healthcare Research and Quality (AHRQ), which was founded in 1996, and which offers services to public and private bodies. For Medicare and Medicaid, Centers for Medicare and Medicaid Services (CMS) evaluate services on the basis of HTA reports. Private insurance companies quite regularly follow the CMS's decisions. Maybe the most interesting development in the context of decisions about benefit packages, however, is the development of health maintenance organizations (HMOs) and other forms of managed care. HMOs provide a high degree of vertical control over providing units and professionals, also with respect to the benefit catalogue. Thus, managed care gives room for a hierarchical element in privately managed care.

With respect to the regulation of the *benefit package* we observe another 'meta-trend': the heralding of health technology assessment as a standardized procedure for the determination of benefit packages. While responsible institutions vary between countries, the criteria and procedures for determining benefit packages became more similar. Interestingly, in the UK, the respective responsibilities were not given to state agencies but to an independent institute that represented all stakeholders of the system in a quasi-corporatist structure, thus strengthening the bargaining mode and marking a partial retreat of the state. In Germany, we once again observe state intervention to strengthen corporatist self-regulation. The US case, finally, is more difficult to judge, due to the high level of fragmentation.

Conclusion: towards a 'mixed model'?

In this essay we have developed a conceptual framework for the description of the role of the state in healthcare systems as it pertains to financing, service provision, and regulation. Utilizing this underlying framework, we then presented some tentative evidence to answer the two major questions raised in this contribution: first, is there an overall retreat of the state and, second, is there some convergence between the three types of healthcare systems, i.e. the national health system, the social insurance system, and the private system?

The analysis of the *financing* dimension of all countries under consideration showed that public health expenditures increased at a higher rate than GDP even after 1975. Moreover, we observed a decreasing share of public health expenditures in total health expenditure, leading to a partial shift from public to private financing. Since this relative retreat of the state is the highest in NHS countries, which had the highest public share at the beginning, and since there is an increase of public financing in the US, this leads to a limited convergence based on a 'catch-up process' of laggards. However, major differences in the role of the state with regard to healthcare financing remain between the three types of healthcare systems.

OECD healthcare data provide very limited information on the public–private dichotomy of *healthcare provision*. The data that are available, however, show neither signs of a retreat of the state nor do they point to a convergence of systems. The average share of public hospital beds as a percentage of total hospital beds, for example, remains above 80% in NHS-systems, at about 55% in social insurance systems, and at about 20% in the private US system.

As far as our third dimension, *regulation*, is concerned, we find a general tendency to introduce into each type of healthcare system such modes of coordination that are unfamiliar to that type. More specifically, internal markets and thus an element of market competition and negotiation were introduced into the traditionally hierarchical mode of Britain's NHS, while competition was also introduced into the German social insurance system, which traditionally rests on bargaining and self-regulation by the stakeholders of the system. In the US, the dawning of managed care introduced an element of hierarchical coordination into a market system. While in the UK and Germany, those major developments were promoted by the state, the US development was introduced by market forces and only later fostered by government. In effect, the role of the state in regulation

Table 2. The changing role of the state in healthcare systems.

Type of healthcare system of data	Financing (all countries)	Service Provision (all countries)	Regulation (UK, Germany, US as representatives for distinct types)
National health service	Decreasing share of public health expenditure on total health expenditure	No clear tendency can be found, possibly due to lack of data	Still high degree of state control but amended by the introduction of competition via 'internal markets' and some corporatist elements through NICE
Social insurance system	Constant share of public health expenditure on total health expenditure		Still predominance of collective bargaining, but complemented, in the 'shadow of hierarchy', with competition as a new principle
Private (insurance) system	Increasing share of public health expenditure on total health expenditure		Introduction of hierarchy through managed care, higher state potential through increase in public coverage
All countries	Slight reduction of public share after 1980; slight convergence tendencies	Distinct patterns of different types remain	Convergence to mixed modes of regulation replace 'pure types'

decreased in the United Kingdom in favour of more market coordination, while in Germany the state continues to act as a referee who intervenes whenever deemed necessary. For example, it was the state that supplemented still powerful self-regulation mechanisms by some element of competition. In the US, finally, we see some retreat of the state from direct intervention, but at the same time, a strengthening of hierarchical regulation, which is executed through the private sector.

These changes should not, however, lead to the conclusion that system-specific characteristics have disappeared. The British NHS is still based upon a hierarchical planning and control system, for example when setting cash limits or deciding on the number and location of general practitioners. In Germany, the corporate structure of the social insurance system was even strengthened with respect to the access of service providers to the healthcare market, or with respect to the regulation of the benefit package. The private US system, lastly, experienced some de-regulation for the private insurance sector.

In Table 1, the role of the state in different types of healthcare systems was outlined. Table 2 sums up which changes happened from the early 1970s onwards.

By and large, we see a slight reduction in public healthcare financing, combined with a tendency towards convergence in this dimension. With respect to regulation, convergence is even more prominent, but we do not have sufficient data to evaluate changes in service provision. Although these observations are based on preliminary data analyses, they lead to the hypothesis that a shift occurs from distinct types of healthcare systems to mixed types. This shift and the spread of gate-keeping, managed care and DRG models around the world would indeed emphasize the role of policy learning and best practice as a yardstick of reform, while the still remarkable differences between the types of healthcare systems point towards inertia and path dependency as the main reasons for the slow pace of this convergence process.

References

1. B. Abel-Smith and E. Mossialos (1994) Cost containment and health care reform: a study of the European Union. *Health Policy*, **28**(2): 89–132.
2. J. Alber (1988) Die Gesundheitssysteme der OECD-Länder im Vergleich. In: M. G. Schmidt (Ed) *Staatstätigkeit. International und historisch vergleichende Analysen* (Opladen: Westdeutscher Verlag): 116–150.
3. J. Alber (1989) Die Steuerung des Gesundheitssystems in vergleichender Perspektive. *Journal für Sozialforschung*, **29**(3): 259–284.

4. K. Behaghel (1993) Kostendämpfung und ärztliche Interessenvertretung. Ein Verbandssystem unter Stress (Köln: Universität Köln, Wirtschafts- und Sozialwissenschaftliche Fakultät): 229.

5. E. R. Brown (2001) Public policies to extend health care coverage. In R. M. Andersen, T. H. Rice and G. F. Kominski (Eds) *Changing the US Health Care System: Key Issues in Health Services, Policy, and Management* (San Francisco, CA: Jossey-Bass): 31–57.

6. F. G. Castles (2004) *The Future of the Welfare State: Crisis Myths and Crisis Realities* (Oxford, UK: Oxford University Press).

7. A. Comas-Herrera (1999) Is there convergence in the health expenditures of the EU Member States? In: E. Mossialos and J. L. Grand (Eds) *Health Care and Cost Containment in the European Union* (Aldershot, Hants., UK: Ashgate): 197–218.

8. A. J. Culyer (1990) Cost containment in Europe. In: OECD (Ed) *Health Care Systems in Transition. The Search for Efficiency* (Paris: OECD): 29–40.

9. M. Döhler and P. Manow (1992) Korporatisierung als gesundheitspolitische Strategie. *Staatswissenschaften und Staatspraxis*, **3**(1): 64–106.

10. M. G. Field (1999) Comparative health systems and the convergence hypothesis. The dialectics of universalism and particularism. In F. D. Powell and A. F. Wessen (Eds) *Health Care Systems in Transition. An International Perspective* (Thousand Oaks, CA: Sage): 35–44.

11. P. Flora (1986) Introduction. In: P. Flora (Ed) *Growth to Limits. The Western European Welfare States Since World War II* (New York/Berlin: Walter de Gruyter) vol. 1, pp. xi–xxxvi.

12. S. Giaimo (2002) *Markets and Medicine. The Politics of Health Care Reform in Britain, Germany, and the United States* (Ann Arbor, MI: University of Michigan Press).

13. H. Glennerster and M. Matsaganis (1994) The English and Swedish health care reforms. *International Journal of Health Services*, **24**(2): 231–251.

14. S. Greß, D. Niebuhr, H. Rothgang and J. Wasem (2004) Benefit decisions in German social health insurance. In: T. S. Jost (Ed) *Health Care Coverage Determinations* (Maidenhead, UK: Open University Press, forthcoming): 115–131.

15. J. S. Hacker (2002) *The Divided Welfare State: The Battle over Public and Private Social Benefits in the United States* (Cambridge, UK: Cambridge University Press).

16. C. Ham (1999) *Health Policy in Britain. The Politics and Organisation of the National Health Service* (Basingstoke: Macmillan, 5th edn. 2004).

17. B. Jönsson and P. Musgrove (1997) Government financing of health care. In: G. J. Schieber (Ed) *Innovations in Health Care Financing* (Washington, DC: World Bank): 41–64.

18. M. Kautto and J. Kvist (2002) Parallel trends, persistent diversity. Nordic welfare states in the European and global context. *Global Social Policy*, **2**(2): 189–208.

19. R. Klein (2001) *The New Politics of the NHS* (London: Prentice Hall).

20. J. J. Kronenfeld (2002) *Health Care Policy: Issues and Trends* (Westport, CT: Praeger).

21. M. A. Laschober and J. C. Vertrees (1995) Hospital financing in the United States. In: U.S. Congress and Office of Technology Assessment (Eds) *Hospital Financing in Seven Countries* (Washington, DC: US Government Printing Office, OTA-BP-H-148): 135–151.

22. T. R. Marmor and K. G. H. Okma (1998) Cautionary lessons from the West: what (not) to learn from other countries' experience in the financing and delivery of health care. In: P. Flora, P. R. de Jong, J. Le Grand and J.-Y. Kim (Eds) *The State of Social Welfare, 1997. International Studies on Social Insurance and Retirement, Employment, Family Policy and Health Care* (Aldershot, Hants., UK: Ashgate): 327–350.

23. R. J. Mills and S. Bhandari (2003) *Health Insurance Coverage in the United States: 2002* (Washington, DC: US Census Bureau, US Department of Commerce).

24. W. Newbrander and R. Eichler (2001) Managed care in the United States: its history, forms, and future. In: A. Ron and X. Scheil-Adlung (Eds) *Recent Health Policy Innovations in Social Security* (New Brunswick, NJ: Transaction Publishers): 83–106.

25. OECD (1994) *Health: Quality and Choice*, (Paris: OECD, OECD Health Policy Studies No. 4).

26. OECD (1995) *New Directions in Health Care Policy*, (Paris: OECD, OECD Health Policy Studies No. 7).

27. OECD (1996) *Health Care Reform. The Will to Change*, (Paris: OECD, OECD Health Policy Studies No. 8).

28. OECD (2002) *OECD Health Data 2002. A Comparative Analysis of 30 Countries* (Paris: OECD).

29. C. Perschke-Hartmann (1994) *Die doppelte Reform. Gesundheitspolitik von Blüm zu Seehofer* (Opladen: Leske + Budrich).

30. P. Pierson (2001) Coping with permanent austerity: welfare state restructuring in affluent democracies. In: P. Pierson (Ed) *The New Politics of the Welfare State* (Oxford, UK: Oxford University Press): 410–456.

31. PKV-Verband (2000) *Die private Krankenversicherung, 1999/2000* (Köln: PKV).

32. R. Robinson and J. Le Grand (1995) Contracting and the purchaser-provider split. In: R. B. Saltman and C. v. Otter (Eds) *Implementing Planned Markets in Health Care. Balancing Social and Economic Responsibility* (Buckingham, UK: Open University Press): 25–44.

33. H. Rothgang (1996) Auf dem Weg zur Effektivitäts- und Effizienzsteigerung? Der 'Umbau des Sozialstaats' in der gesetzlichen Krankenversicherung. *Zeitschrift für Sozialreform*, **42**(11/12): 725–754.

34. H. Rothgang, D. Niebuhr, J. Wasem and S. Greß (2004) Das National Institute for Clinical Excellence – Staatsmedizinisches Rationierungsinstrument oder Vorbild für die evidenzbasierte Bewertung medizinischer Leistungen. *Das Gesundheitswesen*, **64**(5): 303–310.

35. M. E. Rushefsky and K. Patel (1999) *Health Care Politics and Policy in America* (Armonk, NY: M. E. Sharpe).

36. M. G. Schmidt (1999) Warum die Gesundheitsausgaben wachsen. Befunde des Vergleichs demokratisch verfasster Länder. *Politische Vierteljahresschrift*, **40**(2): 229–245.

37. H. Stapf-Finé and M. Schölkopf (2003) *Die Krankenhausversorgung im internationalen Vergleich: Zahlen, Fakten, Trends* (Düsseldorf: Deutsche Krankenhaus Verlagsgesellschaft mbH).

38. J. Wasem (1995) Gesetzliche und private Krankenversicherung – auf dem Weg in die Konvergenz? *Sozialer Fortschritt*, **1995**(4): 89–96.

39. J. Wasem (2000) Die Zukunft der Gesundheitspolitik – Was erwartet die Bevölkerung? In: S. Leibfried and U. Wagschal (Eds) *Der deutsche Sozialstaat. Bilanzen – Reformen – Perspektiven* (Frankfurt a.M.: Campus): 427–438.

40. C. Wendt (2003) *Krankenversicherung oder Gesundheitsversorgung – Gesundheitssysteme im Vergleich* (Wiesbaden: Westdeutscher Verlag).

41. C. Wendt, S. Grimmeisen and H. Rothgang (2004) Convergence or divergence in OECD health care systems?, Paper presented at the Eleventh International Research Seminar of the Foundation for International Studies of Social Security (FISS) on Issues in Social Security, Sigtuna, Sweden, 19–21 June, 2004.

About the Authors

Heinz Rothgang is Assistant Professor at the Research Centre on Transformations of the State (TranState) and at the Centre for Social Policy Reseach (CeS) at the University of Bremen. Together with **Mirella Cacace** (case study: United States), **Simone Grimmeisen** (case study: United Kingdom), and **Claus Wendt** (case study: Germany; plus international comparison) he belongs as a principal investigator to the TranState research group on 'The changing role of the state in OECD health care systems'. Recent articles by some of the authors are: H. Rothgang, Providing long-term care for the elderly in Germany. Projections on public long-term care insurance financing. In: G. Hullen (Ed) *Living Arrangements and Households – Methods and Results of Demographic Projections* (Wiesbaden: Bundesinstitut für Bevölkerungsforschung, 2003): 95–112; S. Greß, D. Niebuhr, H. Rothgang and J. Wasem, Benefit decisions in German social health insurance. In: T. S. Jost (Ed) *Health Care Coverage Determinations* (Buckingham: Open University Press, 2004): 115–131, forthcoming; C. Wendt and T. Thompson, The need for social austerity versus structural reform in European health systems: a four-country comparison of health reforms, *International Journal of Health Services*, **34**(3): 415–433 (2004); J. Kohl and C. Wendt, Satisfaction with health care systems. A comparison of EU countries. In: W. Glatzer, S. v. Below, and M. Stoffregen (Eds) *Challenges for the Quality of Life in Contemporary Societies* (Dordrecht, NL: Kluwer Academic Publishers 2004, forthcoming).

European Review, Vol. 13, Supp. No. 1, 213–215 (2005) © Academia Europaea, Printed in the United Kingdom

THE TRANSTATE RESEARCH CENTRE

What is the state of the state? The members of the national Research Centre Transformations of the State (TranState) at the University of Bremen use the contrast with the OECD nation-state during its 'Golden Age' in the 1960s and early '70s to study the rapidly changing interface between international and domestic politics, and between public and private governance. Studies currently underway at TranState confront the changes in the tightly woven fabric of the twentieth-century western, multi-functional state, which emerged after World War II with the functional amalgamation at the national level of the **T**erritorial State, the state that assures the **Ru**le of Law, the **D**emocratic State, and the **I**ntervention State. This functional definition is expressed in the acronym TRUDI.

Both TranState research and the contributions to this volume are aligned along TRUDI's four dimensions of statehood: *resources* (financial, means of force), *rule of law*, (democratic) *legitimacy*, and *welfare*. These dimensions developed over four centuries and merged, during the 'Golden Age', in one institution, the nation-state. Since then, however, processes of globalization, denationalization, privatization as well as individualization have initiated a new dynamic. The finely woven national constellation of the Golden Age state is coming apart – it is unravelling. Yet though an era of structural uncertainty is ahead, not everything is in flux. We may see structured asymmetric change in the make-up of the state, with divergent transformations in each of its four dimensions. TranState aims at accounting empirically for these transformations since the mid-1970s; explaining them and their dynamics; and, finally, determining how these transformations affect the provision of public goods such as security, the rule of law, democratic legitimacy, or welfare provision.

This Centre of Excellence is made up of fifteen (plus two associated) mostly comparatively oriented research projects with some 65 researchers from Political Science, Law, Sociology, and Economics. It was founded in 2003 by three universities in the State of Bremen, namely, the University of Bremen (as the hub with twelve projects), the International University Bremen (IU[B], with two projects) and the University of Applied Sciences Bremen (with one project), and is co-funded by the German Research Foundation, the *Deutsche Forschungs-gemeinschaft* (DFG). The DFG-grant runs for a four-year period, with an option for two additional four-year spans, subject to successful peer review. The national process of awarding grants aims to strengthen internationally outstanding, cutting-edge interdisciplinary research in the German university system; it is highly competitive, and open to all German universities and disciplines. TranState is part of a network of university institutions that provides graduate and post-doctoral training for researchers; it is currently consolidating its links to major national, European and international research institutions, also within the (EU) Network-of-Excellence (NoE) mission GARNET due to start in 2005, with a view to fostering a Europeanization of careers for junior research staff (for details see http://garnet.warwick.ac.uk). For detailed information on TranState see http://www.state.uni-bremen.de.

The Authors

Claudia Bogedan (Sociology), claudia.bogedan@sfb597.uni-bremen.de

Michael Brüggemann (Communiciation Studies), michael.brueggemann@sfb597.uni-bremen.de

Mirella Cacace (Economics), mirella.cacace@sfb597.uni-bremen.de

Dr Philipp Genschel, Professor (Political Science), p.genschel@iu-bremen.de

Dr Edith Gindulis (Political Science), edith.gindulis@sfb597.uni-bremen.de

Dr Christine Godt, Assistant Professor (Law), cgodt@zerp.uni-bremen.de

Simone Grimmeisen (Political Science), simone.grimmeisen@sfb597.uni-bremen.de

Dr Achim Hurrelmann (Political Science), achim.hurrelmann@sfb597.uni-bremen.de

Dr Markus Jachtenfuchs, Professor (Political Science), m.jachtenfuchs@iu-bremen.de

Dr Christian Joerges, Professor (Law), christian.joerges@iue.it

Katharina Kleinen-von Königslöw (Communication Studies), katharina.kleinen-vonkoenigsloew@sfb597.uni-bremen.de

Zuzana Krell-Laluhová (Political Science), zuzana.krell-laluhova@sfb597.uni-bremen.de

Dr Stephan Leibfried, Professor (Political Science), stephan.leibfried@sfb597.uni-bremen.de

Dr Roland Lhotta, Professor (Political Science), lhotta@hsuhh.de

Julia Moser (Political Science), julia.moser@sfb597.uni-bremen.de

Dr Frank Nullmeier, Professor (Political Science), frank.nullmeier@zes.uni-bremen.de

Dr Herbert Obinger, Assistant Professor (Political Science), hobinger@zes.uni-bremen.de

Dr Bernhard Peters, Professor (Political Science), bpeters@barkhof.uni-bremen.de

Dr Heinz Rothgang, Assistant Professor (Economics), rothgang@zes.uni-bremen.de

Dr Steffen Schneider (Political Science), steffen.schneider@sfb597.uni-bremen.de

Stefanie Sifft (Political Science), stefanie.sifft@sfb597.uni-bremen.de

Peter Starke (Political Science), peter.starke@sfb597.uni-bremen.de

Dr Claus Wendt (Sociology), claus.wendt@sfb597.uni-bremen.de

Andreas Wimmel (Political Science), wimmel@uni-bremen.de

Dr Bernhard Zangl, Assistant Professor (Political Science), bezangl@uni-bremen.de

Dr Michael Zürn, Professor (Political Science), zuern@wz-berlin.de

Addresses

Philipp Genschel and *Markus Jachtenfuchs* can be reached directly at the **International University Bremen** (IU^B), Campus Ring 1, D-28759 Bremen, Germany, *Christian Joerges* at the **European University Institute**, Law Department, Via Boccaccio 121, I-50133 Florence, Italy; *Roland Lhotta* at the **Universität der Bundeswehr Hamburg**, Holstenhofweg 85, D-22043 Hamburg, and *Michael Zürn* at the **Wissenschaftszentrum Berlin** (WZB), Reichpietschufer 50, D-10785 Berlin. *All other authors* can be reached at TranState (CRC 597), **Universität Bremen** (UB), Linzer Str. 9a, D-28359 Bremen, Germany. A central fax number is ++49 [0]421 218 8721. Further Information can also be obtained via the Administrative Director of TranState Dr. Dieter Wolf, via Dieter.Wolf@sfb597.uni-bremen.de (phone ++49 [0]421 218 8723).

European Review, Vol. 13, Supp. No. 1, 217–224 (2005) © Academia Europaea, Printed in the United Kingdom

Index